Peter and Cornelius

American Society of Missiology Monograph Series

THE ASM MONOGRAPH SERIES provides a forum for publishing quality dissertations and studies in the field of missiology. Collaborating with Pickwick Publications—a division of Wipf and Stock Publishers of Eugene, Oregon—the American Society of Missiology selects high quality dissertations and other monographic studies that offer research materials in mission studies for scholars, mission and church leaders, and the academic community at large. The ASM seeks scholarly work for publication in the Series that throws light on issues confronting Christian world mission in its cultural, social, historical, biblical, and theological dimensions.

Missiology is an academic field that brings together scholars whose professional training ranges from doctoral-level preparation in areas such as scripture, history and sociology of religions, anthropology, theology, international relations, interreligious interchange, mission history, inculturation, and church law. The American Society of Missiology, which sponsors this series, is an ecumenical body drawing members from Independent and Ecumenical Protestant, Catholic, Orthodox, and other traditions. Members of the ASM are united by their commitment to reflect on and do scholarly work relating to both mission history and the present-day mission of the church. The ASM Monograph Series aims to publish works of exceptional merit on specialized topics, with particular attention given to work by younger scholars, the dissemination and publication of which is difficult under the economic pressures of standard publishing models.

Persons seeking information about the ASM or the guidelines for having their dissertations considered for publication in the ASM Monograph Series should consult the Society's website—www.asmweb.org.

Members of the ASM Monograph Committee who approved this book are:

Bonnie Sue Lewis, University of Dubuque Theological Seminary
Judith Lingenfelter, Biola University
Gary M. Simpson, Luther Seminary

PREVIOUSLY PUBLISHED IN THE ASM MONOGRAPH SERIES

David J. Endres, *American Crusade: Catholic Youth in the World Mission Movement from World War l through Vatican ll*

W. Jay Moon, *African Proverbs Reveal Christianity in Culture: A Narrative Portrayal of Builsa Proverbs Contextualizing Christianity in Ghana*

E. Paul Balisky, *Wolaitta Evangelists: A Study of Religious Innovation in Southern Ethiopia,* 1937–1975

Auli Vähäkangas, *Christian Couples Coping with Childlessness: Narratives from Machame, Kilimanjaro*

Peter and Cornelius
A Story of Conversion and Mission

vanThanh Nguyen, S.V.D.

American Society of Missiology
Monograph Series

VOL. 15

☙PICKWICK *Publications* · Eugene, Oregon

PETER AND CORNELIUS
A Story of Conversion and Mission

Copyright © 2012 vanThanh Nguyen, S.V.D. All rights reserved. Except for brief quotations in critical publications or reviews, no part of this book may be reproduced in any manner without prior written permission from the publisher. Write: Permissions, Wipf and Stock Publishers, 199 W. 8th Ave., Suite 3, Eugene, OR 97401.

Pickwick Publications
An Imprint of Wipf and Stock Publishers
199 W. 8th Ave., Suite 3
Eugene, OR 97401

www.wipfandstock.com

ISBN 13: 978-1-61097-848-4

Cataloguing-in-Publication data:

Nguyen, vanThanh.

    Peter and Cornelius : a story of conversion and mission / vanThanh Nguyen, S.V.D.

    xvi + 194 pp. ; 23 cm. Includes bibliographical references and index.

    ISBN 13: 978-1-61097-848-4

    1. Bible. N.T. Acts X, 1–XI, 18—Criticism, interpretation, etc. 2. Conversion—Biblical teaching. 3. Missions—Biblical teaching. I. Title. II. Series.

BS2625.6 N35 2012

Manufactured in the U.S.A.

The author gratefully acknowledges the permission he has received to use material previously published by Wipf and Stock Publishers:

"Luke's Point of View of the Gentile Mission: The Test Case of Acts 11:1–18," *Journal of Biblical and Pneumatological Research* 3 (Fall 2011) 85–98.

Dedicated

to my mother,

Hoan Thi Nguyen,

and to my religious community,

the Society of the Divine Word

Contents

Acknowledgments · ix

Abbreviations · x

Introduction · xiii

1 The Narrative Unity · 1

2 The Discourse · 11

3 The Settings · 54

4 The Plot · 82

5 The Characters · 107

6 The Theological Significance · 133

   Conclusion · 157

Appendix A: Table of Narrative Codes · 169

Appendix B: Glossary · 171

Bibliography · 175

Index · 189

Acknowledgments

"Có công mài sắt có ngày nên kim" is a Vietnamese proverbial saying that is similar to the English saying, "With time and patience the leaf of the mulberry becomes satin." This book has been an endeavor that could not have come to fruition without the help and support of many people who have journeyed with me along the way. I am deeply grateful to many dedicated confreres of my religious community—the Society of the Divine Word (S.V.D.)—who have formed me in the Word and mentored me on the road of religious and missionary life. These fine missionaries, formators, and friends are: Jim Bergin, Mark Weber, Roger Arnold (deceased), Roger Schroeder, Steve Bevans, Gary Riebe, Bill Shea, Stan Uroda, Quang Duc Dinh, Derek Simon, Ken Anich, Walt Miller, just to name a few. I am especially appreciative of Tim Lenchak, S.V.D., who carefully read through the initial draft of the manuscript and gave insightful suggestions and directions. Finally, I want to express my deepest gratitude to the American Society of Missiology and to the members of the ASM Monograph Series who approved this work for publication.

Abbreviations

ABD	*The Anchor Bible Dictionary.* 6 vols. Edited by David Noel Freedman. New York: Doubleday, 1992
al.	*alli* ("others")
ATR	*Anglican Theological Review*
AUSS	*Andrews University Seminary Studies*
BDAG	Walter Bauer, Frederick W. Danker, W. F. Arndt, and F. W. Gingrich. *Greek-English Lexicon of the New Testament and Other Early Christian Literature.* 3rd ed. Chicago: University of Chicago Press, 2000
Bib	*Biblica*
BK	*Bibel und Kirche*
BTB	*Biblical Theological Bulletin*
BVC	*Bible et vie Chrétienne*
BZ	*Biblische Zeitschrift*
CBQ	*Catholic Biblical Quarterly*
CPDBT	*The Collegeville Pastoral Dictionary of Biblical Theology.* C. Stuhlmueller, et al., eds. Collegeville, Minnesota: Liturgical Press, 1996
Diss.	Dissertation
ed.	editor(s); edited by; edition
EDB	*Eerdmans Dictionary of the Bible.* David N. Freedman, et al., eds. Grand Rapids, Michigan: William B. Eerdmans, 2000
EDNT	*Exegetical Dictionary of the New Testament.* H. Balz and G. Schneider, eds. Grand Rapids, Michigan: William B. Eerdmans, 1990
EQ	*The Evangelical Quarterly*
ETL	*Ephemerides Theologicae Lovanienses*
ExpT	*Expository Times*
Greg	*Gregorianum*
HeyJ	*Heythrop Journal*
HR	*History of Religions*
HTR	*Harvard Theological Review*

Abbreviations

Id.	Idem ("the same")
IDB	*The Interpreter's Dictionary of the Bible*. 4 vols. Edited by George Arthur Buttrick. Nashville: Abingdon, 1962
Int	*Interpretation*
JAAR	*Journal of the American Academy of Religion*
JBL	*Journal of Biblical Literature*
JETS	*Journal of the Evangelical Theological Society*
JSNT	*Journal for the Study of the New Testament*
JTS	*Journal of Theological Studies*
n.	note
N-A^{27}	27th edition of the *Novum Testamentum Graece* (Nestle-Aland)
NovT	*Novum Testamentum*
NTS	*New Testament Studies*
RB	*Revue Biblique*
repr.	reprint
RevistB	*Revista bíblica*
RivB	*Rivista biblica*
RStB	*Ricerche Storico Bibliche*
RSR	*Recherches de science religieuse*
SBLSP	*Society of Biblical Literature Seminar Papers*
SEA	*Svensk exegetisk årsbok*
SNTS	Society for New Testament Studies
SNTSMS	Society for New Testament Studies Monograph Series
SPCK	Society for Promotion Christian Knowledge
SThD	Sacrae Theologiae Doctor ("Doctor of Sacred Theology")
TDNT	*Theological Dictionary of the New Testament*. 10 vols. Edited by Gerhard Kittel and Gerhard Friedrich. Translated by Geoffrey W. Bromiley. Grand Rapids: Eerdmans, 1964–76
tr.	translator
trans.	translation
TRev	*Theologische Revue*
TS	*Theological Studies*
TZ	*Theologische Zeitschrift*
VT	*Vetus Testamentum*

Introduction

THE MISSION TO THE Gentiles and their conversion into the church gave rise to conflict in the early Christian community. Acts 11:1–18 indicates that there was clearly dissension over the issue of Peter having gone to the house of Cornelius and having participated in table fellowship with him. The issue was no small matter, since it could have split the church. How does Luke portray the resolution of the conflict? Instead of writing a philosophical or theological treatise, the author employs the art of storytelling, a method of teaching that is said to be as old as the world.

The study of Luke-Acts has long been dominated by historical-critical methods which focused on Luke as historian and theologian.[1] More recently however a paradigm shift has taken place by looking at Luke as artist.[2] Since narrative criticism is concerned with the work of the writer as artist and since it treats narrative precisely as narrative, the time has come to apply the narrative critical approach to Acts 10:1—11:18.[3] Focusing on Luke

---

1. The two most influential works are: Conzelmann, *Die Mitte der Zeit*; Marshall, *Luke*. For a survey on Luke as historian and theologian, see especially Bovon, *Luc le théologien*; Richard, "Luke—Writer, Theologian, Historian."

2. Three most significant contributions are: Talbert, *Literary Pattern*; Karris, *Luke*; Tannehill, *Narrative Unity*. Other helpful works include: Kingsbury, *Conflict in Luke*; Kurz, *Reading Luke-Acts*; Lee, *Luke's Stories of Jesus*; Parsons, *Luke*.

3. The story of Peter and Cornelius has been thoroughly investigated from various approaches, but none of the monographic studies has applied narrative criticism to our text. The study that comes closest to narrative criticism was done in 1998 by Handy, "Gentile Pentecost." Even in this monographic study, however, the method used is purely a reader-response approach. This thesis, which consists of less than one hundred and twenty pages, focuses primarily on two literary features: the intertextuality of biblical echoes and allusions, and the repetitions and gaps in the narrative. Other monographic studies of Acts 10:1—11:18 apply historical-critical methods: Bovon, *Vocatione Gentium*; Crampsey, "Conversion of Cornelius"; Stuehrenberg, "Cornelius and the Jews"; Lukasz, *Evangelizzazione e conflitto*.

Introduction

as artist does not mean that we ignore his theological significance. Rather this methodology simply employs a different set of questions: What is the story about? How is the story told? What effect does the story have on the reader? And why does it have this effect?

Although narrative criticism is a relatively new approach in New Testament studies, it nevertheless proves to be quite useful and reliable in analyzing and interpreting biblical stories.[4] The emphasis of our investigation will be upon an analysis and interpretation of Acts 10:1—11:18 that hopefully will contribute to the understanding of this wonderful story of conversion and mission rather than upon a critique of methodology. In our analysis we presuppose that the reader is familiar with the general aspects of the narrative approach; however, when it is necessary, technical terms will be defined and clarified.

The aim of this monograph is to contribute to the understanding and interpretation of the Peter and Cornelius (henceforth P-C) episode as a narrative text. By employing dramatic and literary criteria to delimit the text, chapter 1 demonstrates that Acts 10:1—11:18 is a coherent and independent narrative unit with a unifying plot. Chapter 2 examines the *discourse* or the "how" of the narrative, which includes the arrangement of the events into acts, scenes and sub-scenes; the narrator; point of view; and style and rhetorical techniques.

Chapters 3, 4, and 5 focus on the *story* or the "what" of the narrative. Since setting is often integral to a story, it will become clear in chapter 3 that the narrative settings (spatial, temporal, and social-cultural) of the P-C episode heighten the interest and tension of the story. Chapter 4 examines the plot of the narrative. The analysis will reveal that the events of Acts 10:1—11:18 are skillfully arranged in a meaningful way in order to arouse the reader's interest and emotional involvement and more importantly to communicate the essential message of the story. Understanding the characters is also important to comprehending the story. In chapter 5 we will examine the two main characters (Cornelius and Peter) and the two minor characters (Cornelius' messengers and the circumcised Christians). By giving flesh and color to these characters we will discover not only their function in the story but also their impact upon the reader.

---

4. See Pontifical Biblical Commission, *Interpretation of the Bible*, (I.B.2) 46–48; Powell, *What is Narrative Criticism?*; Merenlahti and Hakola, "Reconceiving Narrative Criticism," 13–48; Rhoads, "Narrative Criticism," 264–85.

Introduction

Since it is not enough just to analyze the "what" and the "how" of the narrative, chapter 6 focuses on the theological significance or motif(s) behind Acts 10:1—11:18. The examination of Luke's portrait of God and especially of his justification of the Gentile mission and integration will help to establish the criteria for interpreting the story.

Finally, the conclusion will gather the results together—*story* and *discourse*, form and content, theology and technique—in order to discover the intention and message of the implied author and the anticipated response of the implied reader. Without doubt the author of our narrative is a master storyteller. Well versed in the Greek language, in rhetoric, and in the art of storytelling, the implied author creatively and effectively guides the implied reader not only to conform to his ideological worldview—namely to his norms, values, and beliefs—but also to align with the standard judgment of God. Since the mission to the Gentiles and their integration into the people of God is prophecy-fulfillment and in accordance with God's salvific will and plan, the events of Acts 10:1—11:18 have been initiated and legitimated by God. Since this is the evaluative point of view of the implied author and of God's, the reader must accept it as the normative interpretation of the story and hence should respond appropriately.

1   *The Narrative Unity*

WHERE DOES A STORY begin and where does it end? Children's fairy tales clearly begin with the formula "Once upon a time" and end with "And they lived happily ever after." Modern literature on the other hand uses typographic devices such as paragraph indentations, blank lines between paragraphs, section headings of various kinds, and other similar devices to establish its boundaries. Unlike modern prose, however, biblical texts in their original form are written as one continuous literary unit. As a result, establishing the narrative boundaries, namely the beginning and the end, can often be quite challenging. Yet the decision which a reader makes to begin at a particular point and to end at a particular point is extremely important, because the delimitation of the text is already "a first interpretive act which, by making out a unit that makes sense, opens the reading and programmes its regulation."[1]

So where does the narrative of Peter and Cornelius begin and where does it end? Furthermore, what criteria must one use to determine that the story of P-C is an independent narrative episode (micro-narrative) containing a unifying plot within the literary work of Acts as a whole (macro-narrative)?[2] By means of two literary criteria, namely dramatic criteria and literary (or stylistic) criteria, the present chapter sets out to delimit the text of Acts 10:1—11:18 by demonstrating that the episode of P-C is indeed an independent micro-narrative with a unifying plot.

---

1. Marguerat and Bourquin, *How to Read*, 30.

2. A narrative episode or micro-narrative is often made up of successive scenes while a narrative sequence is composed of several micro-narratives, linked together by a common theme or the presence of the same principal character. See Marguerat and Bourquin, *How to Read*, 30–39; Walsh, *Style and Structure*, 117–43.

DRAMATIC CRITERIA

The essential criteria for the delimitation of a micro-narrative are the dramatic criteria: change of place, change of time, change of characters, and change of action or plot.[3] Normally the transition from one narrative sequence or scene to another occurs through one or more of these changes; therefore, it is necessary to be attentive to these indicators. When two or more criteria converge, the micro-narrative probably has a clean closure.[4] However, in narrative criticism the delimitation of a micro-narrative rests essentially on the changes in dramatic action or plot.[5] When this occurs, the delimitation of the text is fully established.

Change of Place

The episode of P-C is part of the larger narrative sequence of Acts 9:32—11:18, which contains three stories about Peter, also known as the Petrine narratives: 9:32–35 ("Peter Heals Aeneas"); 9:36–43 ("Peter Restores Tabitha to Life"); and 10:1—11:18 ("The Episode of Peter and Cornelius"). The spatial setting of the first micro-narrative (9:32–35) is situated in Lydda, a Judean town between Jerusalem and Joppa, and the second (9:36–43) in Joppa, which is on the Mediterranean coast. The changes in locale and in characters clearly signal an end of one unit and the beginning of another.

At the beginning of the P-C episode (10:1) the spatial setting is again changed to Caesarea and to Joppa (10:9), back to Caesarea (10:24) and then to Jerusalem (11:2). Obviously the spatial transition at the beginning of this episode signals a break from the previous unit to begin a new unit, while the changes that follow are breaks in scenes or sub-units.

In the sequence that follows the episode of P-C (11:19–26), the spatial setting has changed to Antioch, a completely new and far-away location which again signals a new unit. Although the spatial changes are indicated quite clearly, and although these changes can signal the end of one sequence or scene and the beginning of another, we cannot yet determine with certitude the boundaries of our episode. Since more information is needed, let us now examine the criterion of time.

---

3. Ska, "Our Fathers," 1.

4. A closure is defined as "The totality of narrative indicators which fix a beginning and an end to the narrative, thus delimiting a space where meaning is produced" (Marguerat and Bourquin, *How to Read*, 31).

5. Ska, "Our Fathers," 2.

The Narrative Unity

Change of Time

Time, like space, is a narrative component that can unify a sequence or scene and can also signal a change in a sequence or scene. A close examination of Acts 10:1—11:18 shows the following temporal framework:[6]

- 10:1–8   Day One
- 10:9–23a   Day Two
- 10:23b   Day Three
- 10:24–48   Day Four
- 11:1–18   Some Days Later

The temporal framework of Acts 10:1—11:18 clearly marks its boundaries and unifies it as one independent episode while the previous units (9:36-43) as well as the following sequence (11:19-26) are set outside of this cohesive temporal structure.

Change of Characters

In a narrative sequence or scene a departure of one of the main characters and/or the appearance of a new character can signal a beginning of a new unit or sub-unit. The introduction of Cornelius in Acts 10:1 clearly signals the beginning of a new unit since this is the first time that Cornelius has appeared in the book. A close look at Acts 10:1—11:18 reveals the following dynamics of characterization:

- 10:1–8   Cornelius
- 10:9–16   Peter
- 10:17–23a   Peter and the messengers of Cornelius
- 10:23b–48   Peter and Cornelius (and his household)
- 11:1–18   Peter, apostles and brothers

Obviously, while the characters might change from scene to scene, Peter and Cornelius dominate the entire episode. Only in Acts 11:19-26 do all the previous characters leave the scene and a completely new cast of characters is introduced. Thus the change of the characters in Acts 10:1—11:18

---

6. This temporal framework is deduced from the following literary-chronological indicators: *hōsei peri hōran enatēn tēs hēmeras* (10:3); *tē de epaurion* (10:9); *tē de epaurion* (10:23b); *tē de epaurion* (10:24).

reveals a clear break in the narrative sequence both at the beginning and at the end of the unit.

Change of Action/Plot

For a story to be a story, there must be a plot. And since the plot constitutes the core of a narrative, it is an essential component for delimiting a unit. Jean Louis Ska writes, "The delimitation of narrative unit depends on one main criterion: the analysis of the plot or the dramatic action."[7] But what is a plot? "Plot" can simply be defined as the unifying structure which "links the various happenings in the story and organizes them into a continuous account."[8] It is the plot that holds the narrative together. Without this cohesion the story risks disintegration.

The story of P-C is made up of different scenes with a combination of linked plots which are intricately woven into one episodic plot—namely, the conflict and tension of the admission and integration of the first uncircumcised Gentile into the faith. A more detailed discussion on plot shall be dealt with in a later chapter. Here, I would like to point out that the artistry of the narrator's linking of plots through various scenes not only provides the dramatic effect of repetition and tension but also unifies its micro-narrative into one coherent episodic plot by means of two narrative markers: the initial situation (or exposition) and the final situation.[9] It is between these two narrative markers that a plot is developed and transformed.

A close examination of Acts 10:1–8 shows that this scene provides the readers with new information specifying the circumstances of the action (for example, spatial and temporal settings and characters) and the conflict which needs to be resolved. Since Acts 10:1–8 clearly introduces the initial situation of a new episodic plot, it is a clear indication of a change of

---

7. Ska, "Our Fathers," 2.

8. Marguerat and Bourquin, *How to Read*, 40.

9. Initial situation (or exposition) is defined as "the circumstances of the action (setting, characters), if need be a shortage of something is indicated (sickness, difficulty, ignorance); the narrative will show an attempt to remove it." Final situation is the "statement of the new state attained by the subject following the transformation. Structurally this moment corresponds to the reversal of the initial situation by an elimination of the shortage" (Marguerat and Bourquin, *How to Read*, 44). This topic shall be fully dealt with in a later chapter, but for now it is sufficient to know that these two markers are part of the "quinary scheme" which consists of five stages that typically make up the plot. These five stages are: 1) Initial Situation; 2) Complication; 3) Transforming Action; 4) Denouement; and 5) Final Situation.

action/plot from what had taken place previously (9:36–43). Furthermore, the tension and conflict of the plot are increased and will not be completely resolved until Acts 11:18. Since the difficulty is eliminated and the situation returns to normal, Acts 11:18 clearly functions as the final situation of the episodic plot marking an end of the micro-narrative. Consequently, the plot provides clear boundary to the P-C episode.

To sum up, the dramatic criteria of place, time, characters, and action/plot help us to delimit the narrative episode of P-C. Each of these criteria contributes to the delimitation of our text. The spatial and temporal parameters limit our text to a specific setting within its micro-narrative. The change of the characters reinforces these boundaries by distinguishing the text from its larger narrative sequence. Finally, the change of action/plot constitutes a definitive break from what precedes and from what follows. This analysis of the dramatic criteria demonstrates that the P-C episode (Acts 10:1—11:18) is one coherent and independent narrative unit. Let us now see if literary criteria will confirm this conclusion.

LITERARY CRITERIA

While literary (or stylistic) criteria are not essential for the delimitation of a text in narrative criticism, they are nevertheless useful in the process of discerning the beginning and the end of a text. Some literary criteria can also help identify the internal linguistic and stylistic features which strengthen the unity of the micro-narrative. There are four literary criteria relevant to this study which will be examined: transitional summaries, introductory formulae, shift in vocabulary, and change of literary genre.[10]

Transitional Summaries

In a narrative episode transitions play a significant role in connecting a series of scenes to form one micro-narrative. Sometimes a transitional verse(s) can function simultaneously as a summary and as a transitional conclusion of an episode or a scene.[11] At times such a transition is obvious. For instance, Acts 9:31 is clearly a narrative summary and a transitional

---

10. Mlakuzhyil (*Christocentric Structure*, 87–88) classifies the literary criteria under twelve headings: 1) conclusions; 2) introductions; 3) inclusions; 4) characteristic vocabulary; 5) geographical indications; 6) chronological indications; 7) liturgical feasts; 8) transitions; 9) bridge-passages; 10) hook-words; 11) techniques of repetition; 12) change of literary genre (narrative, dialogue, discourse).

11. See Mlakuzhyil, *Christocentric Structure*, 103–4.

conclusion which brings the church's mission to another stage.[12] Likewise, Acts 9:42–43 serves as a summary and a transitional conclusion, possibly to get Peter to Joppa, where he will be near to Cornelius,[13] but more likely to create a smooth transition to the P-C episode.

There are other summary statements which also serve as introductions to new episodes or scenes. Acts 11:19 is one of them. The description in Acts 11:19 ("Now those who were scattered because of the persecution") is clearly a transitional summary marking the beginning of a new scene which refers back to the persecution after the death of Stephen and the scattering of Christians from Jerusalem in Acts 8:1–4.[14]

Introductory Formulae

Attention to the introductory formulae can also be helpful in isolating a micro-narrative from its narrative sequence. The expression *anēr de tis . . . onomati . . .* ("Now there was a certain man . . . named . . .") in the Acts of the Apostles usually indicates the beginning of a new episode or scene (5:1; 8:9; 9:10, 36; 18:24). It is noticeable that the narrator creatively utilizes this type of introductory formula to divide the narrative sequence of Acts 9:32—11:18 into three separate sub-units: 9:32–33 (Aeneas in Lydda); 9:36 (Tabitha in Joppa); 10:1 (Cornelius in Caesarea).

Another introductory formula which the narrator often uses to introduce a new thematic unit is *oi men oun* plus participle (8:4, 25; 9:31; 11:19; 15:30; 23:31). Thus, 11:19 (*oi men oun diasparentes*, "Now those who had been scattered") clearly introduces a new theme with a completely new cast of characters creating a clean break from the previous episode and beginning a new unit.

---

12. See Wall, *Acts*, 154.

13. See Talbert, *Reading Acts*, 104. Although the construction of *egeneto de* plus accusative with infinitive in acts 9:43 often indicates a beginning of a new scene (4:5; 9:32; 14:1), it can also function as a conclusion (11:26). For the grammatical reasons why Acts 9:43 cannot be part of Acts 10:1—11:18, see Lukasz, *Evangelizzazione e conflitto*, 40–41.

14. The dispersion resulting from the persecution led many Christians to preach the word outside of Jerusalem (Judea and Samaria in 8:1, 4; Phoenicia, Cyprus and Antioch in 11:19). Peter and the other apostles seemed to have remained in Jerusalem (8:1). It is from Jerusalem that Peter traveled to Lydda, Joppa, and Caesarea. The Petrine narratives (9:32—11:18) therefore are not part of the evangelization of the word, which was a consequence of the persecution mentioned in 8:1–4 and 11:19.

The Narrative Unity

Shift in Vocabulary

An independent micro-narrative usually has characteristic vocabulary of its own that can be distinguished from the neighboring units. To illustrate this point, I shall highlight some of the characteristic vocabulary of the P-C episode and compare it with the two neighboring units, namely, 9:32–42 and 11:19–26. The typical vocabulary of Acts 10:1—11:18 may be conveniently classified under the following headings: verbs of "saying;" verbs of "movement;" God; and Holy Spirit.

VERBS OF "SAYING"

Since the P-C episode is a relatively long narrative and one which involves a number of dialogues between different characters, the narrator cleverly uses a repertoire of verbs of "saying" to avoid the repetition of using the same verb and to make his narrative more dynamic and captivating for his readers. There are six different verbs of "saying" in the P-C episode: *legō* (13 times); *laleō* (8 times); *phēmi*, (3 times); *apokrinomai* (twice); *eksēgeomai* (once); *egeneto phōnē* (once).[15] These verbs of "saying" appear a total of twenty-eight times in Acts 10:1—11:18, while Acts 9:32–42 features only the word *legō* (twice) and Acts 11:19–26 uses only the word *laleō* (twice).[16]

VERBS OF "MOVEMENT"

Verbs of "movement" such as "going in," "going out," "standing up," "drawing near," and so forth, are found very frequently in the P-C episode. There are sixteen different verbs of movement employed thirty-seven times in this episode alone. Statistically speaking, almost every other verse describes some kind of movement through the use of one of these verbs. The list below will give us a clear picture of the dynamics of the verbs of "movement" that are at work in the P-C episode:

- to go, *erchomai* (10:29; 11:5, 12) = 3x
- to go into, *eiserchomai* (10:3, 24, 25, 27; 11:3, 8, 12) = 7x
- to go with, *sunerchomai* (10:23b, 45; 11:12) = 3x
- to visit, *proserchomai* (10:28) = 1x

---

15. *Legō* (10:3, 4 (2x), 14, 19, 21, 22, 26, 34; 11:8, 12, 13, 16); *laleō* (10:7, 44, 46; 11:3, 4, 14, 15, 18); *phēmi* (10:28, 30, 31); *apokrinomai* (10:46; 11:9); *eksēgeomai* (10:7); *egeneto phōnē* (10:3).

16. *Legō* (9:34, 40); *laleō* (11:19, 20).

Peter and Cornelius

- to go away, *ekserchomai* (10:23b) = 1x
- to go about, *dierchomai* (10:38) = 1x
- to go up, *anabainō* (10:4, 9; 11:2) = 3x
- to go down, *katabainō* (10:11, 20, 21; 11:5) = 4x
- to go, *poreuomai* (10:20) = 1x
- to come near, *engizō* (10:9) = 1x
- to get up, *anistēmi* (10:13, 20, 23b, 26, 41; 11:7) = 6x
- to draw up, *anaspaō* (11:10) = 1x
- to come up, *ephistēmi* (11:11) = 1x
- to travel, *hodoiporeō* (10:9) = 1x
- to raise, *egeirō* (10:26, 40) = 2x
- to take up, *analambanō* (10:16) = 1x

The list indicates a preference for verbs with prefixes, especially when using *erchomai* ("to go"). There are five prefixes added to the verb *erchomai* alone. Such frequent usage of prefixed verbs reveals a stylistic emphasis as well as the movements of certain characters.

Since Acts 9:32-42 is part of the narrative sequence of Peter's missionary journey through Judea, descriptions of movements are also necessary there. However in this episode the only verb used is *erchomai* with three prefixes: *dierchomai* (9:32, 38), *katherchomai* (9:32), and *sunerchomai* (9:39). Another noticeable difference is that movement is one-directional while in Acts 10:1—11:18 movement is more dynamic and contrasting: "going in" and "going out," "going up" and "going down." Similar to Acts 9:32-42, Acts 11:19-26 also employs only *erchomai* (11:20) and its prefixed relatives: *dierchomai* (11:19) and *ekserchomai* (11:25). The movement in this unity is also linear and one-directional rather than contrasting.

God

God (*ho Theos*) is mentioned twenty-two times in the P-C episode.[17] In approximately every three verses the word God (*ho Theos*) appears while in the preceding unit (Acts 9:32-42) there are no references to God, and in the

---

17. See 10:2 (2x), 3, 4, 15, 22, 28, 31, 33, 34, 38 (2x), 40, 41, 42, 46; 11:1, 9, 17 (2x), 18 (2x).

following unit (Acts 11:19-29) God is mentioned only once (11:23). Thus, the P-C episode is highly theocentric, while its surrounding units are not.

Holy Spirit

The Spirit or Holy Spirit plays a major role in the narrative of Luke-Acts. That role is accentuated in Acts 1–12, where the Spirit is mentioned thirty-seven times (the greatest number of occurrences in the New Testament). Acts 13–28, although one-third longer than Acts 1–12, contains only eighteen instances.[18] In the P-C episode the word Spirit (*pneuma*) or Holy Spirit (*pneuma hagion*) occurs eight times (10:19, 38, 44, 45, 47; 11:12, 15, 16). Acts 9:32–43 on the other hand has no reference to the Holy Spirit, while Acts 11:19–26 has only one occurrence (11:24). Clearly, Acts 10:1—11:18 highlights the importance of the work of the Holy Spirit and her role in initiating the evangelization of the Gentiles and their admission into the church.

Change of Literary Genre

In a narrative sequence the change of literary genres (narratives, dialogues, discourses, miracles, parables, and speeches) can serve as useful indicators of a break. In the Petrine narrative of Acts 9:32—11:18 the following changes of genre take place:

- Acts 9:32–35   miracle
- Acts 9:36–43   miracle
- Acts 10:1—11:18   scenic narrative[19]

The first two accounts (9:32–43) describe Peter's miraculous healings of Jewish Christians (one man, one woman), while Acts 10:1—11:18 is scenic narrative genre which intricately weaves together various genres, for example, apparitions (10:1–8, 9–16), dialogues (10:17–23a), and speeches (10:34–43; 11:4–14). In Acts 11:19–26 the literary genre switches to a straight narrative, where the narrator simply reports a series of events and

---

18. Schweizer, "Πνεῦμα," 404.

19. Licht (*Storytelling*, 29–30) distinguishes four modes of narrative: 1) straight narrative; 2) scenic narrative; 3) descriptive narrative; 4) comment narrative. Licht defines scenic narrative in this way: "The action is broken up into a sequence of scenes. Each scene presents the happenings of a particular place and time, concentrating the attention of the audience on the deeds and the words spoken" (29).

persecutions which are completely unrelated to the theme of the previous episode.

To sum up, the four literary or stylistic criteria (transitional summaries, introductory formulae, shift in vocabulary, and change of literary genre) confirm the delimitation of the text of Acts 10:1—11:18 as one independent micro-narrative. The analyses of the transitional summaries and introductory formulae demonstrate that Acts 10:1—11:18 is purposely arranged to separate its micro-narrative from what goes before and what follows. On the other hand the analyses of the characteristic vocabulary and its literary genre demonstrate that the micro-narrative is one coherent entity which is quite distinct from its surrounding units. While literary criteria alone do not validate the delimitation of our text, they contribute to the endeavor to mark the boundaries of the P-C episode.

CONCLUSION

Every story must have a beginning and an end. Similar to modern literature, the beginning of chapter one is clearly marked as "1.1 Introduction" and ends with "1.4 Conclusion." Unfortunately, biblical texts rarely provide titles or other structural indications. As a result dividing a text into independent units can be quite challenging. So where does the P-C narrative begin and where does it end? To answer this question I have employed dramatic and literary criteria to delimit our text. Analysis of the four dramatic criteria (change of place, time, characters, and action/plot) provided sufficient evidence that the P-C episode begins at 10:1 and ends at 11:18.[20] Analysis of the literary criteria (transitional summaries, introductory formulae, shift in vocabulary, and change of literary genre) confirmed that Acts 10:1—11:18 is an independent micro-narrative with one unifying plot.

---

20. Ska insists that "the unity is first of all a unity of action, a unity of plot. The narrative section finishes when the action is completed. It is therefore essential to analyse the main aspects of the plot and of its temporal structure to establish the limits of the narrative unit" (*"Our Fathers,"* 3).

2   *The Discourse*

Just as there is no form without content and no content without form, so also how a story is told is just as important as the story itself. The way in which a story is told contributes to its meaning and can evoke in the reader suspense, amazement, fear, surprise, or disinterest. The narrator has to use different literary techniques to hold the reader's interest; otherwise the reader will put down the book after the first few paragraphs or even sentences. Thus, this chapter will focus on how the narrator organizes the narrative discourse or rhetoric of Acts 10:1—11:18 in order to effect its meaning on the reader.

Applying the dramatic criteria of change of time, locale, character, and particularly plot (just as I have done in chapter 1), I will divide the P-C story into scenes, and in each scene I will analyze its modes of discourse and its point of view. Before I delve into text itself, it is important to discuss the theoretical elements of narrative (namely *story* and *discourse*) and the structure of narrative communication in order to grasp the mechanism of narrative criticism and to comprehend its approach.

THE NARRATIVE: STORY AND DISCOURSE

Every narrative is composed of two essential elements: the *story* and the *discourse*.[1] Although these two elements are intricately connected and cannot be completely separated in any narrative, distinguishing between these terms at the outset of this chapter is not only useful but necessary. In his highly acclaimed work on fiction and film, Seymour Chatman writes:

> [E]ach narrative has two parts: a story (*histoire*), the content or chain of events (actions, happenings), plus what may be called

---

1. Powell, *What Is Narrative Criticism?*, 23; Genette, *Narrative Discourse*, 27.

existents (characters, items of setting); and a discourse (*discours*), that is, the expression, the means by which the content is communicated.[2]

To simplify the matter, Chatman refers to the *story* as the "what" of the narrative and to the *discourse* as the "how" the story is told in order to achieve certain effects upon the reader.[3] Of the two aspects of the narrative, the discourse or the text is the only one available to the reader. Thus it is only through the discourse that the reader can acquire knowledge of the story.[4]

As the title of this chapter already indicates, it is exactly the *discourse* or the "how" of the story of Peter and Cornelius that will be examined in this chapter.[5] Jan Fokkelman is correct in saying that "when we learn more and more about how a story has been constructed and by what means, and learn to understand what the purpose is behind all those techniques and structures, we will have penetrated deeply into the meaning and values of the text."[6] But before we actually analyze the narrative discourse of Acts 10:1—11:18, allow me to examine the structure of narrative communication to see how it fits in with the narrative unity of Luke-Acts.

THE NARRATIVE COMMUNICATION OF LUKE-ACTS

One of the fundamental questions that narrative critics seek to answer is: How does the author or the sender communicate his message to the reader or the receiver? Although this question deals with the theoretical model of narrative communication, I will not go into this, since many narrative

---

2. Chatman, *Story and Discourse*, 19.

3. Ibid. Unfortunately the usage of the terms "story" and "discourse" are not used uniformly among narrative critics. The French critics who follow Genette, for example, use "histoire" and "recit," while the Russian Formalists use "fabula" and "sjužet." The Anglo-American new critics (for example, Chatman and Sternberg) use "story" and "discourse." To help clarify the confusion, Ska provides a chart of the terms used by different authors. See Ska, *"Our Fathers,"* 6.

4. Rimmon-Kenan, *Narrative Fiction*, 4.

5. There is also another element in narrative which Genette calls *"narration"* (*Nouveau Discours*, 10). Rimmon-Kenan translates Genette's three narrative aspects as: story, text, and narration (*Narrative Fiction*, 3). On the other hand, Funk refers to narrative as: story, discourse, and performance. Funk defines performance as the act of narrating or telling. See Funk, *Poetics*, 3.

6. Fokkelman, *Reading Biblical Narrative*, 28.

critics have already dealt sufficiently with it.[7] However, a good point of departure would be to clarify the technical terminology in order to show how the narrative of Luke-Acts is transmitted from the sender to the receiver.

The narrative transaction can simply be divided into two "facets": the facets of the sender or the teller (real author, the implied author, and the narrator) and the facets of the receiver (the narratee, the implied reader, and the real reader).[8]

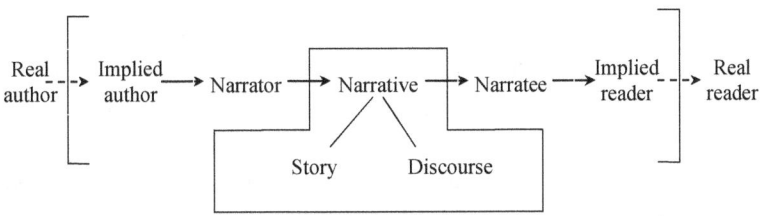

Figure 2.1

The diagram above shows how a story is transmitted from the author to the reader. Although the real author and the real reader fall outside of the narrative transaction (as indicated by the brackets), they are nevertheless indispensable in the narrative transaction in a practical sense (as indicated by the arrow with the dotted lines).[9] To help understand the dynamics of the narrative transaction of Luke-Acts, I will first define each of these elements in an elementary way in order to lay the ground work for the analysis of the narrative discourse of the P-C episode.

THE FACETS OF THE SENDER

The "Real" Author

The real author is the historical figure, whether an individual or a group, who is actually responsible for writing the story and who exists outside of

---

7. See Chatman, *Story and Discourse*, 15–42; Culpepper, *Anatomy*, 6–11; Rimmon-Kenan, *Narrative Fiction*, 86–105; Marguerat and Bourquin, *How to Read*, 3–17.

8. The term "facet" is borrowed from Funk, *Poetics*, 29 and 34. Synonymous to the term "sender" is "dispatcher." See Marguerat and Bourquin, *How to Read*, 4; Grilli, "Autore e lettore," 447–59.

9. For further explanation, see Chatman, *Story and Discourse*, 146–51; Rimmon-Kenan, *Narrative Fiction*, 86–89. For a more complete diagram, see Culpepper, *Anatomy*, 6.

the narrative or text; as such he or she does not enter into the field of narratology. In the case of Luke-Acts, the real author is none other than Luke himself.[10]

The "Implied" Author

Unlike the real author, the implied author is not a real flesh-and-blood figure but rather the image of the real author which can be reconstructed by the reader from the narrative strategy that the real author uses, such as in his structure and style, description of the characters, and systems of values, judgments and world-views. Obviously one can discover and reconstruct the portrait of the implied author only through an analysis of the text.[11] So who is the persona projected by the real author in the text of Luke-Acts? William Kurz, in his pioneering analysis of the works of Luke-Acts through the view of the narrator, has deciphered four essential aspects: 1) *histor*; 2) Christian apologist; 3) master of Hellenistic and biblical styles; and 4) travel companion of Paul.[12]

The first aspect of his persona that the real author of Luke-Acts reveals is that of an historian. As stated in the prologue of Luke 1:1-4, he is a careful historical investigator who, after having collected the evidence, arranged it into a unified narrative. Secondly, the repeated use of the first-person plural throughout Luke-Acts, for example, "events fulfilled among us,"[13] reveals that the implied author is an insider or a Christian. The third aspect of his persona revealed in Luke-Acts is his self-presentation as a master of both Hellenistic and biblical styles of Greek. The elegant Greek of Luke-Acts, particularly in the prologues, demonstrates that he is well educated and a professional writer. The fourth and final aspect of the persona that the real author reveals about himself is found in the "we-sections" of

---

10. Since the discussion of the authorship of Luke-Acts has been a focus of scholarship and research over the centuries, I will not contribute to this debate. For details concerning this topic, see the bibliographies of Fitzmyer, *Acts*, 162–87; and Powell, *What Are They Saying about Luke?* 141–51.

11. Booth (*Rhetoric of Fiction*, 71–76) coined the term "implied author." See also Ska, "Our Fathers," 41; Marguerat and Bourquin, *How to Read*, 12–15; Culpepper, *Anatomy*, 15.

12. Kurz, *Reading Luke-Acts*, 10–12. For the social location of the implied author, see Robbins, "Social Location," 305–32.

13. Luke 1:1; especially in the "we-sections" of Acts 16:10–17; 20:5–15; 21:1–18; 27:1–28.

Acts 16:10—28:16, where the implied author becomes an eyewitness and a companion on Paul's later journeys.[14]

The Narrator

The narrator is not the author but a literary device which the author uses to tell the story and to tell it in a certain fashion.[15] In other words the narrator is the "voice" which the real author uses to guide the reader in the narrative and which provides a proper perspective from which to view a certain action or event.[16] Fokkelman creatively describes the role of the narrator as follows:

> The narrator draws those lines and selects those details, right down to the smallest, that suit him. He is the boss of a complete circus. He is like a juggler who keeps a lot of balls in the air at the same time. He structures time, sketches space, brings characters on and takes them off again, misleads the reader at times, and enforces his point of view through thick and thin.[17]

The narrator of Luke-Acts is creative and dynamic. First of all, he makes himself known explicitly in the prologues as a *self-conscious narrator* speaking to the reader in the first-person singular ("I," Luke 1:1-4; Acts 1:1-2) and in the first-person plural ("we," Acts 16:10—28:16).[18] In the prologues and the "we-sections," the narrator of Luke-Acts utilizes the strategy of telling that interrupts the flow of the narrative; in other words, he is *intrusive*.[19] Outside of the prologues and the "we-sections," however, the narrator switches to the strategy of showing which is characteristic of biblical narratives whose narrators are omniscient as well as omnipresent.[20]

---

14. For a more detailed discussion, see Kurz, *Reading Luke-Acts*, 10-12; Witherington, *Acts*, 51-60.

15. Rhoads et al., *Mark as Story*, 39.

16. For a discussion on the different aspects of the narrator, see Booth, *Rhetoric*, 169-209; Chatman, *Story and Discourse*, 196-262; Culpepper, *Anatomy*, 15-49.

17. Fokkelman, *Reading Biblical Narrative*, 55.

18. Sternberg, *Expositional Modes*, 254. See also Culpepper, *Anatomy*, 17; Kurz, "Narrative Approaches," 205-6.

19. See Abrams, *Glossary*, 134: "With this mode the intrusive narrator is one who not only reports but freely comments on his characters, evaluating their actions and motives and expressing his views about human life in general; ordinarily, all the omniscient narrator's reports and judgments are to be taken as authoritative."

20. Kurz, "Narrative Approaches to Luke-Acts," 206. Culpepper describes omniscient narrators as those who give the reader inside views of what a character is thinking,

Although omniscient and omnipresent, the narrator of Luke-Acts is not unreliable; as a matter of fact, he actually appears "as an authoritative, trustworthy guide, and serves as a model witness to and for the reader."[21] The final characteristic of the narrator in Luke-Acts is that he is oral. Influenced by the oral traditions of many biblical narratives, the narrator of Luke-Acts composes his narratives in ways which are most effective for oral communication through proper sound, harmony, and rhythm for the story is intended to be heard rather than to be read silently.[22]

THE FACETS OF THE RECEIVER

The Narratee

As in the case of the sender, the receiving end of the narrative transaction can also be divided into three facets, the first of which is the narratee. The narratee is the one whom the narrator addresses (either explicitly or inexplicitly) in the text. For example, in Luke 1:1–4 and in Acts 1:1–2 the narrator addresses his two-volume work to "Theophilus," an "overt narratee,"[23] who after the prologues disappears completely from the narrative. Although Theophilus is probably a historical person and is the overt narratee of Luke-Acts, he simply symbolizes a wider audience.[24] It seems obvious that the real author wants his narrative to be read by more readers than just Theophilus.

The "Implied" Reader

Similar to the implied author, the implied reader is not a real flesh-and-blood figure but rather the image or the ideal reader who shares the same perspective and values of the author and whom the author invites to

---

feeling, or intending which none of the characters could easily convey to the reader (*Anatomy*, 21–26). Chatman defines omnipresence as "the narrator's capacity to report from vantage-point not accessible to characters, or to jump from one to another, or to be in two places at once" (*Story and Discourse*, 103).

21. Darr, "Narrator as Character," 57. See also Tannehill, *Narrative Unity*, 2:7. For an opposing view see, Dawsey, *Lucan Voice*; Dawsey, "Literary Unity," 46–66.

22. Perhaps the P-C story is composed intentionally for oral communication; unfortunately however it is beyond the scope of this thesis to dwell on this issue. For further discussion, see Dawsey, *Lucan Voice*, 32; Kurz, *Reading Luke-Acts*, 178.

23. Tannehill, *Narrative Unity*, 2:9. Other examples can be found in Mark 13:14; John 19:35; 20:30–32.

24. Kurz, "Narrative Approaches," 211–12.

perform the act of reading.[25] The narrative of Luke-Acts gives us numerous clues about the implied readers.[26] William Kurz's analysis of the narrators and narrative gaps in Luke-Acts has revealed that the intended readers of Luke-Acts are primarily Christians.[27] Furthermore, in order to understand the implications of the many narrative gaps in Luke-Acts, the intended readers must have had a good knowledge of Christian doctrine and catechesis as well as familiarity with the Greek Old Testament. Otherwise they could not fully understand the indirect allusions nor supply the necessary connections in order to fill in the gaps.[28]

The "Real" Reader

The real reader is the one who actually engages in the act of reading or listening whether or not he or she is explicitly addressed by the real author.[29] Like the real author, the real reader remains outside of the field of narratology.

In summary, since every act of communication according to Roman Jakobson involves a sender (author), a message (text), and a receiver (reader),[30] understanding the structure of narrative communication will reveal the focus of our analysis. The results of an investigation depend largely on where one's focus is located on the axis of communication. Historical-criticism, for example, seeks to discover the intention of the author by reconstructing the world behind the text by means of various traditional methods such as source, form, and redaction criticism. In other words, the historical-critical reading of a text focuses on the author.

Narrative criticism on the other hand does not focus on the author but on how the author communicates the message to the reader. Narrative critics are interested in investigating the effect of the text on the reader by asking: How does the narrator compose and structure the scenes? What

---

25. See Iser, *Implied Reader*; Culpepper, *Anatomy*, 205–27.

26. Since the topic of the Lukan audience and its social location has been thoroughly explored by historical and redaction critics, I will not contribute to this debate. For a detail discussion, see any of the standard commentaries.

27. Kurz, *Reading Luke-Acts*, 12–16.

28. Ibid., 16. See also Dawsey, *Lucan Voice*, 15–32.

29. If the one who is reading is addressed directly by the real author, for example "Theophilus," that person is distinguished as the "first reader-hearer."

30. Marguerat and Bourquin, *How to Read*, 3–17; Powell, *What is Narrative Criticism?*, 1–10.

is the function of dialogue in the narrative? What is the purpose of the repetitions? What knowledge is communicated to the reader and what is concealed? How does the narrator introduce the characters and how are they developed? What is the point of view of the narrator and of the characters? What are the modes of its discourse? Answering these questions is the first step in discovering the meaning and the purpose of the P-C story to which we now turn.

THE ANALYSIS OF THE DISCOURSE OF ACTS 10:1—11:18

Being one of the longest narrative units in the New Testament, the P-C story has a structure which is multifaceted and therefore quite complex to decipher.[31] While some scenes are easy to distinguish, others are more complex, especially when the narrator uses subtle narrative devices. For this reason, the first task of our analysis is to divide our text into its proper scenes using the dramatic criteria of change of time, locale, character, and plot. The text of each scene appears below, line by line.[32] All the direct speeches are indented. On the right side of the text I will list various narrative codes to identify the characters that are involved and some of the important rhetorical nuances and techniques. During the course of this analysis these narrative codes will be identified and fully explained; however, to avoid potential confusion it is highly recommended that the reader consult the Table of Narrative Codes whenever one is not clear.[33]

Scene i—"The Vision of Cornelius" (10:1–8)

Characters:	C =	Cornelius
	A =	Angel
	(M) =	Messengers of Cornelius
Time:		Day One (ninth hour)
Place:		Caesarea (in Cornelius' house)

---

31. One only has to examine different commentaries to see that the structure proposed by different authors reveals the complexity of this narrative. For a good presentation of these structures, see Lukasz, *Evangelizzazione e conflitto*, 43–47; Handy, "Gentile Pentecost," 5, n. 8.

32. The translation is my own.

33. The Table of Narrative Codes is found in appendix A. Many of these narrative codes are borrowed from Funk, *Poetics*, xiii–xv.

The Discourse

Introduction

10:¹ Now in Caesarea	*lchg/ls*
there was a man named Cornelius,	C
a centurion from the Italian Cohort,	*desc*
²a devout and God-fearing man	*com*
along with all his household,	
who gave alms generously to the people	
and prayed to God constantly.	

Nucleus

³About the ninth hour of the day,	*ts*
he clearly saw in a vision	
an angel of God coming in	A
and saying to him,	
"Cornelius."	
⁴He stared intently at him with fear and said,	C
"What is it, Lord?"	
And he said to him,	A
"Your prayers and your alms	
have ascended as a memorial before God.	
⁵Now send men to Joppa	
and summon a certain Simon who is called Peter.	
⁶He is staying with Simon, a tanner,	
whose house is by the sea."	

Conclusion

⁷When the angel who spoke to him had left,	*dep*
he called	
two of his house servants and a devout soldier	(M)
who were his personal attendants,	
⁸and after he had told them everything,	*recap*
he sent them to Joppa.	*dis*

NARRATIVE CODES

lchg	local change (an explicit shift in locale)
ls	local setting
desc	description

Peter and Cornelius

com	commentary of narrator
ts	temporal setting
dep	departure (often marks conclusion of scene)
recap	recapitulation
dis	dismissal
( )	character is patient rather than agent of the event

SCENIC INDICATORS

This scene begins with an explicit shift in character and in locale (*lchg*). A complete new character is introduced: Cornelius. The local setting is now Caesarea. In verse 3 the narrator also informs the reader about the temporal setting of the scene (*ts*), namely the "ninth hour" of the day. At the conclusion of *scene i*, the narrator uses various techniques to bring the scene to closure. First, the narrator tells the reader that one of the characters, namely the angel, departs (*dep*), a clear indicator that the scene is about to end. Secondly, the narrator recapitulates (*recap*) the whole scene, which has the function of defocalizing a narrative segment.[34] Thirdly, the narrator ends the scene by dismissing (*dis*) the characters. These literary indicators demonstrate that *scene i* (10:1–8) is a coherent and unified scene with a new set of characters, located in Caesarea (in the house of Cornelius), and taking place on a certain day (for practical reasons I identify it as day one) at the "ninth hour."[35]

MODES OF DISCOURSE

Scene i is a self-contained scene with an *introduction* (vv. 1–2) which serves as the "focalizing process,"[36] a *conclusion* (vv. 7–8) which serves as the "defocalizer," and a *nucleus* (vv. 3–7) which consists of a series of actions that constitute an event (for example, "the vision of Cornelius"). The modes of the discourse of *scene i* are composed of a mixture of "showing" (*mimesis*)

---

34. See Funk, *Poetics*, 116–17. Defocalizing process reverses the focalizing process by dispersing the characters, expanding the space, lengthening the time frame, or introducing a terminal function. See Funk's glossary, 304.

35. The ninth hour (three in the afternoon) is believed to be a set time for prayer. See Johnson, *Acts*, 182.

36. Funk describes the function of the "focalizing process" as bringing a set of participants together in a specific time and at a particular place, while the "defocalizer" is a narrative device that reverses the focalizing process and brings the story to narrative rest (*Poetics*, 60–74).

The Discourse

and "telling" (*diegesis*).³⁷ The introduction is clearly narrated in the "telling" mode. Right from the start (vv. 1–2) the narrator gives a description (*desc*) of who Cornelius is, "a centurion from the Cohort called the Italica." Beginning in verse 3, however, the mode of discourse changes to "showing." In other words, instead of continuing to tell us who he is, the narrator shows the reader who Cornelius is by describing the scene in vivid detail, allowing the reader to witness and experience what Cornelius himself experiences. In the *conclusion* (vv. 7–8) the narrator returns to the "telling" mode to summarize the scene and to disperse its characters in order to prepare for the next scene.

POINT OF VIEW

The term "point of view" can be broadly defined as the position or perspective from which a story is told.³⁸ To borrow a metaphor from cinema, biblical narratives are like film filtered through the eye of a camera. The camera may zero in on a particular character or object, or it may zoom out to give a panoramic view of the event or situation. Similar to the eye of the camera, biblical narrators employ various techniques to give the reader different points of view of the story.³⁹ Discovering the perspectives of the narrator therefore will allow the reader to enter into a deeper level of the story. According to Jean-Louis Ska, one enters into the "third dimension" of the narrative.⁴⁰

There are three major perspectives or points of view in a given narrative: external focalization, internal focalization, and zero focalization.⁴¹ In

37. The classical terms of "showing" and "telling" are *mimesis* and *diegesis*. For a more in-depth study, see Genette, *Narrative Discourse*, 161–211; Chatman, *Story and Discourse*, 32–34; Ska, "*Our Fathers*," 53; Booth, *Rhetoric*, 67–148; Funk, *Poetics*, 134–61.

38. Berlin, *Poetics and Interpretation*, 46. The discussion on point of view is quite complex (as Ska rightfully points out) partly because the terminology employed by different literary critics is not always consistent (Ska, "*Our Fathers*," 66–67).

39. This metaphor is borrowed from Berlin, *Poetics and Interpretation*, 44. Funk uses the term "point of view" or "perspective" while Genette and Rimmon-Kenan use "focalization."

40. Ska, "*Our Fathers*," 79. Furthermore, Ska writes, "When one misses the "perspective" of a narrative, one sees only a flat, two-dimensional surface."

41. Genette proposes the more abstract term: "focalization" instead of "point of view." See Genette, *Narrative Discourse*, 188–89; Ska, "*Our Fathers*," 66. Different from Genette, Chatman describes point of view in three different senses: perceptual, conceptual, and interest points of view (*Story and Discourse*, 151–53). Uspensky (*Poetics*, 6) on the other hand categorizes point of view according to four "planes": ideological, temporal and

the external point of view the narrator tells the story as an outside observer looking at a scene or at a character; in other words, the narrator says less than the character knows. In the internal point of view the narrator tells the story from the perspective of one of the characters, who reveals what he sees, hears, and feels; in other words, the narrator says only what a given character knows. In zero focalization, the narrator uses his privilege of omniscience to communicate crucial information to the reader; in other words, the narrator knows more than the character or says more than any character knows.[42]

Scene i contains all three points of view. In the *introduction* (vv. 1–2) the narrator acts as an omniscient observer telling (*com*) the reader that Cornelius is a devout and God-fearing man who gives alms to the people and prays to God constantly. This is a perfect example of zero focalization where the narrator intervenes to give essential data to the reader about one of the main characters. Thus right from the start the narrator tries to establish his position as authoritative and reliable. Whether or not the reader accepts him as authoritative and reliable remains to be seen.

At the beginning of verse 3, the narrator abruptly shifts his perspective to an internal point of view, that of Cornelius. This point of view continues throughout the entire *nucleus* (vv. 3–6). In these few verses the narrator gives the reader an inside view of what Cornelius is seeing, hearing and feeling. First, Cornelius "clearly" (*phanerōs*) saw the angel "coming to him." Furthermore, we are told that Cornelius "stared intently" (*atenisas*) at the angel. According to the narrator this was no illusion, for what Cornelius saw took place in broad daylight.[43]

Secondly, the reader gets to hear the dialogue between Cornelius and the angel. Cornelius' question, "What is it, Lord?" shows that he recognizes the angel as someone special. Therefore he addresses him with deep respect. The response of the angel, "Your prayers and your alms have gone up as a memorial before God," confirms the narrator's comments about Cornelius in the introduction. In other words, the reader hears the angel himself commenting on the character of Cornelius. Thirdly, the narrator

---

spatial, phraseological, and psychological points of view. See also Culpepper, *Anatomy*, 21–34. I find Genette's presentation clearer and more useful for interpreting biblical narratives. Since I have adopted Genette's methodology, for consistency's sake I will also adopt his terminology.

42. Genette, *Narrative Discourse*, 188–89; Ska, "Our Fathers," 65–81.

43. Conzelmann (*Acts*, 81) says that "the mention of the time of day shows the reader that a delusion is excluded."

gives the reader a glimpse of how Cornelius felt. We are told that this veteran soldier became "terrified" (*emphobos*).

In the *conclusion* (vv. 7–8) the narrator shifts to an external point of view where the narrator simply describes the scene as an outside observer without giving details as to what Cornelius and the messengers are hearing, thinking and feeling. As a matter of fact the narrator even conceals crucial information from the reader by keeping the reader in the dark as to what Cornelius said to the messengers and why he has to summon Peter. This information will be revealed gradually (10:22, 33; 11:14), giving more suspense to the story.

Scene ii—"The Vision of Peter" (10:9-16)

Characters:	P = Peter
	V = Voice
	(M) = Messengers of Cornelius
Time:	Day Two (sixth hour)
Place:	Joppa (Housetop of Simon the tanner)

Introduction

⁹The next day,	*ellip/tchg*
as they were on their way	(M)
and were drawing near the city,	*lchg*
Peter went up to the housetop	P ls
around the sixth hour to pray.	ts

Nucleus

¹⁰He became hungry	P
and wanted something to eat.	*com*
And while they were preparing for the meal,	
he fell into a trance.	
¹¹He saw the heaven opened	
and a certain object	
like a large piece of cloth descending	
and being lowered to the earth by four corners;	
¹²in it there were all kinds of four-legged animals	
and reptiles of the earth, and birds of the sky.	
¹³Then he heard a voice saying to him,	V

Peter and Cornelius

"Rise, Peter; slaughter and eat."
¹⁴But Peter replied,   P
"Certainly not, sir,
for I have never eaten anything
profane and unclean."
¹⁵The voice again spoke to him a second time,   V
"What God has made clean,
you must not call unclean."

Conclusion

¹⁶This happened three times   *iter*
and immediately the object was taken up to heaven.   *dep*

Narrative Codes

ellip   ellipsis
tchg   temporal change (an explicit shift in time)
iter   iterative narration

Scenic Indicators

This scene opens with the phrase "the next day," which signals an explicit shift in temporal change (*tchg*). Moreover, the temporal setting (*ts*) of this scene is "around the sixth hour." The local setting has also changed (*lchg*) for the scene is no longer in Caesarea but in Joppa, on the "housetop" (*epi to dōma*) of Simon the tanner. The cast of characters in this scene is also different. The two dominant characters are Peter and the voice from heaven. Although the messengers are mentioned in the opening scene, they are not agents but are merely patients who act as narrative links and will play a more active role in the next scene. This scene comes to a closure with the departure (*dep*) of the object "going up to heaven." Thus, all the indicators clearly show that *scene ii* (10:9–16) is one coherent and unified scene focusing on Peter having a vision that takes place in Joppa on the roof top of the house of Simon the tanner around the sixth hour of the second day.

Modes of Discourse

Like the previous scene, *scene ii* is self-contained; it is made of an *introduction* (v. 9), a *nucleus* (vv. 10–15), and a *conclusion* (v. 16), with a mixture of "telling" and "showing." *Scene ii* begins with an ellipsis (*ellip*), since hours have passed within the story world even though the narrator does not report it. The narrator simply tells the reader that it is now "the next day," but the reader must conclude that twenty-four hours have already passed.[44] After having quickly situated the messengers in Joppa and Peter on the rooftop, the mode of discourse abruptly shifts from "telling" (*introduction*) to "showing" (*nucleus*). In the *nucleus* the discourse time is dramatically slowed down to the same pace as the narrative time in order to emphasize its importance and significance.[45] The mode of discourse changes back to "telling" in the *conclusion* (v. 16). In a recounting mode the narrator summarizes Peter's vision through the use of an iterative narration technique (*iter*) which reports only once an experience which happens "three times."[46] This implies that Peter resisted the command of God not once but three times.[47] The effect of the different pace in the narration of this scene is quite noticeable. The less important events are compressed or accelerated (speeded up, e.g. v. 9), whereas the more important events or conversations are given in detail or decelerated (slowed down, e.g. vv. 10–15).[48] Paying attention to these subtle nuances in the narrative can help the reader enter into a deeper level of the story and will pave the way for fruitful interpretation.

Point of View

Like a camera, *scene ii* opens up with a wide-angle shot from above capturing the arrival of Cornelius's messengers and Peter going up to the "housetop" to pray "around the sixth hour." The perspective of the *introduction*

---

44. "Ellipsis" refers to instances when discourse time stops while narrative (story) time continues. Time in narrative has three aspects: order, duration, and frequency. Order deals with the question "when?", duration with "how long?", and frequency with "how often?" For a full discussion, see Genette, *Narrative Discourse*, 33–160. For a good summary, see Rimmon-Kenan, *Narrative Fiction*, 43–58; and Culpepper, *Anatomy*, 53–75. For a concise definition of the elements in narrative time, see Powell, *What is Narrative Criticism?*, 36–40.

45. Narrative (story) time is the duration of the actions and events in the story (measured in seconds, minutes, hours, days, etc.); discourse (narration) time is the material time necessary to tell the narrative (measured in words, sentences, lines, paragraphs, etc.). For an excellent distinction between these potentially confusing aspects of the narrative and a more complete bibliography of this issue, see Ska, "Our Fathers," 7–15.

46. Contrary to iterative narration is "multiple-singular narration" which reports repeatedly an event that happens repeatedly. See Powell, *What is Narrative Criticism?*, 39.

47. Perhaps the narrator is making a reference to Peter's denial of Jesus in Luke 22:34, 54–62.

48. Rimmon-Kenan, *Narrative Fiction*, 56.

Peter and Cornelius

(v. 9) is therefore external, since the narrator simply observes at a distance without revealing Peter's thoughts or motives. The perspective however quickly changes as the camera gradually zeroes in on Peter (v. 10) and reveals even his inner cognition ("becoming hungry") and volition ("wanting to eat"). This is an example of zero focalization, where the omniscient narrator knows the character's thoughts and reveals his desires. Though the comment (*com*) of the narrator is brief (v. 10), he communicates crucial information to the reader, since the knowledge of Peter's hunger and desire to eat appropriately sets the stage for his vision and the meaning behind it.[49] In verse 11 the narrator shifts to an internal point of view and describes the event with vivid details and dramatic effect, showing Peter repeatedly resisting the command of God to eat even though he is famished.[50] Although the narrator does not reveal the inner thoughts and feelings of Peter, the scene ends mysteriously, leaving Peter and also the reader perplexed and confused with the still-echoing words: "What God has made clean, you must not go on calling unclean" (v. 15).

Scene iii—"The Events at Simon's House" (10:17–23a)

Characters:	M = Messengers of Cornelius
	P = Peter
	HS = Holy Spirit
Time:	Day Two
Place:	Joppa (House of Simon the tanner)

Introduction   *(Subscene iiia: "Outside at the Gate")*

¹⁷Now while Peter was greatly puzzled	(P)	tc
about the meaning of the vision that he had seen,		
behold, the men sent by Cornelius	M	
inquired the house of Simon		lc
and stood at the gate.		ls
¹⁸They called out asking,		
"Is Simon, the one called Peter, staying here?"		

Nucleus   *(Subscene iiib: "Up on the Roof")*

¹⁹While Peter was pondering about the vision,	P	lchg

---

49. Haenchen, *Acts*, 347.
50. Johnson, *Acts*, 185.

The Discourse

the Spirit said to him,	HS (P)
"Behold, three men are looking for you.	
²⁰Now, stand up!	
Go down	
and travel with them without hesitation,	
because I have sent them."	

(Subscene iiic: "Down at the Gate")

²¹And Peter went down to the men and said,	P(M)	lchg
"Look, I am the one you are looking for;		
what is the reason for which you have come?"		
²²And they said,	M	
"Cornelius, a Centurion,		desc
a just man and God-fearer,		repet
who is well spoken indeed		
by the whole nation of the Jews,		
was instructed by a holy angel		
to summon you to his house		
and to hear what you have to say."		

Conclusion   *(Subscene iiid: "Inside the House")*

²³ªSo he invited them in	P (M)	lchg
and showed them hospitality.		

Narrative Codes

tc   temporal connective (with link to preceding narrative)
lc   local connective (with link to preceding narrative)
repet   repetitive narration

Scenic Indicators

Like a film in cinematography *scene iii* (vv. 17–23a) is artistically narrated from different locations, angles, and perspectives. Since it is intricately weaved together, it is not easy to notice its subtle indicators and changes. Therefore, I have divided it into four subscenes. *Subscene iiia* (vv. 17–18) begins with a "wide-open shot" which shows Peter still on the roof top (*lc/tc*) pondering the meaning of the vision while the messengers are arriving at the gate (*ls*) and inquiring for Peter. Immediately the eye of the camera zooms in on Peter and on the Spirit, who informs Peter of the arrival of the visitors whom the Spirit has sent. In this *subscene iiib* (vv. 19–20) the characters are Peter and the Holy Spirit, and the location is the rooftop. Obeying the command of the Holy Spirit Peter goes down and outside to the gate.

Subscene iiic (vv. 21–22) takes place at a new location (*lchg*) with a different cast of characters. Then the reader is told that Peter invites the messengers inside (*lchg*) and offers them hospitality. Though this is narrated in very few words, nevertheless it functions as *subscene iiid* (vv. 23a), for the location now has moved inside the house. In short, the spatial arrangement of *scene iii* shows the following movement: outside, up, down, and inside. The following diagrams will help clarify the division of the four subscenes.

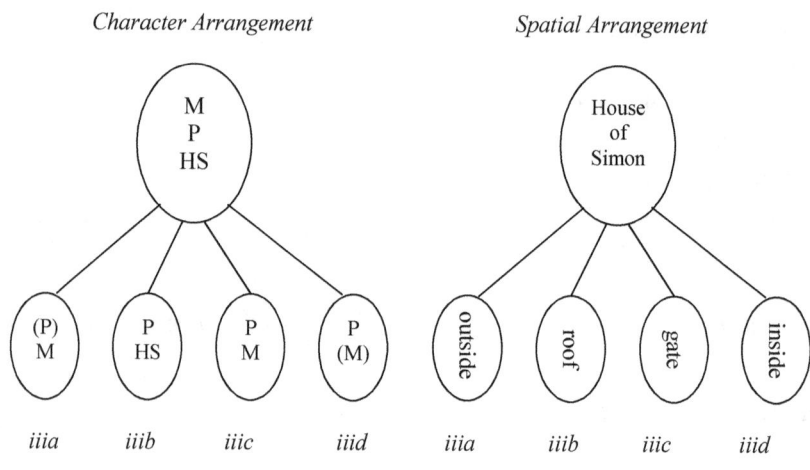

FIGURE 2.2

MODES OF DISCOURSE

The events and actions of *scene iii* are predominantly shown (*mimesis*) rather than told (*diegesis*). In other words, the narrator's role in this mimetic scene is reduced to that of the camera. As such the event is presented with sufficient "objectivity" to allow the reader to witness the event directly and with minimum intervention of the narrator.

In *subscene iiia* (vv. 17–18) the narrator presents the arrival of the messengers of Cornelius with dramatic effect by asking a direct question: "Is Simon, the one called Peter, staying here?"[51] Meanwhile Peter is ponder-

---

51. The *ei* in Greek can be used as a direct question which is intended here in this verse; furthermore, the presence of the adverb *enthade* "here" rather than *ekei* "there"

ing over what he has just seen and heard. This subscene obviously functions as the *introduction* of *scene iii* as well as a bridge that links to the next *subscene iiib* (vv. 19–20). Here Peter is still pondering over the vision when the Spirit intervenes and tells him that "three men" are looking for him.[52]

Again in *subscene iiic* there is direct speech between Peter and the messengers of Cornelius. In this subscene narrative time and discourse time are at an even pace. All of the sudden, however, the mode of discourse switches to "telling" in *subscene iiid* (v. 23a). Although it is short, this subscene is packed with meaning and significance. Earlier I commented that important scenes are ordinarily enacted in detail and sometimes in slow motion; however, what we have here in *subscene iiid* is evidently an exception, for it functions as the "punch line" of the entire scene.

Point of View

In this scene the narrator employs a number of techniques which give the reader a many-faceted perspective to the story. As an omniscient and omnipresent narrator he is capable of reporting from vantage points not accessible to the characters in the story. He jumps from one locale to another and at times is even in two places at once. Thus it is difficult to locate exactly where he stands. In *subscene iiia* the omnipresent and omniscient narrator gives the reader an internal point of view of Peter on the rooftop puzzling over his vision (a "bird's eye" view) and at the same time allows the reader to see (with "split-screen" vision) the messengers arriving at the gate and to hear their direct question. Although the reader hears their question, Peter (still lost in the previous vision) does not hear the question at all.

The omniscient narrator continues to employ the internal point of view in *subscene iiib*. The reader is allowed to experience Peter's perplexity and to hear clearly the command of the Spirit telling Peter to go down to meet the strangers at the gate—whom no one seems to know about except

---

reaffirms that a direct question is intended. See Barrett, *Acts*, 1:510; Conzelmann, *Acts*, 82. For a different view, see Fitzmyer, *Acts*, 457.

52. Instead of *treis* (P⁷⁴ ℵ A C E *al*), Codex B reads *duo* ("two") and a few others (D Ψ *al*) does not indicate any specific number. The reading of codex B is probably influenced by verse 7, where the author considered the soldier as only a guard and not as one of the messengers. As for the shorter text where there is no numerical number, it too is probably influenced by verse 5 where no specific number is mentioned. My preference lies with the present text of N-A²⁷ due to the weight of the attestation of the external evidence. For a more detailed assessment of these variant readings, see Metzger, *Textual Commentary*, 328.

the narrator and the reader. Though Peter still does not understand why, he obeys and goes down and outside to the gate to meet these strangers.

In *subscene iiic* the omniscient narrator skillfully exposes why Peter is summoned to Cornelius' house by having Peter asked the question himself. One must remember that this information has been kept hidden from Peter as well as from the reader. The response of the messengers begins with a repeated description (*repet*) of Cornelius which corresponds closely to what the narrator had said in verse 2—but with some additional information. From the point of view of the messengers the reader now knows that Cornelius is not only "devout" (v. 2) but also "just" (*dikaios*) and "well spoken of by the whole nation of the Jews" (v. 22). The messengers also describe the angel as being "holy" (*hagiou*). Finally the messengers reveal important information which is a direct response to Peter's question: "to hear words (*rēmata*) from you."[53] The meaning of *rēmata* here will be gradually revealed in the following scenes.

The perspective of the final *subscene iiid* changes to an external point of view where the narrator says nothing about what the characters perceive and experience. Like a camera the narrator objectively shows Peter inviting the three messengers in and giving them hospitality. Perhaps the "punch line" here is described minimally and neutrally in order to allow the reader to make an observation and a judgment about Peter's action. An uninformed reader might miss the dramatic effect here. For by inviting the three messengers into the house and showing them hospitality, Peter is clearly breaking the law of purity.[54] Yet at the same time he is also obeying the order of the Spirit, namely to treat them "without discrimination" (v. 20). Is Peter's action justifiable? The narrator hopes that the reader will side with Peter's conclusion that to treat people impartially is in perfect accordance with the will and purpose of the Spirit.

Summary of Act One

As it has been demonstrated *scenes i, ii,* and *iii* are artistically arranged through the use of different scenic indicators, diverse modes of discourse, and various points of view. Each scene is beautifully weaved into the whole while still dependent on the other scenes to provide meaning and

---

53. *Akousai rēmata para sou* can be colloquially translated as "to hear what you have to say."

54. A fuller discussion on the purity system is developed in the next chapter.

The Discourse

progression. Together they tell the first phase of the P-C episode which I call *Act One*.

In Act One the omnipresent and omniscient narrator works like a camera capable of reporting from any angle, locale and perspective (whether internal or external). This allows the reader to observe from the outside or to enter into the narrative and experience what the characters themselves see, hear, feel and even think.

The narrative analysis of the discourse of Acts 10:1–23a reveals that this section functions as the introduction of the main characters and the theme of impartiality. The narrator clearly accentuates this theme throughout the narrative: treating people impartially is fully in accordance with God's will and purpose.[55] Thus Act One can be structured as follows:

Scene i: "The Vision of Cornelius" (10:1–8)
Scene ii: "The Vision of Peter" (10:9–16)
Scene iii: "The Events at Simon's House" (10:17–23a)
    Subscene iiia: "Outside at the Gate" (10:17–18)
    Subscene iiib: "Up on the Roof" (10:19–20)
    Subscene iiic: "Down at the Gate" (10:21–22)
    Subscene iiid: "Inside the House" (10:23a)

Scene iv—"The Journey to Caesarea" (10:23b-24a)

Characters:	P = Peter
	M = Messengers of Cornelius
	B = Brothers from Joppa
Time:	Day Three—Day Four ("the next day and the following day")
Place:	On the road (from Joppa to Caesarea)

23bThe next day,		tchg; ellip
he got up and went away with them,		P
and some of the brothers from Joppa	(M)/B	lc
accompanied him.		
24aAnd on the following day,		tc; ellip
they entered Caesarea.		lchg

---

55. See Johnson, *Acts*, 187; Haenchen, *Acts*, 358; Barrett, *Acts*, 1:491. While following God's will is an overall theme not only of Acts and also of this story, an even more important theme is impartiality.

Peter and Cornelius

Scenic Indicators

This scene begins with the phrase "now on the next day" (*tē de epaurion*) indicating clearly a temporal change (*tchg*) separating this scene from the previous. Verse 24a also has another exact temporal indicator *tē de epaurion*; however this indicator should not be taken as a temporal change but rather as a temporal connection with the first *tē de epaurion* in verse 23b.[56] In other words the narrator has set this scene in a narrative time frame of at least twenty-four hours. During this period of time (day three and day four of our story) Peter, the messengers and the brothers from Joppa spend their time together on the road traveling from Joppa (*lc*) to Caesarea (*lchg*). Though most critics do not consider this as a separate scene, narrative analysis shows that it is a traveling scene which serves as a transition to the next scene. Though it is short and contains few details, it still serves as one coherent scene.[57]

Modes of Discourse

This scene is purely a "telling" (*diegesis*) scene where the narrator uses very few words or discourse time to summarize an event that takes more than twenty-four hours of narrative time. The presence of the two ellipses (*tē de epaurion*, vv. 23b, 24a) gives the pace of the narrative an added acceleration. Obviously the narrator is in a hurry to get the characters to Caesarea, for that is where the central action will take place. Although the narrator doesn't give much detail in this scene, much is implied. While the messengers of Cornelius took less than one day to travel the 50 km to Joppa, the return trip takes nearly two days.[58] Though the narrator does not report it, the reader knows that this caravan must have stayed overnight somewhere along the way.[59] It is interesting that while the narrative discourse is narrated with great speed the characters travel slowly and seem to take their time.

---

56. The *de* here should not be interpreted as an adversative but rather a connecting *de*.

57. Many critics consider this traveling scene as part of scene four (10:23a–33); see Haenchen, *Acts*, 358–59; Bruce, *Acts*, 257–60; Lukasz, *Evangelizzazione e conflitto*, 42–47.

58. Bruce suggests that the messengers left early on day two and rode on horseback to get to Joppa by noon (*Acts*, 254). Haenchen however suggests that the messengers must have walked in the late afternoon of day one and arrived by noon the next day (*Acts*, 347).

59. The narrator informs us later that the number of brothers from Joppa is six (11:12), which makes the company a total of ten people. See Bruce, *Acts*, 258.

Point of View

In this traveling scene the narrator employs an external point of view which observes the characters at a distance without disclosing anything about their thoughts, feelings, and motives. The reader is completely left in the dark as to what went on during this long journey from Joppa to Caesarea. The reader does not know if they conversed with each other, if they ate together along the way, where they spent the night, and how they slept.

Scene v—"The Events at Cornelius' House" (10:24b–48)

Characters:	C = Cornelius
	P = Peter
	HS = Holy Spirit
	(RF) = Relatives and Friends of Cornelius
	(B) = Brothers from Joppa
Time:	Day Four
Place:	At the house of Cornelius

Introduction   *(Subscene va: "The Meeting")*

²⁴ᵇNow Cornelius was waiting for them   C
and had called together
his relatives and close friends.   (RF)

Nucleus

²⁵When Peter entered,   (P)   *Ichg*
Cornelius met him;   C
falling down to his feet, he paid him homage.
²⁶But Peter raised him up and said,   P (C)
"Stand up!
I am only a man."

                              (Subscene vb: "The Dialogue")

    ²⁷As he conversed with him,   P (C)
    he went in   *Ichg*
    and found many people assembled together;   (RF)
    ²⁸so he said to them,
    "You yourselves know that it is forbidden
    for a Jew to associate with or to go to a Gentile,
    but God has shown me   *retro*

Peter and Cornelius

not to call any person profane or unclean.
²⁹For this reason, I came without objection
when I was summoned.
May I ask, then, why you sent for me?"
³⁰And Cornelius replied,   C
"Four days ago at this hour
I was keeping the ninth hour of prayer in my house,   tc/ts
and behold, a man stood before me   recap
in dazzling clothes.
³¹He said,
'Cornelius,   repet
your prayer has been heard
and your alms have been remembered before God.
³²Send therefore to Joppa
and summon Simon
who is called Peter;
he is staying in the house of Simon,
a tanner, by the sea.'
³³So I sent for you at once;
and you were kind enough to come.
Now then we are all present before God
to hear all that you have been commanded by the Lord."

(Subscene vc: "The Speech of Peter")

³⁴Then Peter began to speak   P
and said,
"In truth I realize that God shows no partiality,
³⁵but rather in every nation the one who fears him
and does righteousness is acceptable to him.
³⁶He sent the message to the children of Israel,
preaching the good news of peace through Jesus Christ
—he is Lord of all.
³⁷You know what has happened throughout Judea,
beginning in Galilee after the baptism
that John preached,
³⁸how God anointed Jesus from Nazareth,
with the Holy Spirit and power.
He went about doing good

The Discourse

and healing all those who were oppressed by the devil
for God was with him.
³⁹We are witnesses
of all that he did in the country of the Jews and in Jerusalem.
They killed him by hanging him on a tree.
⁴⁰But God raised him on the third day
and allowed him to show himself,
⁴¹not to all the people,
but to us who have been chosen beforehand by God
as witnesses, who ate and drank with him
after he rose from the dead.
⁴²He commanded us to preach to the people
and to testify that he is the one appointed by God
as judge of the living and the dead.
⁴³To him all the prophets bear witness
that everyone who believes in him
receives forgiveness of sins through his name."

(Subscene vd: "The Outpouring of the Holy Spirit")

⁴⁴While Peter was still speaking these things,
the Holy Spirit fell upon all those   HS
who were listening to the word.
⁴⁵And the circumcised believers   B
who had come with Peter were amazed
that the gift of the Holy Spirit had been poured out
even on the Gentiles,
⁴⁶for they heard them speaking in tongues
and praising God.

Conclusion   *(Subscene ve: "The Baptism")*

Then Peter said,   P
⁴⁷"Can anyone withhold the water
for baptizing these people,
who have received the Holy Spirit just as we have?"
⁴⁸So he ordered them to be baptized   (B)
in the name of Jesus Christ.
Then they asked him to remain for some days.   *termf*

Peter and Cornelius

Narrative Codes

recap   recapitulation
rep   report
retro   retrospective
termf   terminal function

Scenic Indicators

Scene v (vv. 24b–48) might once again remind us of the making of a film. In this long scene the narrator uses various literary techniques to change the angle of presentation, locale and perspective to give it a multi-faceted effect while still remaining one coherent scene.

Scene v opens with a different cast of characters situated in a new locale. The reader is told that Cornelius has been expecting the arrival of Peter and therefore has summoned his relatives and friends (RF) together. It is presumed that the waiting takes place inside the house (*lchg*); however, the initial meeting between Cornelius and Peter, *subscene va*, takes place outside at the entrance of the house of Cornelius. In *subscene vb* the narrator clarifies that Peter and Cornelius move inside the house as they continue their conversation (v. 27). After this subtle shift in locale between *subscenes va* and *vb*, the rest of the scene is situated inside the house of Cornelius. While there is a shift in the cast of characters (the Holy Spirit and the brothers from Joppa) in *subscene vd*, the two main characters throughout this scene are Peter and Cornelius. The temporal setting (*ts*) of this scene is on the fourth day around the ninth hour (v. 30). Finally *scene v* ends with a clean closure where the action is terminated (*termf*) and yet also expanded ("to remain for some days" v. 48b) so that the focus is blurred, and consequently there is a narrative rest.

Modes of Discourse

The narrator employs a mixture of "telling" and "showing" in this scene to draw attention to the meeting of Peter and Cornelius and the events that follow. *Scene v* is very important for it has taken the narrator twenty-five verses of discourse time and four days of narrative (story) time to get these two main characters to meet. The narrator must create a scene that is dramatically appropriate to the characters' anticipation and the reader's expectation. *Subscene va* clearly fulfills both of these requirements. In the *introduction* the narrator tells the reader that Cornelius has been expecting

Peter's arrival. Furthermore, the gathering together of all his friends and relatives shows that Cornelius had made all the necessary arrangements to give Peter a grand welcome. Evidently this is not going to be just a family or private matter but a public affair. The narrator has Cornelius meet Peter personally at the entrance of the house and treat Peter as someone worthy of reverence.[60] And this is described in such a way (*mimesis*) that the reader can see how dramatic this moment is.

Subscene vb also makes good use of the mode of direct discourse. The reader overhears the dialogue between Peter and Cornelius. Peter first gives a brief speech and then asks Cornelius directly why he has been sent for. Cornelius's response is direct discourse in the first person singular. What is particularly significant in Cornelius's response (vv. 30–33) is that it is a recapitulation (*recap*) of his earlier experience of seeing an apparition (10:3–7). This reported speech is actually a scene set within a scene.[61]

Scene within a Scene

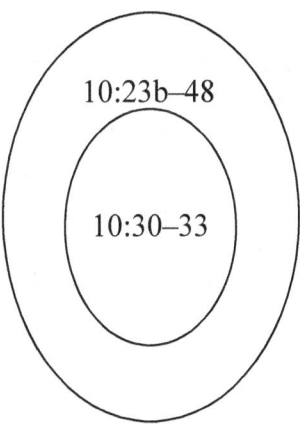

FIGURE 2.3

In this scene within a scene, Cornelius becomes a secondary narrator who narrates his own experience (10:30–33), which repeats what the primary narrator had previously reported (10:3–7). Though Cornelius

---

60. The verb *proskuneō* can mean "adore, worship." See Fitzmyer, *Acts*, 461; Johnson, *Acts*, 189; Bruce, *Acts*, 259.

61. See Funk, *Poetics*, 153.

recounts his earlier experience the scene is nevertheless mimetic, that is according to the "showing" mode of discourse.

Subscene vc (vv. 34–43) switches to *diegesis* or the "telling" mode. In this subscene the eye of the camera zeroes in on Peter as he gives his speech. Though it is in the form of a speech, Peter nevertheless also becomes a kind of second narrator, since he tells the story of Jesus. The discourse time and narrative (story) time in this subscene are noticeably decelerated, highlighting the importance of the message which Peter was summoned to proclaim.

While Peter is still speaking, the narrator interrupts Peter's speech and describes to the reader the event of the "Outpouring of the Holy Spirit." Though *subscene vd* (vv. 44–46) is climatic, it is recounted briefly and with very few details. One would imagine that this scene would be stretched out and portrayed more vividly so that the reader may see and hear what has transpired. Nevertheless, the narrator chose to be succinct and brief, perhaps to give the event more excitement, surprise, and drama.

The *conclusion* which is *subscene ve* (vv. 47–48) has a mixture of "showing" and "telling." Peter asks a rhetorical question which requires a negative response. The question is directed not only at the Christian believers in the scene but also at the reader. Without giving a response the narrator quickly changes the mode of discourse by telling the reader that Peter "ordered them to be baptized" (v. 48a).[62] Furthermore, the reader is told that Peter and presumably also his companions remained at the house of Cornelius "for some days." The discourse time in this subscene is noticeably accelerated. All the details of the baptism as well as what went on during those days at the house of Cornelius are left out. Perhaps the narrator wants to move quickly to the next scene.

Point of View

Subscene va begins with Cornelius and his household anxiously waiting for the arrival of Peter. When Peter finally arrives Cornelius goes out to meet him. So far the focalization is external, for the reader simply observes the scene from without and does not know how Cornelius knew the exact time of Peter's arrival.

---

62. Haenchen rightfully points out that Peter himself does not baptize (*Acts*, 354). Conzelmann also adds that the attitude that the apostles are above the office of baptizing corresponds to the traditional view (*Acts*, 84).

The Discourse

To resolve the issue of Cornelius' knowledge of the time of the arrival of Peter, the variant reading of the Western text (D it^{gig} syr^{hmg} mae)—which is noticeably much longer than the Alexandrian text[63]—adds: "And when Peter drew near to Caesarea, one of the servants ran ahead and announced that he had arrived. And Cornelius jumped up and..."[64] The reason for this elaboration in the Western text is probably to highlight the anxiousness of Cornelius and the importance of this meeting, and to resolve the difficulty of how Cornelius could have known the exact time of Peter's arrival.

When Peter begins to speak, the point of view changes to an internal focalization which allows the reader to hear the words of Peter who humbly explains to Cornelius that he is only a human being.[65] The reader of course is more aware of this than some of the characters in the story; yet by having Peter speak for himself the narrator highlights that even Peter recognizes that he is only an instrument of God.

In *subscene vb* (vv. 27–33) except for verse 27, the narrator employs predominantly an internal focalization through direct speech. This scene zeroes in on Peter and Cornelius. The dialogue begins with Peter acknowledging that he finally understands the meaning of the vision which he had; he is not to treat people with favoritism. Then Peter bluntly asks Cornelius why he was summoned. Cornelius responds by giving his own version of the story and by adding one important detail: "to hear all that you have been commanded by the Lord" (v. 33). In this dialogue the narrator is cleverly disguised behind the voice of the characters to relay new and repeated information to the reader.[66] Though the narrator's voice is not explicitly heard, it is nevertheless never silent.

---

63. Two texts of the Acts of the Apostles traditionally circulated in the early church, the Alexandrian text and the Western text. The former, which is characterized by its brevity and austerity and which is chiefly witnessed to by two very important codices (ℵ and B) is usually considered to be "the best text and the most faithful in preserving the original" (Metzger, *Textual Commentary*, 5). On the other hand, the Western text, which is chiefly witnessed to by codex D and is known for its fondness for paraphrase and expansion, is nearly ten percent longer than the Alexandrian text. The differences between these two texts are sometimes enormous and perplexing and therefore have provoked much discussion and conjecture over the centuries. For the most recent surveys of this discussion, see Metzger, *Textual Commentary*, 223–36; Strange, *Problem of the Text*, 1–34; Plümacher, "Acta Forschung 1974–82," 113–20.

64. Metzger, *Textual Commentary*, 329.

65. Cornelius' gesture demonstrates that Cornelius saw Peter as a heavenly figure. See Haenchen, *Acts*, 350; Barrett, *Acts*, 1:513.

66. For a discussion on "disguised narrator," see Booth, *Rhetoric*, 152.

Peter and Cornelius

In *subscene vc* (vv. 34–43) the narrator zeroes in on Peter and allows the reader to hear his full speech. This speech contains more information about the ministry of Jesus than Peter's earlier speeches had (Acts 2, 3 and 4) and alludes to scriptural references which the narrator presumes that the hearers as well the reader would recognize.[67] An analysis of this speech is forthcoming. For now it is sufficient to note that the speech of Peter is an example of the apostolic *kerygma* which the narrator summarizes.[68] While this speech is from the perspective of Peter, it is nevertheless the reliable and omniscient narrator who is communicating the implied author's ideological and evaluative norms to the reader.[69]

While Peter is still speaking, the narrator interrupts his speech (although obviously Peter has finished what he wanted to say) and dramatically recounts the coming of the Holy Spirit upon Cornelius and his household. In this *subscene vd* (vv. 44–46), the narrator uses his privilege of omniscience to communicate crucial information to the reader. It is zero focalization. First there is a panoramic description of this climactic event from the point of view of the reliable narrator, who immediately recognizes the presence of the Holy Spirit. Secondly, instead of allowing the reader to see and hear what actually happened, the narrator simply relates the event from the perspective of the believers from Joppa. The narrator intervenes to tell the reader that the believers are circumcised Christians. He also comments that they were "amazed" that even the Gentiles receive the gift of the Holy Spirit. Furthermore, the believers heard them "speaking in tongues and praising God."[70] It is interesting to note that this climactic event is told basically from the perspective of the minor characters. This is important, since they will become Peter's defense witnesses in Jerusalem.

In *subscene ve* (vv. 47–48) the narrator shifts to an internal focalization of Peter who asks a rhetorical question that expects a negative response. The question is addressed not only to the six circumcised Christians but also to the reader.[71] Since the outpouring of the Holy Spirit upon the Gentiles is a clear sign of God's acceptance and admission, no response is needed. Thus,

---

67. Tannehill, *Narrative Unity*, 2:141–42; Fitzmyer, *Acts*, 462–66; Dunn, *Acts*, 142–43.
68. Bruce, *Acts*, 261.
69. See Booth, *Rhetoric*, 158; Culpepper, *Anatomy*, 32–34.
70. The event reminds the reader of Pentecost. See Tannehill, *Narrative Unity*, 2:143; Dunn, *Acts*, 146.
71. Haenchen, *Acts*, 354.

The Discourse

Peter "ordered them to be baptized in the name of Jesus Christ."[72] Without much detail the narrator ends the scene with an external focalization allowing the reader to be an objective observer of the baptism and the hospitality that took place inside the house of Cornelius.

SUMMARY OF ACT TWO

Although *scenes iv* and *v* (vv. 23b–48) are two independent segments, they are nevertheless interconnected. Thus they can be grouped together as one act. In Act Two the reliable and omniscient narrator continues to employ various rhetorical techniques to bring Peter and Cornelius together and to recount the important events that take place inside the house of Cornelius. Like the eye of the camera, the narrator depicts different scenes from different angles and perspectives—sometimes close-in shots and sometimes a wide-angle view from a distance. He shifts from one perspective to another even setting aside his privilege of omniscience in order to adopt the perspective of one of the characters or to tell the events as a neutral observer.

The narrative analysis of the discourse of Acts 10:23b–48 can be structured as follows:

Scene iv: "The Journey to Caesarea" (10:23b–24a)
Scene v: "The Events at Cornelius' House" (10:24b–48)
    Subscene va: "The Meeting" (10:24a–26)
    Subscene vb: "The Dialogue" (10:27–33)
        Embedded Narrative: "Vision retold by Cornelius" (10:30–33)
    Subscene vc: "The Speech of Peter" (10:34–43)
    Subscene vd: "The Outpouring of the Holy Spirit" (10:44–46a)
    Subscene ve: "The Baptism" (10:46b–48)

Scene vi—"The Case in Jerusalem" (11:1–18)

Characters:	P = Peter
	AB = Apostles and Brothers
	CC = Circumcised Christians
Time:	Some time later
Place:	Jerusalem

---

72. In Acts baptism usually comes before the reception of the Holy Spirit (8:16), but here the order is exceptional. See Barrett, *Acts*, 1:530; Dunn, *Acts*, 146.

Peter and Cornelius

Introduction

11:¹Now the apostles and the brothers	AB
who were in Judea heard	lc
that the Gentiles had also accepted the word of God.	
²So when Peter went up to Jerusalem,	P ts/lchg
those who were circumcised took issue with him	CC
³saying,	
"Why did you go to the uncircumcised people	
and eat with them?"	

Nucleus

⁴Then Peter began to explain to them in order,	P
saying,	
⁵"I was in the city of Joppa praying,	repet
and in a trance, I saw a vision.	
A certain object like a great cloth	
descended and being lowered	
by its four corners from the sky,	
and it came close to me.	
⁶When I looked closely at it,	
I noticed and saw	
four-legged animals, wild beasts,	postpone
reptiles of the earth, and birds of the sky.	
⁷Then I also heard a voice saying to me,	
'Get up, Peter!	
Slaughter and eat.'	
⁸But I responded,	
'By no means, Lord,	
for nothing profane or unclean	
has ever entered my mouth.'	
⁹But the voice answered	
a second time from the heaven,	
'What God has made clean,	repet
you must not call profane.'	
¹⁰This happened three times,	
and then everything was drawn up again into the sky.	
¹¹Suddenly at that moment,	
three men, sent to me from Caesarea,	

The Discourse

appeared at the house where we were.
¹²The Spirit told me to go with them
without discrimination.
So the six brothers also went with me,   *postpone*
and we entered into the man's house.
¹³He told us
how he saw the angel standing in his house
and saying,
'Send to Joppa and summon Simon,
the one who is called Peter,
¹⁴who will tell you words by which
you and all your household will be saved.'   *postpone*
¹⁵As I proceeded to speak,
the Holy Spirit fell on them
just as it had upon us at the beginning.
¹⁶And I recalled the word of the Lord
how he had said,
'John baptized with water,
but you will be baptized by the Holy Spirit.'
¹⁷Therefore, if God gave them the same gift
as he had given us,
when we believed in the Lord Jesus Christ,
who was I to be able to hinder God?"

Conclusion

¹⁸When they heard this,
they became silent   CC   *termf*
and began to glorify God,
saying,
"God has granted even to the Gentiles   *constop*
the repentance unto life."

NARRATIVE CODES

postpone	postponement of information
constop	conversation stopper

Peter and Cornelius

SCENIC INDICATORS

This scene introduces a different cast of characters: apostles and brothers (*AB*), Peter (*P*), and the circumcised Christians (*CC*). The local setting has also changed from Judea to Jerusalem (*lchg*); however, by mentioning Judea, the narrator makes an explicit local connection (*lc*) between this scene and the previous. Although there is no temporal indicator, it is presumed that this event takes place some days or even weeks later. Just as this scene has a clean break in the *introduction*, it also has a clean closure at the *conclusion*. The phrase "they became silent and began to glorify God" (v. 18) clearly signals a closure. Furthermore, it is followed by another phrase, "God has granted even to the Gentiles the repentance unto life" (v. 18), which functions as a conversation stopper (*constop*) to bring the issue to a complete closure.[73] In short, the dramatic criteria clearly indicate that Acts 11:1–18 is a unified and coherent scene.

MODES OF DISCOURSE

Similar to previous scenes, *scene vi* is a self-contained scene with an *introduction* (vv. 1–3), a *nucleus* (vv. 4–17), and a *conclusion* (v. 18). In this scene the narrator likewise employs a mixture of "telling" and "showing." In the *introduction* the narrator simply reports the news that "the Gentiles had also received the word of God."[74] The reader is also informed that when Peter went up to Jerusalem, the circumcised Jewish Christians were concerned not over the issue of baptism but over Peter's going into the house of uncircumcised people and eating with them. Peter defends his case not by logical argument but simply by recounting both his own vision and the vision of Cornelius.

The "order" (*katheksēs*) in 11:4 is a narrative order of Peter's experiences that led him to change his mind about Gentile admission and integration. It is not the same order of events that occurred in chapter 10.[75] Although Peter is retelling the story, the mode of discourse is nevertheless mimetic—which makes the account vivid, real, and dramatic. While Peter's personal rendition of the story adds several important details which have been postponed until now, it is nevertheless very repetitive—almost to the

---

73. For more examples of conversation stoppers, see Funk, *Poetics*, 130.
74. According to Haenchen, this is a Lukan formula used to highlight that this conversion is not "an unimportant isolated case, but . . . a fundamental turning-point" (*Acts*, 354).
75. Tannehill, *Narrative Unity*, 2:144; Witherington, *Acts*, 363.

point of being redundant.⁷⁶ While Peter's vision is narrated only for the second time (in 10:9–16 by the narrator and in 11:5–10 by Peter), the vision of Cornelius has been told and retold four times.⁷⁷ The only difference is that this time it is told by Peter (11:13–14).

Besides being repetitive, Peter's personal account of his own vision is an embedded narrative, that is a scene within a scene.

Scene within a scene

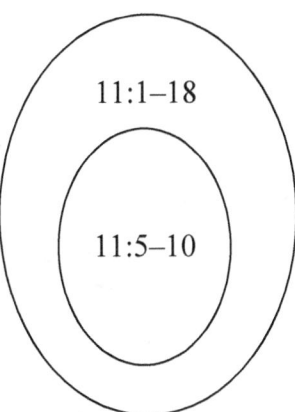

FIGURE 2.4

Thus there are two level narrative layers, for Peter is a secondary narrator who recounts his vision to the Jerusalem community in 11:5–10, which was first told by the primary narrator in 10:9–16.⁷⁸ Similar to *scene ii* (10:9–16) this scene within a scene is also narrated in the mode of showing (*mimesis*) "in the presence of an overt narrator."⁷⁹

The vision of Cornelius retold by Peter in 11:13–14 on the other hand is a scene within a scene within another scene.

---

76. For a full analysis of the repetitious details of this scene, see Witherup, "Cornelius," 45–66; Marin, "Essai d'analyse structurale," 39–61.

77. First by the narrator (10:1–8); second by the messengers (10:22); third by Cornelius himself (10:33–34); and finally the fourth time by Peter (11:13–14).

78. The narrative layers of this scene within a scene is similar to *scene vb* (see figure 2.3).

79. Funk, *Poetics*, 156.

Peter and Cornelius

Scene within a scene within a scene

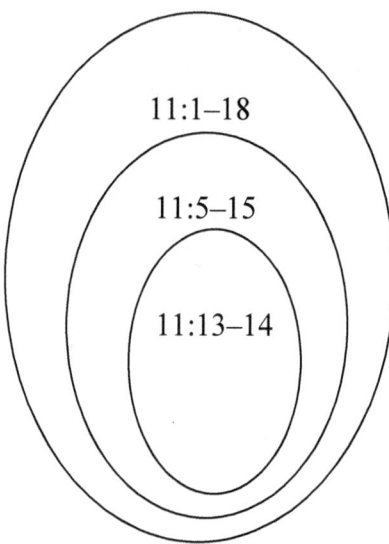

FIGURE 2.5

First, the narrator recounts the event in Jerusalem (11:1–18). Within this scene Peter recapitulates his own story of the event that has transpired in Judea to the circumcised party in Jerusalem (11:5–15). Finally, within this particular account Peter repeats Cornelius' vision (11:13–14). Though Peter's account of Cornelius' vision is an embedded narrative, it is still in the mode of *mimesis*.

By having Peter narrate Cornelius' vision, the narrator has created a complex scene with multiple levels of narration.[80] Consequently we are no longer dealing with a two-level narrative but with three. On the first level the author of Acts, who is an extradiegetic narrator, narrates the original event (10:1–8); on the second level Cornelius, who is an intradiegetic narrator, rehearses that event (10:30–33); and finally on the third level Peter, who is also an intradiegetic narrator, repeats Cornelius' account (11:13–14).[81]

---

80. For further detail on narrative layers, see Funk, *Poetics*, 30–34.

81. The "extradiegetic" narrator is the primary narrator who is external to the story; the "intradiegetic" narrator is the secondary narrator who is internal to the story. See Marguerat and Bourquin, *How to Read*, 27; Genette, *Narrative Discourse*, 228. Being unhappy with these two terms, Funk coined another three terms to describe the multiple

The Discourse

The levels of Cornelius' vision may be represented graphically in the following diagram.[82]

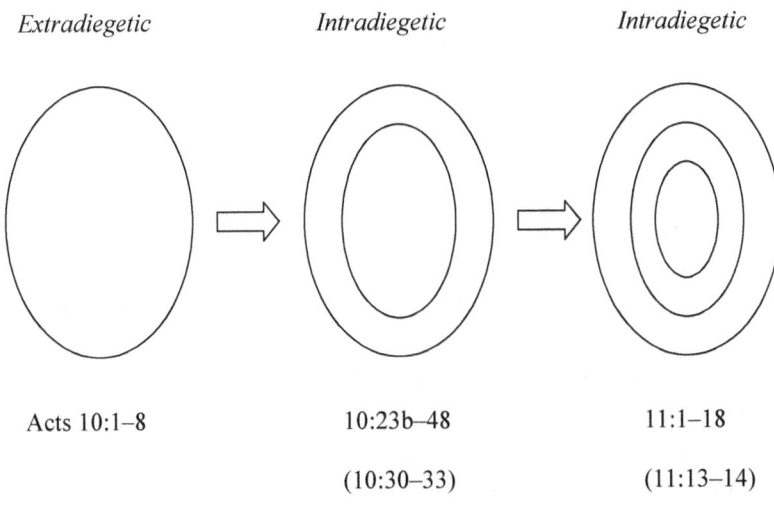

FIGURE 2.6

This illustration not only gives us a picture of the narrative layers of the vision of Cornelius but also of Acts 10:1—11:18. Briefly, when we speak of narrative layers we are dealing with narrative embedding (scenes within scenes) and with the relation of the narrators who tell the story. It should be recalled that when a narrator recounts his tale, he always belongs to the layer above the narrative being narrated.[83] Thus, in the P-C episode, Luke (an extradiegetic narrator) is above the first or the primary narrative; Peter (an intradiegetic narrator), while belonging to the first narrative, actually narrates a second or embedded narrative; and finally, Cornelius (another intradiegetic narrator) belongs to the second narrative but actually narrates a third narrative or the scene within a scene within another scene. This layering can be summed up in the following chart.

---

narrative layers: *hyperdiegetic, intradiegetic,* and *hypodiegetic.* For further clarification, see Funk, *Poetics,* 154, n. 33. I personally find Funk's terminology not very helpful.

82. This diagram is adopted from Funk, *Poetics,* 155.

83. For a fuller discussion on narrative layers, see Funk, *Poetics,* 30–34; Genette, *Narrative Discourse,* 227–31; Rimmon-Kenan, *Narrative Fiction,* 94–96.

Peter and Cornelius

Narrator	Narrative Layers
1. Luke (*extradiegetic*)	
2. Peter (*intradiegetic*)	1. The Episode of P-C (first narrative)
3. Cornelius (*intradiegetic*)	2. Peter's Defense (second narrative)
	3. Recap of Cornelius' Vision (third narrative)

There is another important element at work in these narrative layers which is the status or narrative authority that the narrator gives himself in relationship to the text. For example, if a narrator is present or makes himself explicitly known in the story that he relates, he is said to be *homodiegetic*. If however the narrator does not participate in the narrative or is absent from the story that he narrates, he is said to be *heterodiegetic*.[84] Thus, in relation to the P-C episode (Acts 10:1—11:18), Luke is an *extradiegetic/heterodiegetic* narrator who, although the primary narrator, remains absent from the narrative.[85] On the other hand, in Acts 11:1–18 Peter and Cornelius are *intradiegetic/homodiegetic* narrators, for although they are secondary narrators, they are present in the story that they relate.[86]

Point of View

Different from previous scenes where the omniscient narrator employs a mixture of internal and external perspectives, the presentation of *scene vi* (11:1–18) is predominantly internal focalization. In this scene the voice of the privileged omniscient narrator remains silent and unobtrusive, allowing the story to be told from the perspective of the characters. Outside of the *introduction* (vv. 1–3) and *conclusion* (v. 18), the internal focalization

---

84. *Homodiegetic* literally means "belonging to the same story," and *heterodiegetic* means "belonging to another story." See Funk, *Poetics*, 32; Rimmon-Kenan, *Narrative Fiction*, 95; Marguerat and Bourquin, *How to Read*, 25–28.

85. While it is true that Luke is an *extradiegetic/heterodiegetic* narrator for most of the narratives of Acts, he is also a *homodiegetic* narrator who makes himself explicitly known in the prologue (Acts 1:1–2) and the "we-sections" (16:10–17; 20:5–15; 21:1–18; 27:1—28:16).

86. See Funk, *Poetics*, 32–33. For a concise explanation of the levels and relationships of narrators, see Ska, "Our Fathers," 46–47.

is predominantly that of the *intradiegetic/homodiegetic* character-narrator, namely Peter (vv. 4–17).

In the *introduction* the narrator begins by giving the reader an internal focalization of what the apostles and the brothers have heard, namely "the Gentiles had also received the word of God." Then the eye of the camera zeroes in on the circumcised Jewish Christians, who in direct speech ask Peter: "Why did you go to the uncircumcised people and eat with them?"[87] Interestingly enough, the accusation does not come from the apostles and the brothers but only from the "circumcision party." Furthermore, the issue is not about baptism but about table fellowship with Gentiles.[88]

Now the eye of the camera focuses on Peter as he begins to recount his vision and the following events. Since the perspective is that of Peter, the order is according to the sequence that he had experienced and not necessarily the order of events recorded in chapter 10 (which was narrated by the primary narrator).[89] In this scene the reader is led through the sequence of events as Peter had experienced them so that he/she can share Peter's new insight and experience a similar change of mind about discrimination against the Gentiles.[90] From Peter's personal account the reader discovers three crucial details that have been postponed until now. First, the animals lowered from the sky included "wild beasts" (v. 6); secondly, the brothers from Joppa are "six" in number (v. 12); thirdly, the reason Peter was summoned was to speak "the words of salvation" (v. 14). Furthermore, though the charge was directed against him, Peter makes it quite clear through the

---

87. Instead of *eisēlthes . . . sunephages* some MSS read *eisēlthen . . . sunephagen* (P⁴⁵ B L 33 81 453 614 1175 *al*). The reason for this variant reading might be that copyists failed to recognize the idiomatic *hoti* which in later Greek may stand for *ti* ("Why . . . ?"). Therefore they changed the verb into the third person, where *hoti* can function as recitative introducing direct discourse, either as a statement (NAB, NIV) or as a question (RSV, NRSV). Taking this into consideration, I have chosen to follow the text of N-A²⁷ and to translate the *hoti* as an idiomatic *ti*. See Metzger, *Textual Commentary*, 338; and *BDAG*, 732.

88. Johnson might be correct in saying that, "The sting in the charge, of course, is found in the ancient symbolism of table-fellowship: to eat with someone is to share spiritually with them as well; by implication to eat with Gentiles is to collude to idolatry" (*Acts*, 197).

89. The order narrated by Peter is: 1) Peter's vision; 2) the arrival of the messengers and the Spirit's instruction; 3) Peter's meeting with Cornelius; and 4) Cornelius' vision. See Kurz, "Effects of Variant Narrators," 582.

90. Tannehill, *Narrative Unity*, 2:144.

usage of first person plural "we" (v. 12) that he was not the only one who entered the house of Cornelius.

Peter's recollection of the events inside the house of Cornelius differs greatly from what the primary narrator has reported. First of all, whereas the narrator says that the Holy Spirit fell upon the listeners "while Peter was still speaking" (10:44), Peter less accurately says, "as I began to speak" (11:15).[91] This minor discrepancy is probably due to the fact that as a character-narrator Peter can only relate his own perspective, which is limited and restricted in comparison to the privileged omniscient narrator. There is also another example where Peter is a restricted narrator. In the outpouring of the Holy Spirit, the omniscient narrator recounts the interior "amazement" of the witnesses from Joppa that "the gift of the Holy Spirit had been poured out even on the Gentiles" (10:45). In this particular scene Peter as a character-narrator could only relate his own perspective and could not probe into the minds and thoughts of the other characters. As a result, the outpouring of the Holy Spirit led Peter to remember the word of the Lord, "John baptized with water, but you will be baptized by the Holy Spirit" (v. 16). In short, although the narration of the repeated accounts by the omniscient narrator and the restricted character-narrator produces different results and explanations and thus might even cause some confusion and discrepancies, the combination of the two perspectives nevertheless enriches the reader's understanding of the one event.[92]

Another interesting element in the character-narrator is the usage of the "I-you-us" perspective. In verse 15 Peter points out that the Holy Spirit fell "upon them" (the Gentiles) in Caesarea in the same way as the Spirit fell "upon us" (the Jews) in Jerusalem. Furthermore, Peter reiterates in verse 17 that "if God has given *them* the same gift as he had given *us* when *we* believed in the Lord Jesus Christ, who was *I* to be able to hinder God?" Though the character-narrator is a third-person narrator, the "I-you" perspective of this limited narrator nevertheless adds a new dynamic to the

---

91. There are many explanations for this discrepancy. According to Haenchen, Luke does it in order to create an "unexpected and decisive effect" resulting from the coming of the Spirit (*Acts*, 355). Others propose that it serves to highlight the "divine initiative"; see Conzelmann, *Acts*, 86; Barrett, *Acts*, 1:541; Fitzmyer, *Acts*, 472. Kilgallen ("Did Peter Actually Fail?," 407) on the other hand proposes that *ērksato* (aorist of *archomai*) with infinitive of speaking never merely means "he began" but rather "he proceeded (to do)"; thus, Kilgallen concludes that "Acts 11,15 is to be understood, not to indicate the beginning moment of Peter's speech, but to say that Peter had entered upon his speech, when the Spirit descended."

92. Kurz, "Effects of Variant Narrators," 580.

story which the omniscient narrator could not do. An advantage of the character-narrator is the ability to be more personal and inclusive. When the character-narrator is reliable, which Peter certainly is, his testimony is solid, persuasive, and convincing.[93]

Peter's personal testimony leaves those who have accused him of breaking the law completely stunned, for they "became silent" and even "began to glorify God." The *conclusion* (v. 18) ends with the internal focalization of the circumcised Christians, acknowledging, "God has granted even to the Gentiles the repentance unto life."

SUMMARY OF ACT THREE

Scene vi (11:1–18) is clearly an independent scene separating itself from what comes after. While it has a clean closure indicating a narrative rest, it is nevertheless thematically connected to the previous scenes (Acts 10:1–48). The narrative analysis of this scene reveals that *scene vi* has two embedded narratives and so contains three narrative layers. The structure of Act Three can be summarized as follows:

> Scene vi—"The Case in Jerusalem" (11:1–18)
> Embedded Narrative: "Peter's Testimony" (11:5–17)
> Embedded Narrative: "Cornelius' Vision Recounted" (11:13–14)

In *scene vi* the primary narrator (*extradiegetic/heterodiegetic*) sets aside his privilege of omniscience by utilizing Peter as a reliable character-narrator (*intradiegetic/homodiegetic*) to recount the events that have transpired to the members of the church in Jerusalem. Although he is a limited and restricted narrator, Peter's personal testimony nevertheless enriches the story in ways which the omniscient narrator could not do. Furthermore, as a leader of the church he is reliable and therefore was able to persuade his accusers and the whole assembly in Jerusalem to change their minds and to declare publicly that Gentiles should be admitted into the church

---

93. Having thoroughly analyzed the effects of the various narrators in Acts 10–11, Kurz concludes: "The primary narrator has the dominant perspective, which in Acts bears a close relationship to the perspective of the implied author. The perspectives of the characters narrators like Peter and Cornelius are restricted to the perspectives appropriate to those characters, which are not necessarily those of the author. Yet repetitions by reliable narrators like Peter can contribute further perspectives more finally approximating the implied author's than the initial report by the primary narrator provided" ("Effects of Variant Narrators," 585).

and integrated into its life and practice. And as such, Jewish Christians are now free to associate and eat with Gentiles, for God shows no partiality. To refute this is to go against the will and purpose of God.

CONCLUSION

The narrative analysis of the discourse of Acts 10:1—11:18 has revealed that the style and structure of the P-C story can be divided into three acts with six scenes. Some scenes are subdivided into subscenes and/or contain embedded narratives. Thus, our analysis demonstrates the following narrative structure:[94]

Act One: The Visions

    Scene i: "The Vision of Cornelius" (10:1–8)
    Scene ii: "The Vision of Peter" (10:9–16)
    Scene iii: "The Events at Simon's House" (10:17–23a)
        Subscene iiia: "Outside at the Gate" (10:17–18)
        Subscene iiib: "Up on the Roof" (10:19–20)
        Subscene iiic: "Down at the Gate" (10:21–22)
        Subscene iiid: "Inside the House" (10:23a)

Act Two: The Event

    Scene iv: "The Journey to Caesarea" (10:23b–24a)
    Scene v: "The Events at Cornelius' House" (10:24b–48)
        Subscene va: "The Meeting" (10:24b–26)
        Subscene vb: "The Dialogue" (10:27–33)
            Embedded Narrative: "Cornelius' Vision Recounted" (10:30–33)
        Subscene vc: "The Speech of Peter" (10:34–43)
        Subscene vd: "The Outpouring of the Holy Spirit" (10:44–46a)
        Subscene ve: "The Baptism" (10:46b–48)

---

94. The division of the structure of Acts 10:1—11:18 differs greatly from one scholar to another, ranging from four, five, six, seven, and to eight scenes. For a comprehensive view and bibliography, see Lukasz, *Evangelizzazione e conflitto*, 42–47. For structure giving five subsections, see Fitzmyer, *Acts*, 447; for a seven-scene division, see Haenchen, *Acts*, 357–60; Lukasz, *Evangelizzazione e conflitto*, 45–47; Witherington, *Acts*, 146–365; and Witherup, "Cornelius," 51.

The Discourse

Act Three: The Debate and Resolution
> Scene vi: "The Case in Jerusalem" (11:1–18)
>   Embedded Narrative: "Peter's Testimony" (11:5–17)
>   Embedded Narrative: "Cornelius' Vision Recounted"
>   (11:13–14)

In general, the P-C episode can be compared to a Hollywood film. Like the eye of a camera, the narrator depicts different scenes from different angles—sometimes giving close-in shots and sometimes a "bird's eye" view from a distance. Using a "split-screen" technique he can even be in two places at the same time. Employing a mixture of the modes of discourse, he can either describe (telling or *diegesis*) the event as an objective observer or he can show (*mimesis*) the actions as they appear on the movie screen. Furthermore, he is capable of reporting from any perspective—from an external focalization which allows the reader to observe from the outside or from an internal focalization which allows the reader to enter into the narrative and experience what the characters themselves see, hear, feel and even think. The narrator can even set aside his privilege of omniscience to become a neutral observer and to allow a character-narrator to enrich the story in ways which an omniscient narrator could not employ without being intrusive.

The narrative analysis Acts 10:1—11:18 demonstrates that Luke as the primary narrator (*extradiegetic/heterodiegetic*) is omniscient and completely reliable. As an authoritative and unobtrusive narrator he shows that it is the will and purpose of God that Gentiles like Cornelius and his household should be admitted and integrated completely into the life and activity of the church without restriction. Since his perspective parallels that of the implied author, his point of view is completely trustworthy and therefore should be accepted by the reader just as it was accepted by the Peter and eventually by the Jerusalem church.

3   *The Settings*

EVERY NARRATIVE OCCURS WITHIN certain settings, and how the settings are arranged can determine the action of a story. Narrative settings can be described as the literary space within which characters move and act. As such, literary critics compare settings to adverbs in grammar: they designate where, when and how the action takes place—in the town or city, in the morning or the afternoon, with a man or a woman.

Likewise, the narrative settings of the P-C episode are not "incidental backdrops to events"[1] but rather serve multiple purposes and functions: creating the occasion for conflict through geographical movement, generating the mood and rhythm of narration, providing the appropriate social and cultural context for the plot and the actions of the characters. To disregard the settings of the P-C episode is to miss a great deal of the story as well as the intention of the implied author. Thus, in the present chapter we will analyze the P-C episode under three aspects of narrative settings: spatial, temporal, and social-cultural. It will become clear that a close scrutiny of the narrative settings of Acts 10:1—11:18 will heighten the interest and tension of the plot of the story.

SPATIAL SETTINGS

The P-C narrative is intricately arranged within multiple spatial settings. Each of the following verses defines the spatial location of the narrative action in a different way; each contributes to the spatial order:

- "Now there was a man in *Caesarea* named Cornelius . . ." (10:1).
- "And he saw the *heaven* opened and a certain object like a large piece of cloth descending and lowered upon the *earth* by four corners" (10:11).

1. Rhoads et al., *Mark as Story*, 63.

- "... and we entered into the man's *house*" (11:12).²

In 10:1 Caesarea, a city or a geopolitical location, is specified. In 10:11 two topographical features, heaven and earth, are mentioned. In 11:12 an architectural enclosure, the house, is cited. These three examples demonstrate the three types of spatial settings at work in the P-C episode: geopolitical space (regions, cities, towns), topographical space (physical features of the earth, such as the sea, wilderness, mountains, heaven, earth), and architectural space (human-made structures, such as house, synagogue, the temple).³

In this section, an analysis of the spatial settings of the P-C episode will be examined in great detail. Under each aspect I will do the following: identify the spatial markers (narrative facts), give some general observations of the semantic field, and examine their theological significance and functions.

Geopolitical Space

Elizabeth S. Malbon classifies the geopolitical space as "areas of the earth (*geo-*), which are defined by human-made boundaries of civic or governmental units (*-political*)."⁴ These spatial areas are named village, city, country, and region.

Narrative Facts

A careful examination of the narrative of Acts 10:1—11:18 reveals the following geopolitical facts:

- Caesarea (10:1, 24; 11:11)
- Joppa (10:5, 8, 23b, 32; 11:5, 13 [near the city, 10:9; 11:5])
- Judea (10:37, 39; 11:1)
- Galilee (10:37)
- Nazareth (10:38)
- Country of the Jews (10:39)
- Jerusalem (10:39; 11:2)

2. Translations and italics are mine.

3. For an excellent description of these three aspects of spatial settings, see Malbon, *Narrative Space and Mythic Meaning*, 15–140. See also Powell, *What is Narrative Criticism?*, 70–72; Marguerat and Bourquin, *How to Read*, 80–81.

4. Malbon, *Narrative Space and Mythic Meaning*, 15.

Peter and Cornelius

The list shows that there are seven geopolitical locations with a total of nineteen geopolitical references. The P-C episode begins by situating the narrative "in Caesarea" (10:1) where Cornelius and his household are residing. It is in this gentile city that the angel appears to Cornelius and sets the story in motion. The narrator then shifts the location to Joppa where Peter is praying on the rooftop of the house of Simon the tanner (10:9). It is here that Peter receives his vision and hosts the messengers of Cornelius (10:9–23a).

In 10:24 the geopolitical space is again shifted back to "Caesarea." It is in Caesarea that Peter and Cornelius meet face to face for the first time. In this pagan territory, Peter declares God's impartiality toward Gentiles (10:34) and witnesses the descent of the Holy Spirit poured out on the uncircumcised. As a result Peter does not hesitate to baptize these Gentiles and join them in table fellowship, an action which is ritually unacceptable. It is precisely because of Peter's table fellowship with Gentiles that the Jewish Christians will criticize him when he goes up to "Jerusalem" (11:2).[5]

Semantic Field and Significance

The three major geopolitical locations that have significant theological implications in the narrative settings of Acts 10:1—11:18 are: Joppa, Caesarea, and Jerusalem. In order to grasp their connotative significance, it is necessary to examine them.[6]

Joppa. The name Joppa is derived from the Phoenician word meaning "beauty" or "the beautiful." Joppa is located thirty-five miles west of Jerusalem and about thirty miles south of Caesarea.[7] Since antiquity the city

---

5. There are a few other geopolitical references which do not play an important role in the P-C episode. These geopolitical indicators are found in Peter's speech at Cornelius' house. In this speech Peter situates the ministry of Jesus Christ in a specific geopolitical location. Peter tells Cornelius and his household that Jesus is from "Nazareth" (10:38). Jesus came and proclaimed the good news of peace "beginning from Galilee" (10:37) and then "throughout the whole of Judea" (10:37). Peter also testifies all that Jesus did "in the country of the Jews" and "in Jerusalem" (10:39).

6. Since the semantic field of Joppa, Caesarea, and Jerusalem can be found in any major Bible dictionary, our examination will be brief and will be more on their significance in relation to the P-C episode.

7. Joppa is situated on the top of a hill along the coast of the Mediterranean Sea on the edge of the region of Judea, just south of modern Tel Aviv. In biblical times Joppa probably had a larger and better protected harbor which was formed by a natural breakwater. See Gold, "Joppa," 970.

When Solomon built the Jerusalem temple, timbers were shipped from Lebanon to

has been an oasis for travelers from Egypt heading north or those northern countries heading south. It was also the first stop for pilgrims on their way to Jerusalem.[8] Joppa is mentioned eleven times in the New Testament, and all references are exclusively found in Acts (four times in Acts 9 and seven times in the P-C episode).[9] It is to this far end of the region of Judea (practically the edge of the Jews' homeland) that Peter is summoned from Lydda to heal a disciple named "Tabitha, which means Dorcas" (9:36). In Joppa Peter stays "for many days with one Simon, a tanner" (9:43) which sets the stage for the P-C episode.[10]

Caesarea. Caesarea[11] is mentioned fifteen times in the New Testament, and all the references occur in the Acts of the Apostles.[12] According to Luke it was Philip the evangelist who first brought Christianity to Caesarea (8:40). Years later he and his four unmarried daughters, who apparently made up the nucleus of the Caesarea Christian community, hosted Paul before he went up to Jerusalem (21:8–9). For Paul, Caesarea is "the gateway" to the world and to universal mission (9:30; 18:22; 21:8, 16). It was in Caesarea that Paul was imprisoned for two years (57–59 CE) before he was judged by Festus and then sent to Rome for trial (23:33—27:1).[13]

While there were certainly Jews living in Caesarea in the first century, the population was predominantly Roman, and the culture and religion

---

Joppa, where they were unloaded and then transported overland to Jerusalem (2 Chr 2:15). The same procedure occurred when the Temple was rebuilt in the postexilic period (Ezra 3:7). It was in Joppa that the prophet Jonah ran away "from the presence of the Lord" (Jonah 1:3) by embarking on a ship to Tarshish. See Kaplan and Kaplan, "Joppa," 946.

8. Kaplan and Kaplan, "Joppa," 946.

9. Acts 9:36, 38, 42, 43; 10:5, 8, 9, 23b, 32; 11:5, 13.

10. R. W. Wall suggests that having situated Peter in Joppa Luke clearly alludes to the Gentile mission of Jonah in the Old Testament. Wall argues that the parallels between the two narratives are more than mere coincidence; they draw attention to the theological basis of the early church's Gentile mission. Furthermore, the function of Luke's allusion is to allow the audience "to understand and appreciate why Peter as bar Jonah would respond to God, to Cornelius, and to Jerusalem the way he did." See Wall, "Peter, 'Son' of Jonah," 82–84.

11. Known also as "Caesarea of Palestine," it was a major Greek and Roman port city on the Mediterranean Sea built by Herod the Great in honor of Caesar Augustus. When the Romans annexed Judea in 6 CE, Caesarea became the headquarters of the Roman administration and eventually the capital of Palestine. See Holum, "Caesarea," 206.

12. Acts 9:30; 10:1, 24; 11:11; 12:19; 18:22; 21:8, 16; 23:23, 33; 25:1, 4, 6, 13, 23 (literally the *city*).

13. Lukasz, *Evangelizzazione e conflitto*, 49-50; Hohlfelder, "Caesarea," 800.

were pagan.[14] As such, Luke portrays Caesarea as a distant land that does not even belong to the geographical territory of Israel.[15] According to Czeslaw Lukasz, Luke doesn't seem to include Caesarea within the three divisions of the land of Israel—Judea, Samaria, and Galilee. Lukasz writes,

> The "summary" in 9:31, which concludes the evangelization of "Judea, Galilee and Samaria," confirms that Luke does not directly connect Caesarea with the geographical regions of Israel. Being distant from both Judea and Samaria, it shows the historic truth that Caesarea was really a Hellenistic city, a city of the Gentiles, which was felt as foreign by the Jews.[16]

Therefore, it is not unusual for the reader to sympathize with Peter's hesitation when he is told by the angel to travel "without hesitation" (*mēden diakrinomenos*) from Joppa to this strange and foreign territory of Caesarea (10:20).

Jerusalem. Jerusalem plays an important theological role in Luke-Acts.[17] Luke's gospel begins (1:9) and ends (24:53) in the Temple of Jerusalem. The whole thrust of the Gospel is a "journey" toward Jerusalem: "When the days drew near for him to be taken up, he set his face to go to Jerusalem" (9:51; NRSV). The focus of Jesus' ministry is situated in the city of Jerusalem and the events that take place there.[18] Jesus' mission, including his passion, resurrection and ascension, is fulfilled in Jerusalem (24:50).

---

14. According to Josephus' description, Caesarea had all the principal elements of an up-to-date Hellenistic city: markets, paved streets, a theater for drama, pagan temples, elaborate sewer and water systems, a stadium for races (hippodrome), amphitheaters for gladiators, and an expansive harbor which was built to protect vessels from powerful coastal storms and currents. See Josephus, *JW* 1.408–415; *Ant* 15.331–41. See also Holum, "Caesarea," 206; Hohlfelder, "Caesarea," 798–802; Conzelmann, *Acts*, 81; Handy, "Gentile Pentecost," 110–11.

15. Hengel, "Luke the Historian," 116–19.

16. Lukasz, *Evangelizzazione e conflitto*, 50. The original Italian text is as follows: "Il "sommario" 9,31 che conclude l'evangelizzazione della "Giudea, Galilea e Samaria", conferma che Luca non collega direttamente Cesarea con le regioni geografiche d'Israele. Distanziandola sia dalla Giudea che dalla Samaria, rende la verità storica che Cesarea era una πόλις ellenistica, una città dei gentili, sentita come "straniera" dagli ebrei."

17. The name Jerusalem occurs more than 650 times in the Old Testament and more than 140 times in the New Testament (34 times in Luke; 66 times in Acts). Among the Synoptic Gospels, Luke gives far more prominence to Jerusalem than Matthew or Mark.

For the historical and theological significance of Jerusalem in the Old Testament, see King, "Jerusalem," 747–66; Burrows, "Jerusalem," 843–66.

18. Johnson, *Luke*, 14.

The Settings

Unlike the other evangelists, Luke narrates all Jesus' resurrection appearances in the vicinity of Jerusalem; furthermore, Jesus instructs his disciples to "stay in the city" (24:49). According to Luke Jerusalem is "the city of destiny for Jesus and the pivot for the salvation of [humankind]."[19]

While Jerusalem forms the geographical bridge that connects the narrative unity of Luke and Acts (Luke 24:47; Acts 1:8), the geographical movement in Acts is away from Jerusalem. Jesus commissions his disciples to bear witness to his name not only in Jerusalem but "in Judea and Samaria and to the end of the earth" (1:8). Nevertheless, Jerusalem is still the starting point of evangelization in the narrative of Acts (Acts 1–7). This evangelization then proceeds to Judea and Samaria (Acts 8–12), then Asia Minor and Europe, and finally Rome (Acts 13–28).[20]

While the programmatic mission of Acts is basically an outward movement from Jerusalem, Jerusalem still serves as the home base for missionaries and as a point of return (Acts 8:14; 11:1–18; 12:25; 15:2; 18:22; 19:21; 20:16; 21:13; 25:1). It is not a surprise therefore to see Peter returning to Jerusalem to report on the events that have transpired (11:1–2). Likewise Paul has to go up to Jerusalem to defend the church's actions in Antioch (15:1–21). Jerusalem obviously plays an important role in the narrative of Luke-Acts. The city with its sacred temple is the symbol of Israel and its people. It should be no surprise that Luke considers Jerusalem "as the city of destiny and the pivot for the word of God's salvation to the nations."[21]

The "Journey" Motif

Commentators have keenly pointed out that there is an overarching geographical perspective in Luke which does not merely report movement but rather has deep theological concerns.[22] While the purpose of the travel account (9:51—19:27) is to move Jesus from Galilee to Jerusalem, Luke also theologically depicts Jesus as the Son of Man "going his way, as it has been determined."[23] Likewise, in the Acts of the Apostles Luke frequently narrates the events of the Christian movement through the typical Hellenistic literary device of the "journey" motif. Luke relates a series of journeys made

19. Fitzmyer, *Luke I–IX*, 164.
20. Johnson, *Acts*, 15.
21. Fitzmyer, *Luke I–IX*, 168.
22. Robinson, *Der Weg des Herrn*; Conzelmann, *Die Mitte der Zeit*, 21–86; Bottini, *Introduzione*, 49–58.
23. Fitzmyer, *Luke I–IX*, 166.

by Peter (2:14—5:42; 9:31—11:18), Philip (8:4-40) and Paul (13:4—14:28; 15:36—18:1; 18:18—19:1; 20:1—21:16). Luke calls Christianity the "Way" (Acts 9:2; 16:17; 18:25-26; 19:9, 23; 22:4; 24:14, 22). The "journey" motif in Luke-Acts therefore "becomes a factor in the divine plan of salvation."[24]

A closer analysis of the geopolitical movements in the P-C episode reveals that the journey motif is highly accentuated, since the number of verbs of movement here is remarkable. The following verbs of movement (that is those indicating direction, such as "go, come, arrive, approach, travel") occur in the P-C episode:

- to go (*erchomai*) (10:29; 11:5, 12)
- to enter (*eiserchomai*) (10:3, 24, 25, 27; 11:3, 8, 12)
- to go away (*aperchomai*) (10:7)
- to go out (*ekserchomai*) (10:23b)
- to go with (*sunerchomai*) (10:23b, 45; 11:12)
- to go to (*proserchomai*) (10:28)
- to go around (*dierchomai*) (10:38)
- to come (*paraginomai*) (10:33)
- to go on the way (*hodoipoeō*) (10:9)
- to go (*poruomai*) (10:20)
- to come near (*eggizō*) (10:9)
- to have come (*pareimi*) (10:21)
- to come up (*enphistēmi*) (11:11)

Peter's journey in Judea. At the beginning of the Petrine narrative sequence (9:32—11:18) the narrator informs the reader that before Peter ends up in Lydda, a town situated between Joppa and Jerusalem, he first *travels* "here and there among all the believers" (9:32). Obviously Peter was going around Judea encouraging the faith of the new members of the nascent church. From Lydda Peter then *journeyed* to the farthest boundary that separates the Jewish homeland from gentile land—Joppa. It is in Joppa that Peter heals Tabitha, a disciple devoted "to good works and acts of charity" (9:36). Interestingly Peter does not stay with this model disciple but rather with a tanner named Simon. And so, it is from the edge of the Jewish

24. Ibid., 165.

homeland that Peter is summoned *to cross over* to the foreign and unclean land of the Gentiles—Caesarea.

Peter's journey to unclean territory. Peter certainly does not venture into the unfamiliar and risky territory of the unclean on his own initiative. Luke makes it clear that it is the Spirit who commands Peter: "Stand up! Go down and journey (*poreuou*) with them without hesitation for I have sent them" (10:20). The narrator does not tell the reader exactly when the messengers leave Caesarea, but they reach Joppa about noon, for Peter goes up to the housetop "around the sixth hour to pray" (10:9).[25] While the Spirit commands Peter to go "without hesitation," Peter does not embark upon the journey until the next day (10:23b).

Traveling with Peter and the three messengers are the six brothers from Joppa. Although the distance from Joppa to Caesarea amounts to only thirty miles (fifty kilometers), which can easily be covered in a day's journey, this odd group of travelers spends twenty-four hours together on the road.[26] Certainly Peter and his Jewish companions were hesitant in abandoning their familiar and sacred homeland in order to venture into unfamiliar and unclean territory. For Peter and his companions this journey was not just a geographical movement across a landscape but had theological significance and implications, namely, the breaking of traditional boundaries set by the purity code that separated clean and unclean territory, people and things.[27]

Peter's journey back to Jerusalem. Peter's missionary journey begins (2:14) and ends (11:2) in Jerusalem. Having traversed beyond the borders of the Jewish homeland and having witnessed the extraordinary works of the Holy Spirit in the land of the Gentiles, Peter is now ready to return home. Jerusalem is his home base (11:2; 15:7), the point of departure and the point of return. Overjoyed by what he has witnessed, Peter is anxious to report back to the community the wonders that God has done in the land of the Gentiles. Little does he know that his journey into unclean territory stirs up problems and creates tensions within the faith community. Peter therefore has to defend his maverick actions, but in the end he succeeds in convincing his fellow Jewish Christians that it is in accord with the divine

---

25. Some suggest that the messengers left in the afternoon and therefore traveled through the night; see Haenchen, *Acts*, 334; Fitzmyer, *Acts*, 454. Others say that they left early in the morning; see Bruce, *Acts*, 254; Barrett, *Acts*, 1:504.

26. Wight (*Manners and Customs*, 271–72) says that an average day's journey was around twenty to thirty miles, but when a large group traveled, the distance was half that.

27. A full discussion on the issue of purity can be found in the next chapter under "the social-cultural and religious settings."

plan that the Gentiles be fully admitted into the Christian community and—more importantly—that Christian Jews be allowed to participate in table fellowship with Gentiles who are not yet proselytized.

Topographical Space

Topographical space is defined strictly as that which is part "of, or relating to, the physical features of the earth."[28] They are spatial features that can normally be observed in an aerial photograph or on a relief map— roads, rivers, lakes, seas, wilderness, mountains, cities and villages (although not their names), and the earth. Since in the Bible heaven is conceived of as a layer or zone above the earth, it is also included in topographical space.[29]

Narrative Facts

A careful examination of Acts 10:1—11:18 reveals the following topographical details:

- sea (*thalassa*) (10:6, 32)
- city (*polis*) (10:9; 11:5)
- country (*chōra*) (10:39)
- heaven (*ouranos*) (10:11, 12, 16; 11:5, 6, 10)
- earth (*gē*) (10:11, 12; 11:6)

Although the P-C episode is one of the longest narratives in the New Testament, the description of its topographical space is quite restricted. Only five spatial areas are mentioned in the narrative. Of these five, however, three—sea, city, and country—are references to geopolitical space. Simon's house is "by the sea" (10:6, 32), a clear reference to the Mediterranean Sea. The "city" mentioned in 10:9 and 11:5 is obviously Joppa. The expression "in the country of the Jews" (10:39) most likely refers to Galilee and Judea. Obviously the two most important topographical areas are heaven and earth which, as we shall see, are more than mere stage settings for the dramatic action of the P-C episode.

---

28. Malbon, *Narrative Space and Mythic Meaning*, 51.
29. Ibid., 50–62.

SEMANTIC FIELD AND SIGNIFICANCE

Heaven. The word "heaven" (in Hebrew *shamayim*; in Greek *ouranos*) has two primary meanings in the Old Testament. First, heaven is referred to as "the firmament" or "sky" over the earth. According to ancient cosmology, heaven contains windows and floodgates through which rain, snow, hail, and wind descend upon the earth (Gen 7:11; 2 Kgs 7:2; Mal 3:10; Job 38:22; Jer 49:36). Although the Old Testament clearly asserts that God created heaven (Gen 1:1; 2:4; Isa 42:5; Ps 33:6), nevertheless God also dwells there. Heaven is considered "the dwelling place of God" and the sphere of God's activity.[30] Thus it was natural for people to regard it as the source of all divine blessings (Gen 49:25; Deut 33:13; 1 Kgs 8:35).[31]

The word "heaven" occurs 284 times in the New Testament (thirty-seven times in Luke; twenty-six times in Acts). Focusing on other theological and soteriological concerns, New Testament authors (particularly the author of Luke-Acts) show no interest in the cosmological structure of heaven. Rather they emphasize heaven as the abode of God (Matt 5:16, 45; 18:35; Luke 11:13; 15:18) and of Christ (John 3:13; Acts 3:21), the "locus for Christ's activity on behalf of the Church, and from which he comes at the Parousia."[32] Heaven is not merely a state but a place of perfect bliss where Christians hope to arrive one day. Paul teaches that "our citizenship is in heaven, and from it we also await a savior, the Lord Jesus Christ" (Phil 3:20). The Book of Revelation describes it as the "new Jerusalem" (Rev 3:12; 21:3). Heaven is the real home of God's angels, the just, and the holy ones (Luke 2:13, 15; 10:20; 15:17).

If heaven is believed to be the abode of Christ and the holy ones, why does Peter in his vision see the heaven opened and all kinds of animals, clean as well as unclean, coming down from and then going back up to heaven? Since the animals obviously represent human beings, Jews as well as uncircumcised Gentiles have equal access to heaven. However this is too much for Peter to fathom. He is thoroughly shocked by what he has just witnessed (10:17).

Earth. Ancient Israel's view of the world did not differ much from that of other ancient Near Eastern peoples. Israel perceived the earth as a flat disk (Isa 42:5) surrounded by the ocean (Pss 24:2; 136:6) and supported by various pillars (Job 9:6). It has four corners (Isa 11:12; Ezek 7:2; Job 37:3;

30. BDAG, 738.
31. Hensell, "Heaven," 427.
32. Kirk-Duggan, "Heaven," 564.

Peter and Cornelius

38:13) and an edge (Isa 24:26) or ends (Isa 40:8; Job 28:4). It also has a center or navel (Ezek 38:12) which is believed to be Jerusalem.[33]

In the New Testament, particularly in Luke-Acts, the Greek word *gē* ("earth") has more than one meaning; its references range from "earth" (Luke 5:24; 12:49; 18:8; Acts 1:8; 11:6; 13:47; 17:26), to "soil" (Luke 6:49; 8:8, 15), to "ground" (Luke 22:44; Acts 7:33; 9:4; 10:11; 26:14), to "land" (Luke 5:11; Acts 7:29; 27:39).[34] In the P-C episode *gē* occurs three times (10:11, 12; 11:6), and all are translated as "earth" in connection with or in contrast to "heaven" or "sky" (*ouranos*).

CROSSING THE BOUNDARIES OF SACRED SPACE

Descents and ascents. The P-C episode is full of movements on the vertical plane (up and down). The following verbs of vertical movement occur in this narrative:

- to go up (*anabainō*) (10:4, 9; 11:2)
- to go down (*katabainō*) (10:11, 20, 21; 11:5)
- to draw up (*anaspaō*) (11:10)
- to lower down (*kathiēmi*) (10:11; 11:5)
- to take up (*analambanō*) (10:16)
- to come down (*epipiptō*) (10:44)
- to rise (*anistēmi*) (10:13, 20, 23b, 26, 41; 11:7)
- to fall down (*piptō*) (10:25; 11:15)
- to raise (*egeirō*) (10:26, 40)

There are two sets of vertical movements which play an important theological role in the topographical spatial setting. First, Peter sees heaven open, and a large sheet containing all kinds of clean as well as unclean animals *descends* and *is lowered* upon the earth (10:11; 11:5). The "descent" is counterbalanced by the object being *taken up* to heaven (10:16; 11:10). It is important to note that this scene of "descent" and "ascent" is narrated twice: once by the narrator to the reader (10:11; 10:16) then later by Peter to the Jerusalem community (11:6; 11:10). Second, Cornelius is informed by the angel that his prayers and alms *have gone up* (to heaven) as a memorial

---

33. Hoppe, "Earth," 233–34; see also Gaster, "Earth," 2–3.
34. Darton, *Modern Concordance*, 140–42.

before God (10:4). This "ascent" is counterbalanced by the Holy Spirit *coming down* upon Cornelius and his household (10:44; 11:15).

Between heaven and earth. The vertical movement between heaven and earth, particularly by clean and unclean animals, metaphorically as well as theologically implies that for Luke there is no longer a division between sacred space (heaven) and profane space (earth). In other words, even the topographical spatial boundaries between heaven and earth are now fluid and are no longer defined by ethnic demarcation. Furthermore, the "descents" and the "ascents" of the animals reveal that even the heavenly realm—where traditionally only the holy ones (that is the Jews) dwell—now hosts Gentiles as well.

Architectural Space

The third and final spatial setting is that of architectural space. Architectural markers locate events in relation to artificially enclosed spaces or human-made structures—house, synagogue, temple, door, roof, or housetop.[35]

Narrative Facts

A careful examination of the P-C episode displays the following architectural details:

- home, household (*oikos*) (10:2, 22, 30; 11:12, 13, 14)
- house (*oikia*) (10:6, 17, 32; 11:11)
- roof, housetop (*dōma*) (10:9)
- gate, entrance (*pulōn*) (10:17)

Although there are only three architectural structures mentioned in the P-C episode, there are a total of twelve references. Since the majority of the references are either *oikos* (home or household) or *oikia* (house), our analysis will focus exclusively on this architectural area.

Semantic Field and Significance

Oikos and *oikia*. The Greek has two words for describing either the group of people that make up a household ("residents") or the physical place or building where the family gathers ("residence").[36] Some lexicons make a dis-

---

35. Malbon, *Narrative Space and Mythic Meaning*, 106–40.

36. The word *oikos* occurs 115 times in the New Testament, while *oikia* occurs 93 times.

tinction between the two Greek words, suggesting that *oikos* strictly means household ("residents"), while *oikia* is a dwelling place ("residence").[37] Other lexicons consider these two Greek terms to be synonyms and therefore use them interchangeably.[38] Luke's usage, however, is quite distinct in the P-C episode. Whenever *oikos* appears, it primarily implies "home" or "household," whereas *oikia* strictly means "house" or "building."

Household in Luke-Acts. The term *oikos* appears thirty-four times in Luke and twenty-five times in Acts, while *oikia* appears twenty-five times in Luke and twelve in Acts. Statistically speaking, Luke-Acts contains almost half of the references to "house" in the New Testament.[39] In his article, "Temple versus Household in Luke-Acts: A Contrast in Social Institutions," John H. Elliott points out that not only houses, homes, and households provide the settings for the reception of the good news in Luke-Acts (for instance, teaching, healing, hospitality and table fellowship), but also these private homes or house churches represent "the basic social organization through which the gospel advances from Palestine to Rome."[40] A closer examination of the Acts of the Apostles shows that the Jesus movement spreads literally "from house to house" (Acts 20:20): from the households of Galilee, Jerusalem and Jericho to those of Damascus (9:10–19), Joppa (9:43; 10:6, 17–18, 32), Caesarea (10:1—11:18; 21:8), Tyre (21:3–6), Philippi (16:15, 34, 40), Thessalonica (17:5–7), Ephesus (20:20), Troas (20:7–12), Corinth (18:3, 7–8), and Rome (28:16, 23, 30–31).

Furthermore, Elliott rightly points out that the success of the spread of the Jesus movement was greatly attributed to the early Christian promotion of the household as the Kingdom of God. The Christian household was united by bonds of mercy, faith, hospitality, and friendship, and its

---

37. There is also third possible meaning, "possessions or property." See Liddell and Scott, *Intermediate Greek-English Lexicon*, 546; BDAG, 698–99. Malbon (*Narrative Space and Mythic Meaning*, 107–8) provides a good explanation of the usage by different lexicons. For a good description of and bibliography on the architectural and domestic features of the Israelite house, see Holladay, "House, Israelite," 308–18.

38. Although he uses them interchangeably in his analysis of the Markan text, Trainor considers *oikos* to mean household and *oikia* to mean house; see Trainor, *Quest for Home*, 8; also Malbon, *Narrative Space and Mythic Meaning*, 108. For an alternative view, see Brandt and Lukinovich, "Οἶκος et οἰκία chez Marc comparé à Matthieu et Luc," 525–53.

39. Because of the limitation of this paper, I will focus solely on the semantic field of "house" in Luke-Acts. For a more comprehensive analysis, see Trainor, *Quest for Home*, 5–11.

40. Elliott, "Temple versus Household," 226.

The Settings

boundaries had no social or ethnic limits. It included the marginalized, the outcasts, Samaritans, and Gentiles.⁴¹

Entering Unclean Homes

Entering and exiting. It has already been pointed out that the P-C narrative is full of movement, sometimes ascending and sometimes descending. On the architectural level however there is another kind of movement at work, namely, from the exterior to the interior.⁴² The following verbs of horizontal movement occur in the narrative:

- go in, enter (*eiserchomai*) (10:3, 24, 25, 27; 11:3, 8, 12, 13)
- come in or go to (*proserchomai*) (10:28)
- invite in (*eiskaleomai*) (10:23a)
- go away/out (*aperchomai*) (10:7)

It is noteworthy that the verbs of entering and their occurrences are much more frequent than those of "going out," which actually appears only once. Some of the most intriguing horizontal movements are: an angel of God *entering* Cornelius' house (10:3); the messengers of Cornelius *entering* in the house of Simon the tanner (10:23a); Peter *entering* Cornelius' house (10:27) and then staying with him for several days (10:48). Conversely, there is only one real exit that the narrator explicitly depicts—that of the angel of God (10:7).

The home of Simon the tanner. Besides 9:43, which serves as a transitional verse to link the Petrine sequence together and to situate the locale of the P-C episode, Luke makes two other explicit references to Peter *staying* in the "house of Simon the tanner" (10:6, 32). In addition to the triple mention of Peter lodging with a leather worker, the actions or events that take place in the home of Simon the tanner consume a lot of discourse time (10:9–23a; 11:5–12a).⁴³

What is so intriguing about Peter entering and residing in the home of Simon the tanner? Since tanners work with the hides of dead animals, they

---

41. Elliott, "Temple versus Household," 226–30.

42. I owe these ideas to Marguerat and Bourquin's keen perception and analysis. See Marguerat and Bourquin, *How to Read*, 81.

43. "Discourse time" may be simply defined as the material time which is measured by words, sentences, lines, verses, chapters, etc., that is necessary to tell the narrative. In contrast to discourse time is "story time." These terms have been briefly dealt with in chapter 2, n. 45. A fuller discussion appears in the following section (temporal settings).

are considered unclean by most Jews! Furthermore, because of the odor produced from the tanning process, it is not a pleasant experience to live near a tanner.[44] In fact the Mishnah and Talmud strongly criticize tanners because of their ongoing ritual defilement which is caused by their trade.[45] Thus Peter's decision to reside in the house of Simon the tanner reveals that the apostle is receptive to Jews who are considered marginalized and unclean. This does not mean, however, that Peter is now willing to enter the home of a Gentile. Perhaps Peter's lodging with Simon the tanner serves as a preparation for a more radical move, namely, to venture into a Gentile's house.

The home of Cornelius. All the movements in the P-C narrative seem to be directed toward the home of the Gentile Cornelius. First an angel of God *enters* Cornelius' house (10:3).[46] In his vision Peter is told by the Spirit "to travel with them [Cornelius' messengers] without hesitation" (10:20) or "without making a distinction" (11:12). Moreover, the reader is repeatedly reminded that it was the angel who summoned Peter to the house of the Gentile Cornelius (10:6, 22, 29, 32; 11:13). Thus Peter is not the one who takes the initiative to venture into Cornelius' house. Since the angel not only enters but also commands Peter to do likewise, who is Peter to disobey God's command?

And so Peter *enters* Cornelius' house (10:27).[47] But Peter is not alone, for the six brothers from Joppa also "*enter* into the man's house" (11:12). Nevertheless, Peter is the only one who is criticized for "*going into* the home of the uncircumcised and eating with them" (11:3). According to the Jewish purity laws, Peter has trespassed the boundary of sacred space and therefore has been defiled. The Mishnah clearly states: "The dwelling-places of

---

44. Gaertner, "Tanning," 1275.

45. Jeremias (*Jerusalem*, 301–16) gives many rabbinic references despising tanners and their profession (*m. Ketub.* 7:10; *b. Pesaḥ* 65a; *Qidd.* 82b). According to Jeremias, dung-collectors and tanners go hand in hand, since the former collects the dung needed for fueling and tanning. So detested are these trades that even a wife has the right to seek a divorce if her husband engages in either of these professions. See also Witherington, *Acts*, 333.

46. The exact location of the vision is kept hidden until Cornelius tells Peter that the event actually takes place in his house (10:30). According to Humphrey ("Collision of Modes?," 65–84), Luke's primary argument is that entry into the Gentile domain has been enacted by God and is therefore acceptable.

47. Dunn (*Acts*, 139) appropriately points out that this is the climax to the first half of the chapter.

Gentiles are unclean" (*m. Oholot* 18:7).[48] Peter obviously is familiar with the Jewish purity code, for he says, "You know that it is forbidden for a Jew to associate or to go to a Gentile, but God has shown me not to call any person profane or unclean" (10:28).[49] Peter finally realizes that the clean and unclean animals of the vision refer not only to food but also to people.[50]

In short, by having Peter enter the home of Cornelius Luke no longer regards Gentile homes as unclean and "off limits" for Jewish Christians. Furthermore, since God has opened the door of salvation to Gentiles, there are no more barriers between Jews and Gentiles to full fellowship.[51]

TEMPORAL SETTINGS

According to Bar-Efrat, a narrative "cannot exist without time."[52] "Time," he says, "is like clay in the potter's hand as far as the author is concerned; he moulds it as he pleases, making it an integral part of the form of the work as a whole."[53] Although time plays an integral part of the narrative, the reader does not usually pay much attention to it. Since references to temporal settings in biblical narratives are typically brief and rare, the reader often takes them for granted. However, Mark A. Powell points out that, because temporal descriptions are rare, their occurrences should receive all the more attention. The scarcity of temporal references "may be rich in connotative significance."[54]

There are at least two different types of temporal settings: chronological and typological. In general, chronological references describe the time when the action takes place or indicates an interval or duration of time. On the other hand, typological references indicate the kind of time within which the action occurs—for example at night, in the winter, on the

---

48. Cited in Fitzmyer, *Acts*, 457.

49. According to Fitzmyer (*Acts*, 461) Acts 10:28 states that visiting the house of a Gentile is not only a source of ritual uncleanness, but also *athemiton* ("unlawful"), a word used in 2 Macc 6:5; 7:1; 10:34; 3 Macc 5:20. Furthermore, it is unlawful for a Jew even to come into close contact with a Gentile. See also Dunn, *Acts*, 139.

50. Johnson, *Acts*, 190.

51. Handy ("Gentile Pentecost," 100) holds that the central purpose of Luke's narrative strategy is to legitimate the presence of Jewish believers in Gentile homes.

52. Bar-Efrat, *Narrative Art*, 141. See also Ska, *"Our Fathers,"* 7; Marguerat and Bourquin, *How to Read*, 79.

53. Bar-Efrat, *Narrative Art*, 141.

54. Powell, *What is Narrative Criticism?*, 73.

Peter and Cornelius

Sabbath.⁵⁵ Since the analysis of the temporal settings of Acts 10:1—11:18 are predominantly chronological, we will focus our attention on these.

Chronological Durative Time

Chronological references can be further classified as either *durative* or *locative*. Chronological durative time refers to temporal references that denote an interval or an amount of time in which an action or event has transpired. Some narrative units might take hours, days, weeks, months, and even years. So, how much "story time" does the P-C episode take? The answer is revealed in an analysis of the durative references.

DURATIVE REFERENCES

There are five durative references in the P-C episode:

- the next day (*tē de epaurion*) (10:9)
- the next day (*tē de epaurion*) (10:23b)
- the next day (*tē de epaurion*) (10:24)
- four days ago (*apo tetartēs hēmeras*) (10:30)
- to remain for some days (*epimeivai hēmeras tinas*) (10:48)

The first *tē de epaurion*, which is translated "and on the next day" (10:9), indicates a temporal change and also denotes the second day in the story time. The second *tē de epaurion* (10:23b) tells the reader that it is now the third day. The third *tē de epaurion* (10:24) clearly indicates the fourth day. Just in case the reader has not been able to calculate the time, the narrator also mentions that it was "four days ago" (*apo tetartēs hēmeras*) when the story began to unfold (10:30).

The last chronological durative reference is less precise. The narrator simply tells the reader that Peter remains in Cornelius' house for "some days" (*hēmeras tinas*) (10:48). Perhaps "some days" could mean two to three days or even a week, but unfortunately the narrator is intentionally being imprecise here.⁵⁶ At any rate, Peter stays for "some days" and presum-

---

55. Ibid., 72–74, 78–82.

56. The concept of time is varies from culture to culture. Different people and cultures have different ways of perceiving time. Many cultures, including first-century eastern Mediterranean cultures, have a "social" concept of time rather than a "clock" time, which was invented and meticulously followed by modern western society. Since the Judeo-Palestinian concept of time in the New Testament era was predominantly "social,"

ably takes part in table fellowship with Cornelius and his household before going up to Jerusalem (11:2).

Story Time and Discourse Time of Acts 10:1—11:18

The analysis of the chronological durative references reveals the following temporal structure and narrative rhythm of the P-C episode:

Story Time	References	Discourse Time	Rhythm
Day one	10:1–8	8 verses for one day	*allegro*
Day two	10:9–23a	15 verses for one day	*moderato*
Day three	10:23b	half verse for one day	*prestissimo*
Day four	10:24–48	24 verses for one day	*lentissimo*
Some days later	11:1–18	18 verses for one day	*adagio*

The P-C episode takes about one week of story time and sixty-six verses of discourse time. The pace of the narrative is dynamic, changing from day to day. Day three and four however merit the most attention, since they have contrasting rhythm. The rhythm of day three seems disjointed, since the change from *moderato* to *prestissimo* to *lentissimo* breaks the flow of the narrative. The acceleration in 10:23b indicates that the narrator is quickening the pace in order to move on to something which is more important and suspenseful. Moreover, when the rhythm of the narrative slows down dramatically as in day four (*lentissimo*), it indicates that the narrator is telling the reader to pay special attention to this particular scene. Acts 10:24–48 depicts the climactic events of Peter's speech, followed by the descent of the Holy Spirit and Baptism. All this activity took place in the house of the Gentile Cornelius.

In comparison to the entire Acts of the Apostles the pace of the P-C episode is relatively *lento*. According to Daniel Marguerat's reconstruction of the rhythm of narration in the book, it takes twenty-eight chapters (Acts 1–28) to narrate twenty-eight years (CE 30–58).[57] Since it takes an average of one chapter to narrate one year of story time, the pace of the P-C episode

---

it was measured in terms of social relations and transactions, focusing on the present moment rather than the past or the future. For further discussion on time in the first-century eastern Mediterranean, see Malina, "Christ and Time?," 179–214; see also Fianu, "Narrative-critical and Theological Study," 54–55.

57. Marguerat and Bourquin, *How to Read*, 87.

Peter and Cornelius

is therefore extremely slow. This clearly shows how important and significant the P-C episode is for Luke in the Acts of the Apostles.

Chronological Locative Time

Chronological locative time can be classified as a specific point in time in which a given action takes place. This location in time could be either "broad" (when it is measured in terms of years or centuries) or "narrow" (in terms of days or hours).[58]

Locative References

An analysis of the chronological locative time of Acts 10:1—11:18 reveals the following:

- "about the ninth hour" (10:3)
- "around the sixth hour"[59] (10:9)
- "the ninth hour" (10:30)

These locative markers are all "narrow," for they specify a particular hour ("sixth hour" and "ninth hour") when a given action takes place. Furthermore, these narrow locative references are set within the time of prayer.

Prayer Time

The sixth hour. According to the biblical measurement of time, the sixth hour of the day in modern clock time is equivalent to noon (twelve o'clock).[60] This was perhaps the time for the midday meal in the first century Greco-Roman culture.[61] Although twelve o'clock was not a fixed time for Jewish prayer, pious Jews were highly encouraged to pray privately at

---

58. Powell, *What is Narrative Criticism?*, 72.

59. A few variant readings (A gig l vg^mss) specify that it was the sixth hour "of the day" (*tēs hēmeras*), while a few others (a² 36 *pc*) changed the time of the vision from the sixth to the "ninth" (*evatēn*) hour, making Peter's prayer coincide with Cornelius's prayer (10:3, 30). Considering the weight of its witnesses and its being attested by both the Alexandrian and the Western traditions, the reading of the "sixth hour" is probably more original. See Johnson, *Acts*, 183.

60. In a society without clocks or watches, the three-hour interval—the third, sixth, and ninth hour—was a sufficient designation for time. Though they are not definite, they are similar to our approximate expressions of time: *dawn, mid-morning, mid-day* (or *noon*), *mid-afternoon,* and *sunset.* See Cadbury, "Some Lukan Expressions," 278.

61. Fitzmyer, *Acts*, 454.

least three times a day—the third hour, the sixth hour and the ninth hour (cf. Ps 55:18; Dan 6:11; *Didache* 8:3).[62] In Luke-Acts, Jesus and the Apostles are men who pray often and more frequently than others.[63] Being a model apostle, Peter is depicted here as a man of prayer who prays even "at the sixth hour" (10:9).

The ninth hour. According to Jewish ritual practice, the ninth hour (three o'clock in the afternoon) is the time of the evening sacrifice in the Temple and the appropriate time for evening prayer.[64] In Acts 3:1 Luke portrays Peter and John as observant Jews who go to the temple at the ninth hour for evening sacrifice and prayer.[65] In the P-C episode, the narrator tells the reader that it is "about the ninth hour of the day" (10:3) that Cornelius sees the angel of God entering his house. While it is not yet clear whether Cornelius is praying when he has the vision, in verse 30 Cornelius clarifies that he was actually "keeping the ninth hour of prayer" in his house when the angel appeared. Interestingly Luke depicts this Gentile centurion as a pious Jew and a model Christian who "generously gives alms to people and prays to God constantly" (10:2).

In short, the chronological locative references in the P-C episode demonstrate that divine revelations or visions are connected with prayer. This motif of connecting visions with prayer is prominent in Acts (9:11, 12; 10:2–6, 9–17; 18:9, 10; 22:17–21; 23:11; 16:9, 10; 26:13–19).[66] Various studies have shown that prayer plays an important function in the overall

---

62. Fitzmyer, *Acts*, 454; Haenchen, *Acts*, 374; Bruce, *Acts*, 254. It is also interesting to note that these prayer times coincide with the period of Jesus' crucifixion and death (Mark 15:33; Matt 27:45; Luke 23:44).

63. Jesus prays at his baptism (Luke 3:21), in a deserted place (5:16), all night before choosing the Twelve (6:12), in solitude (9:18, 28), to the Father (11:2), for Peter (22:32), on the Mount of Olives (22:42), and on the cross (23:34). Similarly the apostles imitate the Lord by praying frequently, for example, in the upper room (Acts 1:14); before choosing a successor (1:24); together in communal life (2:42, 46, 47); Peter and John (3:1); Paul (9:11); Peter (10:9); Paul and Barnabas (14:23); Paul and Silas (16:25); Paul (20:36); Paul and other (21:5); Paul (22:17).

64. According to Johnson, the evening temple service is part of the teaching of the Torah (Exod 29:38–42; Num 28:1–8) and also a traditional time for prayer, as suggested by Daniel 6:10; 9:21, and *m. Tamid* 5:1, 6:4. Even Josephus describes the ninth hour as the time for sacrifice and prayer in *Antiquities of the Jews* 14:66. See Johnson, *Acts*, 64. For a fuller discussion on Jewish practices, see especially Cohen, *From the Maccabees*, 62–79.

65. Witherington points out that this is clear evidence that "the earliest Christians continued to live as observant Jews, probably still offering sacrifices in the temple" (*Acts*, 173).

66. Trites, "Prayer Motif," 182–83.

scheme of Luke-Acts.[67] Besides encouraging the reader to pray constantly in order to discern the will of God, the primary function of prayer in Luke-Acts is "a means whereby God directs his divine plan of salvation and those who have a role to play in that plan."[68] Thus, it is through prayer that Cornelius experiences the vision of the angel; furthermore, it is through prayer that Peter discovers the divine plan that the door of salvation has been opened to the Gentiles.

SOCIAL-CULTURAL AND RELIGIOUS SETTINGS

New Testament texts, like all oral or written communication, presuppose an understanding of the social-cultural and religious system in which they were produced and in which they made sense for the authors and their original audience.[69] They presume that the reader is first century eastern Mediterranean, sharing similar social systems and understanding similar cultural patterns. Unless the reader is familiar with the social, religious, historical and cultural environment of the biblical texts, he/she is liable to misunderstand the texts by interpreting them on the basis of one's own social and cultural context. Ethnocentrism and anachronism are the two common pitfalls of modern interpreters. To avoid these pitfalls, modern readers must be consciously aware that their way of thinking, acting and perceiving the world is quite different from that of the biblical world. To understand the biblical authors, the reader must make a conscious effort to learn about the culture and the social norms that form the context of these texts.[70]

The problem for us modern readers is that these texts and their social systems are alien to us. In order to get a glimpse of what these texts possibly mean, we have to "fill in the gaps" and "read between the lines." But how can considerate readers living two thousand years later "read between the lines"

---

67. Recent literature on prayer includes: Longenecker, ed., *God's Presence*; Karris, *Prayer and the New Testament*; Plymale, *Prayer Texts*. All of these works have excellent bibliographies.

68. Plymale, *Prayer Texts*, 4.

69. Anthropologists recognize that New Testament authors, who lived in a "high context" society, produced sketchy texts with limited details spelled out partly because they presupposed that the readers shared similar points of view. Those who live in the United States, for example, belong to a "low context" society that produces detailed texts, spelled out as much as conceivably possible, leaving little to the imagination. See Elliott, *What is Social-Scientific Criticism?*, 10–11.

70. Malina, "Reading Theory Perspective," 9–10.

without making false judgments and erroneous interpretations? Since there is such a big gap between us and the New Testament world, we need to read the New Testament texts with a different set of lenses, that is from the perspective of the first century Mediterranean contexts within which they were written. To achieve this goal, we rely on data already gathered from other interdisciplinary approaches, particularly from social-scientific analysis.[71]

Understanding the social and cultural context of the P-C episode is therefore extremely important in order to grasp the heightened tension and the core conflict in Acts 11:3, where Peter is confronted with the question, "Why did you go to the uncircumcised and eat with them?" Thus, the third aspect of the narrative settings is organized around the key social-cultural issue of "who eats what with whom under which circumstances." But first we must briefly examine the notion of purity and impurity in first century Judaism.

Purity and Impurity

There is no doubt that Jewish purity laws played an important role in early Christianity. New Testament writers devoted much time and energy to deal with this controversial issue in the early church, particularly as the community attracted large numbers of non-Jews.[72]

Purity may be described as the orderly system in which people and objects are in their proper place, whereas impurity is that which is inappropriately out of place. Like "dirt," as anthropologist Mary Douglas has observed, what is impure is *judged* to be "out of place."[73] So purity is a matter of perception, a cultural construct. Rich soil in a farm field is considered clean until it has been transferred to the kitchen floor—where it is dirt! In Israel, purity and impurity, clean and unclean, holy and profane were all determined by whether things, persons, and places were "in place" or "out of place."

---

71. The growing scholarly interest in this approach is attested by numerous publications. For an extensive bibliography, see Harrington, "Second Testament Exegesis," 77–85; Elliott, *What is Social-Scientific Criticism?*, 138–74; Rohrbaugh, ed., *Social Sciences and New Testament*.

72. For a recent discussion, see Poorthuis and Schwartz, eds., *Purity and Holiness*, particularly the following articles: Tomson, "Jewish Purity Laws"; Ottenheijm, "Impurity"; and Koet, "Purity and Impurity." See also Booth, *Jesus and the Laws*.

73. For a more comprehensive discussion, see Douglas, *Purity and Danger*, 7–41. See also Malina, "Clean and Unclean," 149–83.

Peter and Cornelius

The distinction between the pure and the impure was a major concern for Jews in biblical times. They were taught to safeguard the purity laws in order to not offend God's holiness (Lev 10:10–11; Ezek 22:26; 44:23). Moreover, their own call to holiness required a complete separation from the common or the profane (Exod 22:31; Lev 20:22–26; Deut 14:2). As a result, the radicalism of Israel's vocation to holiness led to an insistence on segregation from other people and nations.[74] Such an attitude created serious problems for the early church, particularly in its efforts to carry out the mission mandate of Jesus, "you shall be my witnesses in Jerusalem and in all Judea and Samaria and to the end of the earth" (Acts 1:8).

Purity References in Acts 10:1—11:18

The following semantic references indicate that Luke pays particular attention to purity laws in the P-C episode:

- profane and unclean (*koinos kai akathartos*) (10:14, 28; 11:8)
- to make clean, cleanse (*katharizō*) (10:15; 11:9)
- to make unclean, defile (*koinoō*) (10:15; 11:9)

The adjectives *koinos* and *akathartos* ("profane" and "unclean") occur three times. The first reference is made by Peter who vehemently resists the divine invitation to slaughter and eat, "Certainly not, Lord, for I have never eaten anything *profane* and *unclean*" (10:14). Peter repeats the statement when he reports his vision to the Jerusalem community, "By no means, Lord, for nothing *profane* or *unclean* has ever entered my mouth" (11:8). If unclean animals are "out of place," how much more so must be the mixture of clean and unclean animals in the sheet! Their association causes defilement, since clean and unclean creatures must be kept separate, as dictated by the Torah (Lev 20:24–26; Deut 14:2–21); otherwise the clean creatures too are contaminated.[75] It is not a surprise therefore that Peter was scandalized by what he saw and even more so by what he was asked to eat.[76]

---

74. Lenchak, "Clean and Unclean," 262–63.

75. House, "Defilement by Association," 143–53; see also Douglas, "Impurity of Land Animals," 33–45.

76. According to Tiede ("Acts 11:1–18," 175–80), Peter's vision alludes to the story of Eleazar's torture and death in 2 Maccabees 6, where he dies rather than eat unclean food. Tiede points out that throughout the centuries many Jews have faced torture and certain death rather than violate the dietary observances. Thus, Peter's resistance is quite understandable.

The Settings

The third reference to *koinos* and *akathartos* appears at the beginning of Peter's speech, "You know that it is forbidden for a Jew to associate or to go to a Gentile, but God has shown me not to call any person *profane* and *unclean*" (10:28). Having been directed by the Spirit to come into the home of the Gentile Cornelius, Peter finally understands that the vision of the mixture of clean and unclean animals applies not only to food but also to people. Just as creatures could interact within the sheet and not be defiled, so too Peter could associate with Gentiles without fear of contamination.

The verbal antonyms *katharizō* and *koinoō* are expressed by the heavenly voice, "What God has made *clean*, you must not go on calling *unclean*" (10:15; 11:9). The divine declaration of free association between Jews and Gentiles without defilement is loud and clear. The Old Testament principle of separation and distinction between Jews and non-Jews is finally annulled. The "wall of separation" between "insiders" (chosen Israelites) and "outsiders" (non-Jews) is finally torn down. Furthermore, the theological implication of Peter's acclamation, "God shows no partiality" (10:34), must be that Israel is no longer the unique covenant people.[77] Although this idea may have been too radical for Peter and the Jerusalem community to accept, the narrator highlights that it is in accord with God's plan, since it is God who initiates everything. To resist is to oppose God, as Peter gradually finds out, "Who was I to be able to hinder God?" (11:17).

Lukan Purity Arrangements

In his analysis "The Symbolic Universe of Luke-Acts," Jerome H. Neyrey points out that Luke portrays Jesus and his disciples as drawing new maps of a reformed purity system which is radically inclusive.[78] The new and true map of God's chosen people is not confined to Israelites living in Judea but includes peoples of all countries and cultures. Jesus himself commissions the disciples to go to "Jerusalem, all Judea, Samaria, and the end of the earth" (Acts 1:8). Furthermore, Peter has declared to Cornelius, "Truly I realize that God shows no partiality" (10:34). At the Jerusalem Council Peter again says, "God made no distinction between us and them, but cleansed their hearts by faith" (15:9). According to Neyrey, therefore, the Lukan purity arrangements are not based on the Old Testament notion of "holiness"

---

77. Wenham, "Theology of Unclean Food," 13. According to Jervell ("Law in Luke-Acts," 133–51), the Mosaic law relates not only to salvation but to Israel's "identity" as the people of God.

78. Neyrey, "Symbolic Universe," 271–304.

but on "mercy," which is inclusive and impartial. Furthermore, the only boundary or fence that separates true members of God's covenant, whether they are Jews or Gentiles, is essentially "faith in Jesus."[79]

According to Luke-Acts faith in Jesus is the criterion for salvation—not participation in the Old Testament purity system that indicates who is "in place" and who is "out of place," what belongs and what does not. For Christians, there exists only one marker: people are either "in Christ" or they are not.

Food, Meals, and Table Fellowship

Having established Luke's category of who's "in" and who's "out," we now turn our attention to the criticism of Peter by the circumcised Christians: "Why did you go to the uncircumcised and eat with them" (11:3)? In a nutshell the question centers around the social and cultural dynamics of food, meals, and table fellowship.

Food/Meal References

The topic of food, meals and table fellowship occurs frequently in Luke-Acts.[80] The following references appear in the P-C episode:

- "he became hungry and wanted to eat" (10:10)
- "preparing a meal" (10:10)
- "slaughter and eat" (10:13; 11:7)
- "I have never eaten anything" (10:14; 11:8)
- "who ate and drank" (10:41)
- "eat with them" (11:3)
- "showed them hospitality" (10:23a)

---

79. Ibid., 296–97; Malina, *New Testament World*, 172–81.

80. The following are just a few occurrences of meals and table fellowship in Luke-Acts: Luke 5:29–39 (a tax collector named Levi invites Jesus to a feast in his house); 7:36–50 (Jesus is invited to dine in a Pharisee's house); 10:38–42 (Martha and Mary receive Jesus into their home); 11:37–52 (Jesus eats in the house of a Pharisee); 14:1–24 (Jesus eats with the Pharisees on the Sabbath); 22:7–38 (Jesus has table fellowship with his disciples before Passover); 24:36–49 (Jesus appears in the midst of the disciples and eats before their very eyes); Acts 2:42–47 (the first Christian community breaks bread together); 9:19 (Paul is strengthened through table fellowship); Acts 10:1—11:18 (the story of Peter and Cornelius and their conversion through the sharing of a meal).

Social Boundary Markers

The topic of food, meals and table fellowship has been a major focus of recent studies of Luke-Acts, particularly from social-scientific and anthropological approaches.[81] These studies conclude that meals or the sharing of food are highly complex social events. Mary Douglas speaks of food as a "code" that communicates a multi-layered message:

> If food is treated as a code, the message it encodes will be found in the pattern of social relations being expressed. The message is about different degrees of hierarchy, inclusion and exclusion, boundaries and transactions across boundaries. Like sex, the taking of food has a social component, as well as biological one. Food categories therefore encode social events.[82]

From an anthropological point of view, meals/food serve as social boundary markers distinguishing what one eats, where one eats, when one eats, how one eats and with whom one eats.[83] In his analysis of table fellowship, Philip Esler provides literary and historical evidence for the Jewish ban on dining with Gentiles. After having examined classical as well as Jewish sources, Esler concludes that Jews in the first century CE "were zealous in keeping themselves apart from the Gentiles by means of definite boundaries which were perceived as originating in the Mosaic code."[84] Consequently the Jewish antipathy toward dining with Gentiles affected the mission of the early church so much so that Jewish-Gentile table fellowship became a matter of intense controversy and a major concern for Luke-Acts.[85]

The Test Case of Acts 10:1—11:18

In the article "Meals and the New Community in Luke," Halvor Moxnes notes that Luke portrays Jewish society as extremely concerned with

---

81. Neyrey, "Meals, Food, Table Fellowship," 160-82. Neyrey provides an excellent survey of the most important studies on "meals, foods, and table fellowship" in the past twenty years, especially those using social-scientific and anthropological approaches. He also provides an excellent bibliography.

82. Douglas, "Deciphering a Meal," 36.

83. For a discussion on food laws and the theological reasoning behind it, see Wenham, "Theology of Unclean Food," 6-15; Grant, "Dietary Laws," 299-310. See also Neyrey, "Ceremonies in Luke-Acts," 361-87; Elliott, "Household and Meals," 102-8.

84. Esler, *Community and Gospel*, 84.

85. See Yao, "Dismantling Social Barriers," 29-36.

boundaries around meals. By frequently eating with tax collectors and sinners, Jesus literally threatens "the sanctity of Jewish society as the people of God, breaking taboos by including unclean people, outsiders, in the meal fellowship."[86] By eating with outsiders, Jesus challenges the rules which were the basis for the unity and identify of the Jewish people. For that reason the Pharisees and scribes strongly criticize Jesus' actions (Luke 15:30). Peter is similarly criticized for his inexcusable social and religious insensitivity (Acts 11:3).

Consequently Peter knows the encoded message of meals and foods. In the P-C episode he repeatedly resists the commands of God to eat, even though he is quite hungry. But gradually he gives in to the guidance of the Spirit. He enters unclean homes and participates in table fellowship with uncircumcised Gentiles. It is precisely the Jewish-Gentile fellowship meal that gets Peter into trouble with his Jewish brethren in Jerusalem (11:3). Esler correctly points out that the central issue in the P-C episode is "not that the gospel has been preached to Gentiles, but the far more particular fact, of great ethnic and social significance, that Peter has lived and eaten with them."[87] In other words, the focus and function of the P-C episode is not just the legitimacy of the Gentile mission or admission into the church but the legitimacy of complete integration of Jews and Gentiles in the Christian community which included table fellowship. Interestingly enough, the fourfold requirement of the Apostolic Council in Acts 15 (avoiding things polluted by idols, incest, strangled meat, and blood) was established only after the practice of full integration and table fellowship had been tested and implemented by Peter in Acts 10:1—11:18.

The P-C episode therefore was the test case *par excellence* for genuine mission to the Gentiles. With the divine abolition of the Jewish purity systems, Christian evangelists were now free to journey beyond the Jewish homeland and to enter into homes which were once socially and religiously off-limits. Furthermore, since Christian community was now based on faith in Jesus Christ, Jews and Gentiles were permitted to sit down at the same table to share common Eucharistic meals. Obviously the Christian community could not return to its old ways but had to move forward. The Spirit had been poured out. The Gentiles were baptized. And table fellowship was celebrated without a distinction between Jews and the uncircumcised. Having been tested by the apostle Peter (10:48) and approved by the

---

86. Moxnes, "Meals and the New Community," 161.
87. Esler, *Community and Gospel*, 93.

Jerusalem church (11:18), the mission to the Gentiles could finally carry out Jesus' missionary mandate to its logical conclusions: "You shall be my witnesses in Jerusalem and in all Judea and Samaria and to the end of the earth" (Acts 1:8).

CONCLUSION

While the narrative settings of the P-C episode provide the context for the plot and the actions of the characters, they are also highly charged with symbolism and theological significance. The spatial settings of geopolitical space (Joppa, Caesarea, and Jerusalem), topographical space (heaven and earth) and architectural space (house) set the narrative within a certain locale and provide an occasion for conflict to take place. The analysis of the spatial settings reveals that crossing boundaries between the sacred and the profane are fluid, whether the movements be horizontal (Jewish homeland to Gentile territory), vertical (heaven and earth), or exterior to interior (entering unclean Gentile homes). Furthermore, the traditional boundaries of the purity code separating clean from unclean have disappeared. Thus movement beyond traditional boundaries is acceptable, since sacred space is no longer confined to fixed geopolitical, topographical, or architectural space.

Although the temporal settings of the P-C episode are brief and scarce, they are nevertheless rich in connotative and theological significance. The analysis of the chronological durative time establishes the temporal structure and reveals the narrative rhythm of the P-C episode. Furthermore, through the chronological locative time the reader discovers that climatic events, such as divine revelation and the descent of the Holy Spirit, occur around the "ninth hour," that is during prayer time.

Finally, the analysis of the social-cultural and religious settings of the P-C episode highlights the climatic tension and conflict of the narrative's plot. Social-scientific analysis of food and meals in first century New Testament times reveals that the readers understood Peter's table fellowship with uncircumcised Gentiles as a great scandal for Jewish-Christians in the early church. Nevertheless, the time had arrived for the church not only to embrace the mission to the Gentiles but also (and more importantly) to legitimate table fellowship between Jews and Gentiles in the Christian community.

4 The Plot

EVERY STORY REVOLVES AROUND three essential elements: settings, events, and characters. While narrative settings may be compared to adverbs, events are like verbs or predicates in a grammatical sentence. In other words, events are the incidents (acts) or happenings that occur within a story.[1] Without events a story cannot take shape. Consequently there must be events if there is to be a story. But a story is not just a number of random events that are thrown together, for the events have to be arranged in some kind of logical, temporal or causal sequence. They must be "plotted" in a meaningful way in order to arouse the reader's interest and emotional involvement and more importantly to communicate the essential message of the narrative. It is precisely this plotting of events that is the focus of the present chapter.

We will examine the events of Acts 10:1—11:18 with the help of the *quinary* (five-stage) plot structure of a narrative. This analysis of the P-C episodic plot demonstrates that for Luke, Acts 10:1—11:18 is the test case *par excellence* for the mission to the Gentiles and their integration into the church. The decision to accept Gentiles is again tested and finally approved by the "Jerusalem Council" in Acts 15.

THE PLOT AND ITS STRUCTURE

Aristotle defined plot (*muthos*) as "the combination of the incidents of the story" (*Poetics* 6).[2] From this classical definition modern literary critics

---

1. For a comprehensive study of "story as events," see Chatman, *Story and Discourse*, 43–95; Rimmon-Kenan, *Narrative Fiction*, 6–28; Powell, *What is Narrative Criticism?*, 35–50.

2. Aristotle, *Poetics*, 231.

The Plot

have developed their own explanations of plot.³ I do not intend to examine the definition of plot here, since that is not the focus of this present study. Rather I will focus on the structure of plot. Every narrative plot follows a certain causal order which connects various events or happenings and organizes them into one coherent story. The order of a unified plot, Aristotle pointed out, contains three moments: "beginning, middle, and end" (*Poetics*, 7).⁴ Many critics today however have amplified this into a more complex structure by adding various elements to Aristotle's three moments.⁵

Of the various options available, I find the *quinary* (or five-stage) scheme⁶ most helpful in analyzing the plot structure of Acts 10:1—11:18. The *quinary* scheme basically follows Aristotle's three moments of plot (beginning, middle, and end; or complication, climax, and resolution). In

---

3. Abrams (*Glossary*, 139) states that "the plot in a dramatic or narrative work is the structure of its actions, as these are rendered and ordered toward achieving emotional and artistic effects." Bar-Efrat (*Narrative Art*, 93) says that "if the characters are the soul of the narrative, the plot is the body. It consists of an organized and orderly system of events, arranged in temporal sequence. In contrast to life—where we are invariably confronted by an endless stream of incidents occurring haphazardly and disparately—the plot of a narrative is constructed as a meaningful chain of interconnected events." Marguerat and Bourquin (*How to Read*, 41) define plot as the "systematization of the events which make up the story: these events are linked together by a causal link (configuration) and inserted into a chronological process (sequence of events)."

For other helpful definitions of plot, see Aletti, *L'art de raconter*, 242; Crane, "Concept of Plot," 141–45; Brooks, *Reading for the Plot*, 3–36.

4. According to Aristotle, "a beginning is that which is not itself necessarily after anything else, and which has naturally something else after it; an end is that which is naturally after something itself, either as its necessary or usual consequent, and with nothing else after it; and a middle, that which is by nature after one thing and has also another after it. A well-constructed Plot, therefore, cannot either begin or end at any point one likes; beginning and end in it must be of the forms just described" (*Poetics* 7). See Aristotle, *Poetics*, 233.

5. Utilizing Aristotle's moments of plot, Freytag (*Technik des Dramas*, 100–101) created a pyramid structure consisting of the following elements: *exposition, inciting moment, complication, climax, turning point, falling action, resolution, last delay, denouement* (conclusion). Cited from Ska, "Our Fathers," 20–21.

Adele Berlin, being influenced by William Labov's socio-linguistic model, adopts a narrative structure containing six elements: abstract, orientation, complicating action, evaluation, result or resolution, coda. See Berlin, *Poetics and Interpretation*, 101–110.

Others, on the other hand, follow Aristotle's three basic categories. See Fokkelman, *Reading Biblical Narrative*, 76–78. Gunn and Fewell (*Narrative*, 102) divide the plot structure into exposition, conflict, and resolution.

6. The Latin term and scheme are attributed to Marguerat and Bourquin (*How to Read*, 43–44). Amit (*Reading Biblical Narratives*, 47–48) also adopts a five-stage narrative arrangement which she calls "the pediment structure."

addition to these three essential stages, the *exposition* (initial situation) and the *final situation* are added, giving plot a five-stage structure. Furthermore, the *quinary* scheme is arranged symmetrically and can be illustrated with the form of a pyramid. At the apex of the pyramid structure is situated the climax or the turning point of the story.

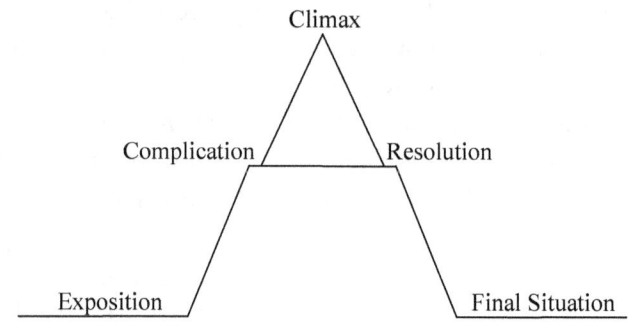

FIGURE 4.1

THE QUINARY PLOT STRUCTURE OF ACTS 10:1—11:18

The P-C episode embodies the five stages of the *quinary* scheme:

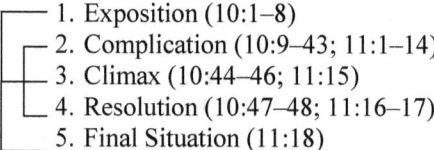

FIGURE 4.2

In the *exposition* (10:1–8) the narrator gives the background information of the story, specifying the who, what and how of the action. Next comes the *complication* or crisis (10:9–43) in the narrative. Following the conflict, the third stage (which is the heart of the story) is the *climax* (10:44–46). After the pivot or turning point of the plot is revealed, the fourth stage brings about the *resolution* (10:47–48). Though the P-C episode comes to a moment of rest in 10:48, the episodic plot of the story is not completely over. There is, however, a *second complication* (11:1–14), a *second climax* (11:15), and a *second resolution* (11:16–17) before the *final situation* (11:18) which brings the narrative to a state of equilibrium.

Exposition (10:1–8)

The exposition (or the initial situation) provides the readers with indispensable information and with the basic background necessary to enter the world of the story.[7] The exposition may introduce the main character(s), specify the time and/or place of the action, or depict an obstacle or negative aspect (sickness, ignorance, difficulty) that the narrative attempts to remove. In short, the exposition answers questions like: Who? Where? When? And sometimes how?[8]

The expositional information is usually placed at the beginning of a narrative; however, in some cases information is gradually revealed during the course of the story.[9] While the exposition of the P-C episode occurs at the beginning of the narrative, some indispensable information is withheld—only to be revealed at some appropriate moment in the course of the narrative. This literary technique is called "delayed exposition."[10]

Cornelius and the "Delayed Exposition"

In 10:1–8 the narrator introduces Cornelius, one of the main protagonists. The reader not only knows his name but also his traits (devout and almsgiver), military status (centurion), and religious piety (a God-fearer who constantly prays).[11] Furthermore, the exposition sets the narrative in the

---

7. In narrative criticism events that are essential and could not possibly be removed without destroying the logic of the narrative are called, "kernels." On the other hand, "satellites" are events which are not fundamental to the development of the plot and therefore can be deleted without destroying the basic plot of the story. Since there are few objective criteria for determining kernels and satellites, Powell (*What Is Narrative Criticism?*, 36) correctly points out that the distinction between them should be applied with caution. For a different perspective, see Chatman, *Story and Discourse*, 53–56.

8. See Marguerat and Bourquin, *How to Read*, 43–44; Amit, *Reading Biblical Narratives*, 33; Ska, "Our Fathers," 21; Bar-Efrat, *Narrative Art*, 111. For a more in-depth study, see Sternberg, *Expositional Modes*, 1–34.

9. Bar-Efrat, *Narrative Art*, 112 and 121.

10. See Sternberg, *Expositional Modes*, 14; Ska, "Our Fathers," 23; Alter, *Art of Biblical Narrative*, 81; Bar-Efrat, *Narrative Art*, 112. According to Abrams, "The beginning (the "initiating action," or "point of attack") need not be the initial stage of the action that is brought to a climax in the narrative or play. The epic, for example, plunges in *medias res*, many short stories begin at the point of the climax itself, and the writer of a drama often captures our attention in the opening scene with a representative incident, related and close in sequence to the event which precipitates the central situation or conflict" (*Glossary*, 141).

11. Since all of these details have been thoroughly discussed in the previous chapters, it is not necessary to reexamine them.

pagan city of Caesarea at about the ninth hour, the appropriate time for Jewish sacrifice and prayer. The exposition of the character of Cornelius does not end here. In 10:22 the three messengers report Cornelius' vision to Peter and describe the centurion as "upright" (*dikaios*) and "well spoken of by the whole nation of the Jews." Moreover, when Cornelius gives his own account of the vision to Peter (10:30–33), he admits that he was "keeping the ninth hour of prayer" when the angel appeared to him in his house. Undoubtedly the effect of such a positive and extensive presentation of Cornelius is to make him an attractive figure and therefore a worthy candidate for admission to and fellowship in the Christian community.

Suspense and Drama

Despite the fact that the narrator provides extensive background information about Cornelius and repeatedly recounts his vision (10:3–6, 22, 30–33; 11:11–14), one crucial piece of information has been concealed. The reader has no idea what the angel said to Cornelius nor what Cornelius told the messengers about why Peter was being summoned. This indispensable information is revealed gradually in bits and pieces throughout the narrative (10:22, 33; 11:14), adding suspense and interest to the story.

In 10:22 the messengers simply tell Peter that the reason is "to hear words (*rēmata*) from you." The reader knows that Peter is being summoned to relay a message, but the content of that message is still unclear. When Cornelius and Peter finally meet face to face, the centurion tells the apostle that he is eager to hear all that Peter has been "commanded to say by the Lord" (10:33). This is rather ironic, because Peter had not received any such message. The anticipation of Cornelius and the uncertainty of Peter leave the reader wondering what Peter will say. The message is finally revealed when Peter reports Cornelius' vision to the Jerusalem community. Peter reiterates the words of the angel, who promised Cornelius that the apostle will tell him words by which "he and his household will be saved" (11:14). By delaying this indispensable information until the end, the narrator has created suspense and added drama to the story.

Complication (10:9–43)

When narrative tension breaks the equilibrium of the story, conflict begins. This is the moment of complication. The indicator of tension "can be the statement of a difficulty, a conflict, an incident, a hindrance in the way of the resolution of a problem."[12] The complication or conflict may occur at various levels—with nature, with society, with God, with oneself, or with other characters. Complication is integral to a narrative, for without it "stories would be only a sequence of events strung together without tension or suspense or struggle on the part of the characters."[13] Furthermore, through conflict core values and beliefs are revealed, making this moment the "heart of most stories."[14] In the P-C episode, the protagonist Peter experiences three conflicts or oppositions: with the Spirit (that is, with God), with himself, and with Cornelius and his household.

Peter in Conflict with God

It is around "the sixth hour" when Cornelius' messengers approach Joppa, where Peter was residing (10:9). Their arrival disrupts the equilibrium of the narrative, introducing tension and triggering (off) a series of actions. The scene begins with Peter going up to the "housetop" of Simon the tanner to pray. While praying, he becomes hungry and wants to eat. It is in the context of food and meal preparation that Peter receives his vision of clean and unclean animals first descending from and then ascending back to heaven. Although he is hungry, three times Peter resists God's invitation "to slaughter and eat"—despite the fact that each time God declares, "What God has made clean, you must not go on calling unclean." Clearly Peter's persistent resistance reveals an internal struggle with God. God's command to eat unclean food is an abomination to Peter's social-religious values and beliefs. Furthermore, since the vision is not about unclean food but about people, the central obstacle therefore is "gentile uncleanness, which prevents Jews from associating freely with Gentiles."[15] The focus of the P-C episode is to remove this obstacle.

Peter in Conflict with Himself

The second major complication concerns Peter's conflict with himself. Acts 10:17–23a portrays Peter in a state of incomprehension. The narrator tells the reader that Peter "was greatly puzzled" (v. 17) over the meaning of the

---

12. Marguerat and Bourquin, *How to Read*, 44.

13. Rhoads et al., *Mark as Story*, 77. Sternberg (*Poetics*, 173) states, "No ignorance, no conflict; and no conflict, no plot."

14. Rhoads et al., *Mark as Story*, 77; Berlin, *Poetics and Interpretation*, 104.

15. Tannehill, *Narrative Unity*, 2:135.

Peter and Cornelius

vision.[16] Two verses later Peter continued "to ponder" over the vision (v. 19).[17] Peter's mental struggle over the message of the vision occurs simultaneously with the arrival of the messengers. Engrossed with his thoughts, Peter does not even hear the messengers' loud cry at the gate. Hence the Spirit intervenes and orders Peter to go down and to travel with them without hesitation. Interestingly, Peter does not immediately carry out the Spirit's request; rather he first asks the reason for their arrival, then invites them in and shows them hospitality.[18]

Peter is confused by these events—by the mysterious vision, by the arrival of the messengers, and by the command of the Spirit to go with these Gentile strangers while he is famished. The reader can easily sympathize with Peter, who is acted upon and does not yet know what is going on. At this point complication occurs not only in the narrative but also in Peter's life!

Peter in Conflict with Cornelius

The third complication involves the relationship between Peter and Cornelius. In this Jewish-Gentile interaction, tension and conflict heighten and rise to a climax. Peter, his six companions from Joppa, and the three messengers set off on the long journey to the pagan city of Caesarea. Although the discourse time is short (barely more than one verse), the story time takes twenty-four hours. So, Peter and company spent a lot of time on the road. Certainly traveling in the first century was not a pleasant experience.[19] The journey itself is already a complication, since it requires crossing a boundary—from Jewish to Gentile territory. The tension increases as Peter draws near to Caesarea and to Cornelius' house. The reader must wonder: How will Cornelius treat him? Will he enter a Gentile home? What will Peter say?

The meeting of Peter and Cornelius at the entrance of the house is dramatically portrayed: "And when Peter entered, Cornelius met him, and falling at his feet, worshiped him" (10:25). Although the narrator succinctly

---

16. NASB translates the imperfect active of *diaporeō* as "was greatly perplexed in mind," and NAB translates as "was in doubt."

17. According Johnson (*Acts*, 185), the present participle in the genitive absolute construction of *dievthumeomai* gives the sense of a continuing mental struggle.

18. Witherington (*Acts*, 351) rightfully points out that the narrator does not portray Peter ideally but rather as one who is reluctant and resistant to the message of the vision.

19. For traveling in Palestine, see Wight, *Manners and Customs*, 272–74.

describes this encounter with very few words, the situation is nevertheless tense and dramatic. The Greek verb *proskuneō* can me translated, "to fall down and worship."[20] It is a gesture exclusively shown to God or to Jesus (Luke 4:7, 8 [quoting Deut 6:13]; 24:52; Acts 8:27; 24:11). Cornelius' gesture therefore probably shocked Peter.[21] He must confront Cornelius' unwarranted action, since this kind of gesture is shown only to God and not to any human being.[22] Thus Peter made Cornelius get up, saying, "Stand up; I am only a mortal" (10:26).[23]

Tension remains high and reaches its peak when Peter enters Cornelius' house and says, "You yourself know that it is unlawful for a Jew to associate with or to visit a Gentile; but God has shown me that I should not call anyone profane or unclean" (10:28). Despite his understanding of the vision, Peter nevertheless has crossed a boundary which is prohibited by the Jewish tradition or Jewish interpretation of the Torah and therefore has been defiled. Moreover, Peter knowingly breaks the law, making the narrative more ironic and suspenseful.

Despite Peter's realization that no one can be called profane and unclean, the tension remains high, since Peter still needs to know why he has been summoned (10:29). Furthermore, Cornelius and his household are anxious to hear the message which Peter supposedly "has been commanded

---

20. Other possibilities are: to do obeisance to, prostrate oneself before, do reverence to, welcome respectfully. All of these definitions express an attitude or gesture of complete dependence on or submission to a high authority figure. It is also noted (*BDAG*, 882) that this word is frequently used to designate the custom of prostrating oneself before persons and kissing their feet or the hem of their garment, the ground, etc.; the Persians did this in the presence of their deified king, and the Greeks before a divinity or something holy.

21. Haenchen (*Acts*, 350) says that Cornelius treats Peter like a heavenly visitor. Fitzmyer (*Acts*, 461) states, "Cornelius's reception of Peter in this manner shows his esteem for the heavenly authority attached to Peter's visit and mission." On the other hand, Barrett (*Acts*, 1:513) says, "if Cornelius had to any degree accepted Judaism he could not have thought of Peter as divine; presumably he took him to be an angel."

22. According to Haenchen (*Acts*, 350), by confronting Cornelius' action the narrator demonstrates the exemplary humility of Peter; Conzelmann (*Acts*, 82), on the other hand, says that this is not a matter of humility but rather of an established motif.

23. Instead of *anastēthi*, the D manuscript has Peter shockingly ask: *ti poieis* ("what are you doing?"); likewise, p[(w)] sy[hmg] add the question but also retained the imperative *anastēthi*. After *eimi*, D* E it mae bos[mss] also add a superfluous phrase *hōs kai su*. According to Witherington (*Acts*, 352), Luke goes out of his way to show that Peter is not divine and thus not worthy of reverence or worship. Indeed, Luke portrays Peter as very mortal who three times resisted the heavenly vision.

Peter and Cornelius

by the Lord" (10:33) to give. Peter now proclaims his message (10:36–43), which is a summary of the apostolic *kerygma*—although it contains more information about the ministry of Jesus than Peter's previous addresses had.[24] It is during the course of Peter's proclamation that the plot of the P-C episode reaches its climax.

Climax (10:44–46)

Ska defines climax as "the highest point of a progression, be it dramatic (highest point of suspense, etc.), emotional (the lowest or highest emotional state) or intellectual (the major discovery, for instance)."[25] Thus the climax is the point of greatest dramatic tension. Daniel Marguerat calls this stage the "transforming action" which removes the difficulty, the shortage, or the disturbance announced by the story.[26] The climax of the narrative makes a particular event tellable, since a story is tellable only if it has something extraordinary or uncommon; otherwise it is pointless and boring.[27] The climax of the P-C episode (as we shall see) is certainly extraordinary and makes the tale worth telling.

THE SURPRISE INTERRUPTION OF THE HOLY SPIRIT

In verse 44 the narrator says, "While Peter was still speaking these things, the Holy Spirit fell upon all who were listening to the word." The sudden outpouring of the Holy Spirit upon Cornelius and his household culminates the plot of the P-C episode. The narrator gives the impression that the Holy Spirit interrupted Peter's speech, although actually Peter had already said what he needed to say.[28] Clearly Luke uses this literary technique of interrupting a speech to heighten the dramatic tension of the story and more importantly to illustrate the event as a supernatural phenomenon.[29]

---

24. Bruce, *Acts*, 261; Fitzmyer, *Acts*, 464.

25. Ska, *"Our Fathers,"* 29. Furthermore, Ska writes, "in a Greek tragedy, it is the moment in which the hero reaches the 'apex' of his fortunes" (29).

26. Marguerat and Bourquin, *How to Read*, 44.

27. See Berlin, *Poetics and Interpretation*, 105. Berlin classifies this stage as "evaluation."

28. Barrett (*Acts*, 1:528) points out that the last words of Peter's speech (namely, "everyone who believes in him") are significant. In other words the only qualification required is faith rather than being or becoming a Jew.

29. Luke uses a similar technique in 17:32; 22:22; 23:7; 26:24. Talbert (*Reading Acts*, 110) states that the device of interrupting a speech is widespread in antiquity (Josephus, *Antiquities* 16.11.5 §§ 379–386; Xenophon, *Hellenica* 6.5.37).

The event was "wholly of God's doing."[30] Indeed it was the Spirit who intervened and granted the gift of *glossolalia* to these Gentiles even before baptism. The effect of this phenomenon overwhelmed those who witnessed the event.[31] The narrator describes the reaction, "The circumcised believers who had accompanied Peter were astounded that the gift of the Holy Spirit should have been poured out on the Gentiles also, for they could hear them speaking in tongues and glorifying God" (10:45–46).

The Gentile Pentecost and *Glossolalia*

The description of the outpouring of the Holy Spirit on the Gentiles is very similar to that of Pentecost (2:1–4).[32] The wording is strikingly the same—the "gift" of the Holy Spirit (as in 2:38), being "poured out" (2:17), "speaking in tongues and praising God" (2:4, 11). The narrator clearly wants the reader "to recall the Pentecost scene and acknowledge that Gentiles have been chosen by God to receive the same gift and the same power as Jesus' first followers received at the beginning of their mission."[33] Thus what happened to Cornelius and his household was no different from what happened to the first disciples on the day of Pentecost. Furthermore, Luke demonstrates that "receiving the gift of the Holy Spirit is essential to being a Christian, as is belief in Jesus as the Christ and Lord of all."[34]

The effect of the Holy Spirit, in particular the *glossolalia*, was so visible and so obvious that neither Peter nor the circumcised believers could doubt or deny it. Obviously God had accepted the Gentile Cornelius and his household. This event will therefore become an irrefutable test case for Peter to convince the Jerusalem church to fully accept Gentiles and to integrate them into the Christian community.[35]

---

30. Dunn, *Acts*, 145.

31. From his analysis of the Targum Pseudo-Jonathan, Talbert (*Reading Acts*, 111) suggests that the reason why the Jewish Christians were so astonished is because they believed that the gift of the Spirit is a distinguishing mark solely for Israel. Since Gentiles were not supposed to receive the same gift, their amazement at what had just occurred is not surprising.

32. This is the fourth outpouring of the Holy Spirit in Acts (2:1–4; 4:3; 8:17).

33. Tannehill, *Narrative Unity*, 2:143. Though Acts 2 and 10 have many elements in common, Witherington (*Acts*, 101–2) denies that Acts 10 is the Gentile Pentecost.

34. Witherington, *Acts*, 361.

35. Esler, "Glossolalia," 136; Dunn, *Acts*, 146; Witherington, *Acts*, 359.

Peter and Cornelius

Resolution (10:47–48)

The Webster's *New Collegiate Dictionary* defines resolution as "the point in a literary work at which the chief dramatic complication is worked out." Yairah Amit classifies this stage as "unraveling," since the consequences of the change (or climax) are revealed.[36] In this phase solutions are given to resolve the tension that occurred in the narrative. Hence it is crucial to pinpoint the resolution in the analysis of the plot. According to Ska, "this moment, more than any other, is the one the reader is waiting for."[37] Once the problem is resolved, the dramatic tension drops and brings the narrative to a state of equilibrium (either temporarily or completely).

Peter's Transformation

Having witnessed the sudden outpouring of the gift of the Holy Spirit upon the Gentiles, Peter was finally convinced that God truly shows no partiality. Whatever doubts he may have had previously about the message of the vision, were now dispelled.[38] Furthermore, whatever resistance he may have felt toward associating with Gentiles had now completely dissipated. The action of the Holy Spirit had obviously transformed Peter. His initial resistance to God, his incomprehension about the meaning of the vision, and his conflict with Cornelius were now resolved. As a result Peter could ask, "Can anyone withhold the water for baptizing these people, who have received the Holy Spirit just as we have?" The answer is: No one![39] Since God has clearly accepted the Gentiles, how could anyone disapprove?

---

36. Amit, *Reading Biblical Narratives*, 47; Marguerat and Bourquin (*How to Read*, 44) classify this stage as "denouement." Ska (*"Our Fathers,"* 29) suggests that the term "denouement" refers to the final situation of the narrative, since resolution is the action that resolves the conflict or problem of the plot.

37. Ska, *"Our Fathers,"* 29.

38. This is a good example of a "revelation plot." A revelation plot ends with a gain in knowledge. In Peter's case, he finally realizes God's impartiality. There is another type of plot called "resolution plot," which involves the doing or carrying out of a certain action (at a pragmatic level). The act of dining with Gentiles and associating with them is an illustration of a resolution plot. Thus the P-C episode contains a combination of both revelation plot and resolution plot.

39. The Greek *mēti* expects a negative response. See Zerwick, *Biblical Greek*, n. 447.

Peter's Acceptance of Gentiles

Peter's personal transformation naturally led him to embrace the Gentiles and to offer them baptism so that they might become full Christians—"a sign of the Church's acceptance of God's action."[40] It is noteworthy that the order here is exceptional. Usually baptism precedes the outpouring of the Spirit (see Acts 8:14–17). In the P-C episode the reception of the Spirit precedes baptism. The order demonstrates God's complete acceptance of Gentiles, which leads to Peter's personal acceptance of them—without further reservation and without placing conditions upon them. Dunn points out that, "God had to give so clear an indication of his will otherwise even Peter might have hesitated to take such a step in the case of Gentiles without first requiring them to be circumcised."[41]

Peter's admission of the Gentiles did not end with the ritual of baptism, for now Peter initiates Jewish-Gentile table fellowship. Philip F. Esler writes,

> The fact that Peter can ask in Acts 10:47 whether anyone could refuse baptism to such people, now that they had received the Holy Spirit, raises the possibility that without the gift of the Holy Spirit some might doubt whether baptism was appropriate. Accordingly, the author presents the manifestation of the gifts of the Holy Spirit, especially *glossolalia*, as the critical factor in the acceptance of Gentiles into the Christian community, which acceptance extends ultimately to their being welcomed into Eucharistic table-fellowship with Jewish members of the community.[42]

Presumably Peter accepted Cornelius' invitation "to remain for some days" (10:48) and consequently participated in common Eucharistic (and other) meals without making distinction between Jews and uncircumcised Christians. Although the tension seems to be resolved and the narrative seems to end in a state of equilibrium, its closure is nonetheless deceptive and illusory.

---

40. Johnson, *Acts*, 194. Barrett (*Acts*, 1:530) notes that there was an assumption in the early church that to become a Christian one must be baptized.

41. Dunn, *Acts*, 146.

42. Esler, "Glossolalia," 136–37.

Peter and Cornelius

New Complication (11:1–14)

In the Bible, stories with a double climax and resolution are not uncommon—for example, the Abraham cycle (Gen 21:1–21), the Joseph story (Gen 45–50), the parable of the workers in the vineyard (Matt 20:1–16), the parable of the wedding feast (Matt 22:1–14), and the parable of the lost son (Luke 15:11–32). In these stories the narrative appears to have come to a conclusion when an element of surprise suddenly creates a new crisis.[43]

Illusory Conclusion

This is precisely what happens in the P-C episode. Peter's inexcusable participation in Jewish-Gentile fellowship at Cornelius' house instigated a new crisis and augmented the complication of the episodic plot. The tranquil end in Acts 10:48 is only an "illusory conclusion."[44]

Before Peter went up to Jerusalem, the report about the momentous event in Caesarea had already been circulated. Thus when Peter arrived in Jerusalem "those from the circumcised believers"[45] criticized him, saying, "Why did you go to uncircumcised people and eat with them?" (11:3). First of all, it is interesting to note that the criticism is not against baptizing Gentiles but about Jewish-Gentile table fellowship in which Peter obviously participated. The problem was a real one, since a Jew who ate with a Gentile compromised his or her Jewish identity. By eating with Gentiles, Peter has "gone against his identity as one of God's people, and has, furthermore, jeopardized the identity of the community."[46] Secondly, while the narrator recounts that only "those of the circumcised believers" directly confronted Peter and his actions, this group nevertheless seems to represent "the whole Jerusalem congregation."[47]

Peter in Conflict with the Jerusalem Church

Once again the narrative tension is high. Peter's full acceptance of the Gentiles through baptism and particularly his fellowship with them created a

---

43. Ska, "Our Fathers," 28.

44. Bar-Efrat (*Narrative Art*, 124) notices that several biblical narratives possess the pattern of illusory conclusion.

45. They were a group of Pharisaic Jewish Christians who were very conservative in their approach to the Torah. See Witherington, *Acts*, 362, n. 137.

46. Johnson, *Scripture and Discernment*, 97. See also Johnson, *Acts*, 200.

47. Conzelmann, *Acts*, 86. For a different view, see Johnson, *Acts*, 197.

new crisis in the Jerusalem community. How will Peter resolve this conflict? How will he defend his actions in order to convince the whole Jerusalem assembly that what he did was in perfect accord with God's plan and purpose? Furthermore, how can he prove to his adversaries that it is time to embrace the Gentiles and to integrate them into one Christian community without making distinctions and without demanding restrictions? Interestingly Peter defends his case not by rhetorical argument but simply by recounting both his own vision and the vision of Cornelius. In his analysis of the decision-making process in the early church, Luke T. Johnson states,

> When challenged, he [Peter] does not stand on his authority as an apostle, or argue from the Scripture, for neither really covers the situation. He neither argues nor asserts. Rather, he narrates his own experience. This and this alone moves the others to accept and ratify his decision.[48]

Second Climax (11:15)

In longer narratives there may be more than one climax. Bar-Efrat says, "Instead of rising to the climax and afterwards descending quickly to the tranquil end, they ascend to the climax, descend, but then they rise again to a second climatic point, and only afterwards do they finally fall off to the equilibrium of the end."[49] This is the case with the P-C episode, which contains a second turning point. This second pinnacle appears in Acts 11:15 when Peter says, "As I began to speak, the Holy Spirit fell upon them just as it had upon us at the beginning."

PETER'S POINT OF VIEW

Peter's personal rendition of the climatic account of the descent of the Holy Spirit is dramatic and engaging for the hearer (as well as for the reader). Furthermore, from Peter's point of view the coming of the Spirit was clearly an act of divine initiative. Even though the effect is powerful, stressing God's initiative, the literary device of *archomai* with the infinitive ("as I began to speak") poses difficulty and perhaps contradicts what the narrator had said in Acts 10:44.[50] When did the Holy Spirit actually descend? Was it

---

48. Johnson, *Scripture and Discernment*, 97.

49. Bar-Efrat, "Some Observations," 166. See also Ska, *"Our Fathers,"* 28; Gunn and Fewell, *Narrative*, 104.

50. Haenchen, *Acts*, 355; Conzelmann, *Acts*, 86.

near the end of the sermon, just before he finished (10:44)? Or was it before he had a chance to speak at all (11:15)?

Divine Initiative

John J. Kilgallen has shown (with abundant examples from Greek literature and particularly from Luke-Acts) that *archomai* with the infinitive often has a sense of "proceeding (to do)" rather than "beginning (to do)."[51] Thus Kilgallen concludes that Acts 11:15 "can be understood to represent what Luke has already presented in 10:34–43: Peter had progressed some of the way, but not all of the way, in his discourse to Cornelius—when the Spirit came."[52] Consequently the literary device used by Luke gives the impression that the Holy Spirit interrupted the unfinished speech of Peter making the outpouring of the Spirit more exciting and an act of divine initiative.

Second Resolution (11:16–17)

The turning point of a narrative normally inaugurates the falling point, leading naturally to the resolution. The resolution is the moment in which the central dramatic conflict is worked out. Once the complication is resolved, the dramatic tension drops and the narrative may come to a tranquil end. Just as there is a double climax in the P-C episode, so there is also a double resolution. In this second resolution (11:16–17) Peter's final conflict (namely, with the Jerusalem church) is worked out.

Equality of the Gift of the Holy Spirit

The sudden outburst of the Holy Spirit caused Peter to remember the words of the Risen Lord in Acts 1:5 (originally attributed to John the Baptist in Luke 3:16): "John baptized with water but you will be baptized with the Holy Spirit" (11:16). With these words Peter explicitly connects the coming of the Holy Spirit at Cornelius' house with the Pentecost event in the

---

51. Kilgallen ("Did Peter Actually Fail?," 405–10) has clearly demonstrated that Dibelius was wrong to accuse Luke of contradicting himself in Acts 11:15, for the phrase in question should not be taken literally to mean "as Peter just began to speak." There are three example in the Gospel of Luke where lengthy speeches of Jesus are introduced by *ērksato* (aorist of *archomai*) plus the infinitive of speaking: 7:24 (followed by 82 words); 12:1 (followed by 212 words); 20:9 (followed by 120 words). Thus, *ērksato lalein* can suggest a speech as long as, or longer than the speech in Acts 10:34–43 (181 words) to which Peter refers at 11:15. See also Witherington, *Acts*, 364, n. 147.

52. Kilgallen, "Did Peter Actually Fail?," 409.

upper room in Jerusalem (2:1-4). Surely some of those who are listening to Peter can still vividly remember that event. Furthermore, Peter makes it clear that God gave these Gentiles the same gift (the Holy Spirit) as he gave those in the upper room when they believed in the Lord Jesus Christ.[53] The Gentiles' reception of the Holy Spirit proves God's acceptance and therefore must be an irrefutable test case—unless the church can somehow disprove its legitimacy.

Decisive Factor

Since the gift of the Spirit is the decisive factor for accepting Gentiles into the church, baptism is not an issue in this section of the narrative. Dunn rightfully points out that

> Interestingly, baptism itself is not mentioned in this second telling. For that is not the point: it was the gift of the Spirit to uncircumcised [people] which settled the matter. It was the Spirit, not baptism which rendered circumcision irrelevant.[54]

For Peter and for Luke the gift of the Sprit is the decisive factor for Gentile admission and integration into the Christian church. Furthermore, this acceptance naturally includes Gentile participation in Eucharistic table fellowship with Jewish members of the community.

Without having to bring up the issue of table fellowship with Gentiles, Peter concludes his testimony with an appropriate question, "Who was I to be able to hinder God?" The rhetorical question leaves the Jerusalem assembly speechless. His speech effectively "put an end to all further criticism, especially since Peter has shown how the authority of God has been involved."[55]

---

53. Marshall (*Acts*, 197) points out that the comparison made by Peter is with the experience of the original inner circle of Jesus' followers and not with that of the first Jewish converts on Pentecost. Thus Peter accentuates full equality. See also Witherington, *Acts*, 364.

54. Dunn, *Acts*, 151. According to Dunn, Luke emphasizes repeatedly that it is the Spirit which is the primary mark of divine acceptance and of discipleship. See the Samaritan episode (8:14-17). Furthermore, Dunn (*Acts*, 152) writes, "Even though it is Luke's emphasis, we need not doubt that the heart of Luke's account is firmly rooted in history and that it took such evident manifestations of the Spirit's presence to convince believers so deeply rooted in their Jewish traditions (Gal 2:8)."

55. Fitzmyer, *Acts*, 472.

Peter and Cornelius

Final Situation (11:18)

The final situation of the plot normally gives a tranquil closure to a narrative. At this stage the story reaches "a point of calmness at the end, the tension drops, the story-line descends and life returns to its former pace and daily routine."[56] In a Greek tragedy this stage is commonly called *katastrophe*, a state where suspense and tension are completely eliminated.[57] Some endings, however, describe the resolution in order to provide meaning, fulfillment, and closure to the narrative.[58] This type of ending occurs in the final situation of the P-C episode (11:18).

THE CHURCH'S APPROVAL

Peter accentuates the role of God's initiative in his recounting of the Cornelius episode.[59] He claims no credit, for the event is attributed to God's doing. Furthermore, Peter's rhetorical question at the end gives the impression that he "blamed it all" on God. Clearly God has willed this event to take place; therefore, no one—not even Peter—can oppose it.

Peter's testimony led his adversaries to finally admit that "God has given even to the Gentiles the repentance that leads to life" (11:18b).[60] Interestingly there is no hint about the need of circumcision. No restrictions or conditions are given. The case made by Peter concerning the equality of the gift of the Holy Spirit proved irrefutable. Equality of gift (the Holy Spirit) means equality of salvation, which implies equality among all believers, whether circumcised or uncircumcised, Jews or Gentiles. This equality necessarily includes table fellowship, for that is the heart of Christian unity and fellowship. Thus for the first time the Gentile mission and integration is approved not only by Peter but also by the Jerusalem church.

---

56. Bar-Efrat, *Narrative Art*, 129.
57. Marguerat and Bourquin, *How to Read*, 44; Ska, "Our Fathers," 28–29.
58. Gunn and Fewell, *Narrative*, 105–6.
59. Talbert (*Reading Acts*, 112) notes that Peter's response to the criticism consists of four examples of divine initiative told from the apostle's perspective. The emphasis throughout is on the divine initiative and human obedience.
60. Barrett (*Acts*, 1:543) points out that the plural article in *tois ethnesin* ("to the Gentiles") indicates the Gentiles as a class of people and is not a reference aimed just at Cornelius and his friends alone. Furthermore, Witherington (*Acts*, 364) notes that the reason why Cornelius' name is not even mentioned in Acts 11 is because Luke is emphasizing the broader implications of the events in Caesarea.

The Plot

NARRATIVE REST

The conflict of the P-C episodic plot has been resolved. The references to being "silent" and "praising God" (11:18a) indicate that the plot has come to its narrative rest. Since tension has been released and suspense has been eliminated, the story returns to a state of equilibrium—at least in principle.[61] Unfortunately the issue of the Gentile mission and integration is not yet completely resolved. While the criticism is temporarily silenced and the debate has subsided, the conflict about Jewish-Gentile fellowship—namely, sitting down at the same table and sharing the same loaf and the one cup—is only suspended until Acts 15.

THE ROLE OF THE P-C EPISODE IN ACTS 15

Acts 15 is one of the most important chapters in the book of Acts.[62] Some authors even propose that the chapter is arranged both structurally and theologically at the very center of the Acts of the Apostles,[63] making the Jerusalem Council the climax or turning point of the unifying plot of the entire narrative.[64] Whether or not Acts 15 was intended by Luke to be the center of the Book, it is not our major concern.[65] What is noteworthy is that

---

61. The reader does not know that the issue is not completely settled but only suspended until Acts 15. Johnson (*Acts*, 201) rightly points out that the full implications of the church's approval will not be seen until the Jerusalem Council.

62. Witherington, *Acts*, 439. According to Dunn (*Acts*, 195), Acts 15 is a watershed for both volumes of Luke.

63. Marshall, *Acts*, 242. According to Fitzmyer (*Acts*, 538), chapters 1–14 have 12,385 words, and chapters 15–28 have 12,502 words. Fitzmyer's calculation shows that Acts 15 falls designedly in the center of Acts. Of course not all scholars agree with Fitzmyer's proposal.

64. Marguerat and Bourquin (*How to Read*, 55–56) makes a fine distinction between episodic plot and unifying plot. An *episodic plot* is a plot of a micro-narrative; on the other hand, a *unifying plot* is a plot of a narrative sequence (for example Acts 10:1—15:35 could function as a unifying plot of the inauguration of the Gentile mission) or a macro-narrative (for example the whole book of Acts).

65. Suggestions for the structure of Acts are varied from author to author. For a good survey see Fitzmyer, *Acts*, 119–20.

For a seven-part structure which is different from Fitzmyer, see Betori, "Strut-turazione," 3–34. Developing those of J. Dupont and P. H. Menoud, Betori suggests the following outline for the book of Acts: introduction (1:1–14); first section (1:12—8:4); second section (8:1b—14:28); third section (14:27—16:5); fourth section (15:35—19:22); fifth section (19:20—28:31); conclusion (28:14b–16). Between these seven part division, there exists the following links: 1:12–14; 8:1b–4; 14:27–28; 15:35—16:5; 19:20–22; 28:14b–16. See also his earlier article, Betori, "Alla ricerca," 187–205.

the P-C episode not only is obviously referred to in Acts 15 but also plays a crucial role in the final decision of the Jerusalem Council.

The Situation and the Conflict of Acts 15

The P-C episode had a significant impact upon the Gentile mission. The narrative, as it were, gave Paul the impetus to reach out freely to the Gentiles and to participate in table fellowship with them. Without such fellowship the Gentile mission would have been tremendously jeopardized. Furthermore, the resolution of the P-C episode allowed Paul to inaugurate the third part of Jesus' mission mandate—namely, to be witnesses "to the ends of the earth" (1:8). In Acts 13:1—14:28 the Gentile mission proceeded with great momentum. Many Gentiles were accepted into the church without having to keep the Jewish law or to undergo the ritual of circumcision.

Unfortunately the impact of the P-C episode did not last very long, and its resolution was quickly forgotten. Less than four chapters later the narrator reports that some Christians of Jewish background came to Antioch and insisted that unless Gentiles observe the Mosaic law and be circumcised they will not be saved (Acts 15:1).[66] The intrusion and demand of these Jewish Christians of Pharisaic background created "no small dissension and debate" (v. 2), signs of conflict within the community.[67] Unable to resolve the conflict among themselves, Paul and Barnabas had to go to Jerusalem to settle once and for all the issue of Gentile circumcision with the apostles and elders.[68]

---

66. The demands of circumcision and observance of the Mosaic law are interpretations of God's words spoken to Abraham in Gen 17:10–14 and to Moses in Deut 5:28–33. See Fitzmyer, *Acts*, 545–46.

67. Witherington (*Acts*, 450) notes that "there was not just debate, there was στάσις, conflict, requiring conflict resolution."

68. There is much discussion about the number of visits Paul made to Jerusalem by the time of the Apostolic Council. According to Acts, Paul made three visits to Jerusalem (Acts 9:26–29; 11:27–30; 15:1–5). But from Paul's own account in Galatians, he visited Jerusalem only twice before the Jerusalem Council (Gal 1:18–20//Acts 9:26–29; Gal 2:1//Acts 15). The visit reported by Luke in Acts 11:27–30 is not mentioned by Paul. For a detail discussion on the relationships between Acts 11, 15 and Galatians 1–2 and the historicity of Acts 15, see Witherington, *Acts*, 440–50; Fitzmyer, *Acts*, 539–41; Marshall, *Acts*, 244–47; Wilson, *Gentiles and Gentile Mission*, 178–91.

The Case of the P-C Episode in Acts 15

Apparently the case of Gentile admission and integration into the church without first becoming a Jew was not completely settled in Acts 10:1—11:18. Though the issue had been resolved between Peter and other Jerusalem leaders, it was not officially approved by the whole church. The problem resurfaced, and this time needed to be resolved by a larger assembly of apostles and elders. Thus the so-called "Jerusalem Council" was convened.[69]

The decision of the Jerusalem Council had tremendous ramifications upon the church as a whole and upon the Gentile mission in particular. In a nutshell, the Council decided that circumcision and observance of all the prescriptions of the Mosaic law were not necessary to be a Christian. The only requirements for Gentile Christians were to abstain "from things polluted by idols, and from fornification and from whatever has been strangled and from blood" (15:20). These dietary and moral requirements enabled Jews and Gentiles to associate with one other and to share in table fellowship. This significant decision was the result of two major speeches, first by Peter and then by James. In both of these speeches the P-C episode plays a major role in the argument for the case of the Gentile mission and integration.[70]

Peter's Speech (Acts 15:7–11)

The presence of Paul and Barnabas at the Council provoked tension and debate. The Jewish Christians of Pharisaic background once again insisted that circumcision and observance of the Mosaic law were necessary conditions for salvation (v. 5). If the Gentiles wanted to be admitted into the church, then they have to fulfill these two conditions. During this intense debate, Peter intervened and said,

> 7b "My brothers, you know that in the early days God made a choice among you, that I should be the one through whom the Gentiles would hear the message of the good news and become believers.
> 8 And God, who knows the human heart, testified to them by

---

69. The Jerusalem Council was held sometime late in 49 CE. For a concise summary of the events that took place before the Apostolic Council, see Witherington, *Acts*, 444, n. 361. For varied historical reconstructions of the actual situation, see Marshall, *Acts*, 242–47.

70. Since the aim here is merely to show the role of the P-C episode in Acts 15, the analysis of the two speeches are brief, touching only on the related issues. For a detailed analysis see any basic commentary.

> giving them the Holy Spirit, just as he did to us; ⁹ and in cleansing their hearts by faith he has made no distinction between them and us. ¹⁰ Now therefore why are you putting God to the test by placing on the neck of the disciples a yoke that neither our ancestors nor we have been able to bear? ¹¹ On the contrary, we believe that we will be saved through the grace of the Lord Jesus, just as they will." (NRSV)

Peter began his speech by recalling an event which happened "in the early days" of the church. That epoch-making event was none other than the Cornelius episode. The listeners were reminded of its significance.[71] Looking back at the Cornelius incident, Peter now understood more fully the meaning of his vision and the event that had taken place in Caesarea.

First and foremost, Peter points out (as he did in 11:16–17) that the outpouring of the gift of the Holy Spirit upon the Gentiles "as he did to us" clearly demonstrates that God makes no distinction between Jews and Gentiles. Furthermore, the fact that the Holy Spirit came down upon the Gentiles even before baptism is now interpreted by Peter "as a form of heavenly testimony to Christians of Jewish background about the acceptability of the Gentiles' share in the divine plan of salvation."[72] Moreover, Peter points out that God knew the hearts of these Gentiles and that "they were and would respond in genuine faith to the gospel."[73] Thus God cleansed them without making a distinction between "us and them" because of their faith in Jesus Christ. Since God had accepted these Gentiles without their first becoming Jews, why should they now carry the yoke which "neither our ancestors nor we have been able to bear" (15:10)? According to Peter, imposing circumcision and the observance of the Mosaic law upon the Gentiles would be putting God to the test.

Peter concludes his speech by stating that salvation for both Jew and Gentile comes through grace and faith and not through the law (15:11). Tannehill rightly points out that this is not a minor point, "for 15:11 is the epitome of what Peter has been taught by God through his experience with Cornelius. It is also the central insight that should guide the Jerusalem church in its decision."[74]

---

71. Witherington (*Acts*, 453, n. 384) suggests that as many as ten years may have passed. Thus a reminder was probably necessary. See also Wilson, *Gentiles and Gentile Mission*, 192; Soards, *Speeches*, 90–92; Witherup, "Cornelius Over," 60–62.

72. Fitzmyer, *Acts*, 547.

73. Witherington, *Acts*, 454.

74. Tannehill, *Narrative Unity*, 2:186.

The Plot

Peter's speech had a powerful effect on his listeners. His testimony from past experience, particularly the appeal to the Cornelius episode, changed the atmosphere of the assembly. Previously there was heated debate (15:7), but after Peter's personal testimony everyone (even those challenging table fellowship with Gentiles) grew silent (15:12). Now they seemed willing to listen to Paul and Barnabas, who recounted "all the signs and wonders that God had done through them among the Gentiles" (15:12).

It is noteworthy that Paul's role in Acts 15 is kept to a minimum. His contribution is at most "implied and indirect."[75] While his report confirms what Peter has been saying, Paul seems to have little or no impact upon the final decision of the council.[76] The person with sufficient influence and authority to settle the matter was neither Peter nor Paul, but James.

JAMES' SPEECH (15:13–21)

James begins by summarizing Peter's speech, saying, "My brothers, listen to me. Simeon has related how God first looked favorably on the Gentiles, to take from among them a people for his name" (15:14). The clear reference to Peter's speech indicates his support and approval of Peter's position and yet at the same time it provides new insight into the Cornelius episode.[77]

In order to appreciate the theological implications of James' initial declaration, it is necessary to examine the terminology which he used. The Greek word *laos* ("people"), which in the Old Testament exclusively refers to Israel, is consciously chosen here instead of the normal designation

---

75. Fitzmyer, *Acts*, 552.

76. Many scholars have correctly pointed out that the lack of influence of Paul and Barnabas on the decisions of the council (as narrated by Luke) is quite different from what is reported by Paul in his letter to the Galatians. The discrepancy is quite noticeable. According to Galatians 2, Paul maintains that he resisted the "false brothers." Furthermore, through his effort and persistence the "pillars" of Jerusalem—James, Cephas and John—came to a decision to which Paul himself agreed. Paul reports no conditions placed on Gentile Christians except that they remember the poor. Such a discrepancy has led many scholars to question the accuracy of Luke's narration of Acts 15. According to Fitzmyer (*Acts*, 543–44), Acts 15 consists of two separate stories joined together. The first story (15:3–12) dealt with the issue of the circumcision of Gentile converts and their observance of the Mosaic law; the second story (15:13–33), however, dealt with the issue of dietary laws and took place at a different time. It appears that Paul was not present at the second meeting. Fitzmyer distinguishes these two events by calling the first "the Jerusalem Council" and the latter "the Jerusalem Decree." See also Johnson, *Acts*, 269–70.

77. For a detailed analysis of James' speech, see Soards, *Speeches*, 92–95; Bauckham, "James and Gentiles," 154–84.

ethnē ("nations" or "Gentiles").⁷⁸ By referring to the Gentiles as *laos*, James acknowledges that they have been accepted by God and have become "a people of God" just like Israel. The descent of the Holy Spirit upon Cornelius and his household is irrefutable (15:28). Thus, there is no longer a distinction between Jews and Gentiles—not even in terminology.

This idea is revolutionary, particularly when it comes from James, who represents a more conservative church. To back up this new development, James appeals to Scripture, citing Amos 9:11–12 (Acts 15:16–18). James shows that this Old Testament prophecy—namely, God's restoration of the dwelling of David in order that the Gentiles might seek the Lord—is being fulfilled. Having proved his theological point, James settles the matter by proposing a compromise, requiring the Gentiles "to abstain only from things polluted by idols, and from fornification and from whatever has been strangled and from blood" (15:20).⁷⁹

An Irrefutable Test Case

In short, the P-C episode played a significant role in the final decision of accepting Gentiles into the church without first requiring them to become Jews. Peter made explicit references to the P-C episode in his speech and claimed that God's initiative in pouring out the same gift of the Holy Spirit upon the Gentiles in Caesarea provided an irrefutable test case of God's approval and acceptance (10:44; 11:15; 15:8). To object is to oppose God's will and plan. Peter's personal testimony silenced all dissension at the Council. As an authoritative figure that represented the Jerusalem church, James supported Peter's testimony and backed him up with a Scripture citation. James' fourfold requirements of Gentile Christians served as a compromise which was unanimously accepted and endorsed by the whole church. Consequently the role and function of the P-C episode is to serve as a test case for the acceptance of Gentiles as equal members of the church. Furthermore, Acts 10:1—11:18 helped to resolve once and for all the issue of circumcision and the observance of the Mosaic law.

---

78. *BDAG*, 586–87 and 276–77. See also Bruce, *Acts*, 251; Johnson, *Acts*, 264; Fitzmyer, *Acts*, 554.

79. The four prohibitions come from Lev 17–18 and are binding on the alien who sojourns in the land of Israel. See Bauckham, "James and Gentiles," 172–78; Dunn, *Acts*, 204–6.

CONCLUSION

The structure of the P-C episodic plot embodies the five stages of the *quinary* scheme. In the *exposition* (10:1–8) the narrator introduces the traits, military status, and religious piety of Cornelius. Furthermore, by means of "delayed exposition," the narrator continues to add new information about Cornelius throughout the narrative. While the delaying technique makes Cornelius a more attractive and worthy candidate for admission and fellowship, it also creates greater interest and adds suspense to the plot.

In the second stage, the *complication* (10:9–43), the narrator introduces tension into the story. The protagonist Peter experiences three conflicts: with the Spirit (or God), with himself, and with Cornelius and his household. This dramatic tension increases until the descent of the Holy Spirit. The sudden outpouring of the Holy Spirit upon Cornelius and his household culminates the plot of the P-C episode. This is the *climax* and the major turning point of the whole narrative (10:44–46). Having personally witnessed the outpouring of the Holy Spirit upon the Gentiles, Peter is transformed. In this fourth stage of the P-C episodic plot, the *resolution* (10:47–48), Peter finally and completely accepts these Gentiles by baptizing them and by participating in table fellowship with them. Though the narrative seems to be completely resolved and ends in a state of equilibrium, the closure is deceptive and illusory.

When Peter goes up to Jerusalem the story resumes, and a *new complication* (11:1–14) is introduced. Peter's participation in Jewish-Gentile table fellowship at Cornelius' house instigates a new conflict—namely, with the Jerusalem church. Peter defends his actions by recounting the event all over again, adding more interest and tension to the plot. Furthermore, from his own perspective Peter pinpoints the climatic moment of the plot when "the Holy Spirit fell upon them just as it had upon us at the beginning" (11:15). In this *second climax*, Peter emphasizes the surprise element of divine initiative. According to him, the reception of the same gift of the Holy Spirit (particularly *glossolalia*) by the Gentiles provides sufficient proof that God accepted them. Therefore the church too must not continue to resist God but rather to approve and legitimate Jewish-Gentile fellowship. This is the *second resolution* (11:16–17) of the P-C episodic plot.

In the *final situation* (11:18), the leaders of the Jerusalem church are convinced by Peter's argument. Their silence followed by their praise of God brings closure and rest to the narrative. At this point the issue of Jewish-Gentile table fellowship seems to have been completely resolved. Little does the reader know that it has only been suspended until Acts 15.

Peter and Cornelius

The issue of Jewish-Gentile fellowship reaches another turning point in Acts 15. Some Jewish Christians of Pharisaic background demand that Gentiles be circumcised and observe the Mosaic law in order to be saved. At the Jerusalem Council Peter stands up to defend the case of the Gentiles by appealing to the Cornelius episode. Peter argues that, since God has cleansed their hearts by faith and has poured out the same gift of the Holy Spirit upon them, this test case proves that God has accepted the Gentiles without imposing upon them the yoke of the law. James, the authoritative figure of the Jerusalem church, fully supports Peter and cites Scripture to back up Peter's position. Consequently the P-C episode plays a crucial role in settling the issue and finalizing the decision of the Jerusalem Council. Undoubtedly for Luke, Acts 10:1—11:18 is an irrefutable test case for the mission to the Gentiles and their integration into the church as equal members.

5   *The Characters*

WHILE EVENTS CORRESPOND TO verbs and settings to adverbs, characters are like nouns. In other words, characters are the actors who perform the various activities that make up the plot of a story. Similar to a grammatical sentence which consists of both a subject and a verb, "character and plot are interdependent, and both are essentials of a narrative."[1] The novelist Henry James asks, "What is character but the determination of incident [plot]? What is incident but the illustration of character?"[2]

Rather than entering into the endless discussion about plot-centered or character-centered narrative (which many have already done),[3] it seems more appropriate simply to assume that there is a close interrelationship between character and plot. Each depends on the other to create a meaningful and attractive story. Similar to an umbrella, plot functions like the frame, while characters are like the fabric.[4] Both the frame and the fabric of an umbrella are indispensable for providing shade and shelter.

---

1. Darr, *On Character Building*, 39.

2. James, "Art of Fiction," quoted in Powell, *What is Narrative Criticism?*, 51.

3. Many formalists and structuralists are plot-centered. Their claim that character is subordinate to plot can be traced back to Aristotle's famous dictum: "We maintain, therefore, that the first essential, the life and soul, so to speak, of Tragedy is the Plot; and that the Characters come second" (*Poetics*, 6). For the formalist and structuralist conceptions of character, see Chatman, *Story and Discourse*, 111–13. For a more comprehensive discussion over the complex relationship between character and plot in narratives, see Shepherd, *Narrative Function*, 51–67.

There are narrative critics who are of the opinion that the debate over character-centered or plot-centered priority is futile. They simply acknowledge the fact that character and plot are interrelated and interdependent. See Chatman, *Story and Discourse*, 113; Darr, *On Character Building*, 39; Rhoads et al., *Mark as Story*, 98; Fianu, "Narrative-Critical and Theological Study," 84.

4. I owe this image to Marguerat and Bourquin, *How to Read*, 58.

Peter and Cornelius

In the last chapter we analyzed the plot of Acts 10:1—11:18 and constructed the frame of the narrative. In his chapter we will focus on building the contours of that frame—namely giving flesh to its characters. We will first examine the characterization of the two main characters (Cornelius and Peter) and then of the two minor characters (Cornelius' messengers and the circumcised Christians). By gathering data from both direct and indirect characterization we will be able to give flesh and color to each of the characters and to discover their function in the story.

THE MAIN CHARACTERS

Cornelius and Peter are two indispensable characters to the plot of Acts 10:1—11:18. How do we go about evaluating and reconstructing them? This chapter will approach characterization[5] by asking three essential questions. The first question deals with the *characterization of the characters*: What are their character traits[6] and how are they revealed to the reader? From the character traits, which are found either explicitly in the narrative (direct characterization)[7] or in the clues inferred from the text (indirect characterization),[8] each of the characters may be classified in one of three

---

5. Theories on character and characterization are varied and complex. For different approaches to reconstructing characters in biblical narratives, see Sternberg, *Poetics*, 321–64, 475–81; Alter, *Art of Biblical Narrative*, 114–30; Bar-Efrat, *Narrative Art*, 47–92; Powell, *What is Narrative Criticism?*, 51–67; Marguerat and Bourquin, *How to Read*, 58–76; Darr, *On Character Building*, 16–36.

For a review of scholarship on character in modern literary theory, see Gowler, *Host, Guest, Enemy and Friend*, 29–75; Chatman, *Story and Discourse*, 107–38; Rimmon-Kenan, *Narrative Fiction*, 29–42.

For a discussion on the application of modern literary theory to an ancient document, see Shepherd, *Narrative Function*, 43–97; Burnett, "Characterization and Reader Construction," 3–28; McCracken, "Character," 29–42.

6. Powell ("Religious Leaders," 94) describes character traits as "persistent personal qualities that define the character involved." See also Chatman, *Story and Discourse*, 121–31.

7. Direct characterization may be voiced by the narrator, or by one of the characters, or by the subjects themselves. This literary technique is known as "telling" or *diegesis*. Since biblical narrators are omniscient and reliable (Luke for example is certainly considered a reliable narrator), their judgments and point of view are usually not called into question. However, when one character describes another, or when he/she speaks about him/herself, their characterization has varying degrees of reliability, which must be evaluated in light of their trustworthiness and consistency. See Booth, *Rhetoric*, 67–148; Powell, *What is Narrative Criticism?*, 52; Ska, "Our Fathers," 89; Bar-Efrat, *Narrative Art*, 54.

8. Instead of overtly telling the reader the characters' traits, the implied author may show the reader what the characters are like through statements that present either their

ways: as a *round character*, as a *flat character*, or as a *stock character*.[9] The second question involves the reader's evaluative point of view: What is the reader's perception of the characters?[10] The reader normally reacts to a character or a character group in one of three ways: *empathy*, *sympathy*, or *antipathy*.[11] The third question focuses on the character's reliability: How credible is the presentation of the character?[12]

By asking these three questions we will be able to reconstruct a portrait of the characters and to give flesh to their role and function in the narrative. We begin with Cornelius, since he is the first character introduced by the narrator.

Cornelius

Cornelius possesses multiple traits, for he grows and develops throughout the course of the narrative. His actions and speech surprise the reader as well as the other characters in the story. Since his personality is complex and his behavior is unpredictable, he appears as a "real person" with whom the reader can identify. Being dynamic and having a personality of his own, Cornelius is characterized as a "round" character.[13]

---

own point of view or through the comments of other characters about them. This technique of "showing" or indirect characterization—although more interesting and intriguing—is less precise and therefore unreliable. The reader must gather all the data from the narrative and evaluate them in order to figure out the implied author's portrait of the characters—a process which is not done for the reader by the narrator. Although this detective work is challenging, indirect presentation allows the reader to become involved in the reconstruction of the characters. See Powell, *What is Narrative Criticism?*, 52; Bar-Efrat, *Narrative Art*, 64.

9. These terms will be defined in the course of the presentation; for now see Powell, *What is Narrative Criticism?*, 55. Berlin names these three categories of characters differently: the round character is the *full-fledged character*; the flat character is the *type*; and the stock or functionary is the *agent*. See Berlin, *Poetics and Interpretation*, 23.

10. The "reader's perception" or "evaluative point of view" refers to the norms, values, and general world view that govern the way a character looks at things and renders judgments on them. See Powell, "Religious Leaders," 94.

11. Powell, *What is Narrative Criticism?*, 55–58; Marguerat and Bourquin, *How to Read*, 66–68.

12. Powell, *What is Narrative Criticism?*, 52–53.

13. "Round" characters are dynamic because they change and develop in the course of the narrative. They possess multiple and often conflicting traits. See Powell, *What is Narrative Criticism?*, 55; Ska, "Our Fathers," 83–84; Gunn and Fewell, *Narrative*, 75.

Peter and Cornelius

CHARACTERIZATION

The characterization of Cornelius is quite thorough and significantly positive. The narrator reveals his ethnic and military background, his religious and moral character, and his personal habits and traits. The only thing the narrator does not reveal is his physical appearance![14] The reader receives various evaluations of Cornelius from different characters in the narrative—from the reliable narrator, from the angel (representing the voice of God), from his messengers, and from Cornelius himself. This comprehensive (almost to the point of being redundant) presentation of Cornelius is uncommon in biblical narrative.[15] Hence there must be a reason or a narrative function for such a peculiar characterization of Cornelius; otherwise Luke—a master storyteller—would not have employed such a repetitive technique. The narrator begins by telling the reader (direct characterization) that the character's name is "Cornelius." Cornelius was a very common name, since thousands of slaves freed by Lucius Cornelius Sulla (138–78 BCE) had taken his name.[16] Although Cornelius is a popular name, the narrator gives the centurion an identity and an individuality that the reader can relate to. He is not anonymous like some other characters (for example, the centurions in Luke 7:1–10; 23:47, and the eunuch in Acts 8:26–40).

Cornelius is not just any soldier from the "Italian Cohort" (10:1).[17] He is a Roman centurion (*hekatontarchēs*) with a hundred men under his command. The narrator's precise description of his rank and occupation under-

---

14. For reasons why physical description is sparse in biblical narrative, see Bar-Efrat, *Narrative Art*, 48–53; Gunn and Fewell, *Narrative*, 57–59; Rimmon-Kenan, *Narrative Fiction*, 65–66.

15. Barbi ("Cornelio," 279, n. 11) states, "Luca più volte, presentando un personaggio, ne indica la professione o condizione sociale (cf. Lc 19,2; At 13,6; 19,24; 27,1), la religiosità (cf. Lc 2,25; At 18,7) oppure offre più caratterizzazioni insieme (cf. Lc 1,5–7; 2,36–37; 23,50; At 5,34; 9,36; 16,14; 18,24). Mai però vengono elencati tanti elementi insieme come nel caso di Cornelio soprattutto per quanto riguarda le qualità religioso-morali."

16. Haenchen, *Acts*, 346; Lukasz, *Evangelizzazione e conflitto*, 51.

17. While there is archaeological evidence supporting a Second Italian Cohort stationed in Syria around 69 CE, there is no evidence for the presence of the unit named here in Caesarea for the period 41–44 CE. According to the chronology of Acts the conversion of Cornelius occurred before the death of Herod Agrippa, which was probably in 41 CE. See Johnson, *Acts*, 181; Lukasz, *Evangelizzazione e conflitto*, 52, n. 13; Speidel, "Roman Army," 233–40.

This discrepancy has provoked much discussion about the historicity of the P-C episode. For a historical-critical investigation, see Dibelius, "Die Bekehrung des Cornelius," 96–107; Bovon, "Tradition et redaction," 22–45; Löning, "Die Korneliustradition," 1–19; Haacker, "Dibelius und Cornelius," 234–51; Gaventa, *From Darkness to Light*, 96–129.

scores his identity as a Gentile, "since Jews, from the time of Julius Caesar, were exempt from serving in the Roman army."[18] Moreover, the narrator uses three terms to highlight Cornelius' identity as a Gentile: "Gentile" (*ethnos*, 10:45; 11:1, 18); "foreigner" (*allophulos*, 10:28); "uncircumcision" (*akrobustia*, 11:3).

Cornelius, however, is not just any Gentile. He has a high social status in society. His status is implied throughout the narrative: he has servants and devoted soldiers at his disposal (10:7); he is clearly a patron of a large household (10:2); and he has many relatives and friends (10:24). Thus the characterization of Cornelius' military, ethnic and social status causes the reader to wonder, "What kind of impact will this Gentile veteran soldier make if he is converted to Christianity?"

The reliable narrator specifically describes Cornelius as *eusebēs* ("devout, godly, or pious"), a quality often used in the Greek-speaking world to describe someone who revered the gods but rarely attributed by New Testament authors to a Jew or a Christian.[19] Nevertheless, not only is Cornelius described as "devout" (10:2) but also the soldier who is his messenger (10:7). Cornelius' piety and reverence for the sacred are not only indicated by the reliable narrator but are also exemplified in Cornelius' speech. Cornelius responds to the angel ("What is it, Lord (*kurie*)?") with respect and reverence, even though he does not know who the angel really is. When Peter enters Cornelius' house, the Gentile centurion addresses the apostle courteously: "So I sent for you at once; and you were kind enough to come" (10:33a). Furthermore, the uncircumcised centurion thinks and speaks "biblically"[20] like a believer: "Now then we are all present before God to hear all that you have been commanded by the Lord" (10:33b).

Cornelius also displays religious piety through his actions. We are told by the narrator in verse 2 that this Gentile soldier "prays to God constantly." His perseverance in prayer is praised by the angel (10:4) and confirmed

---

18. Matson, *Household Conversion Narratives*, 104. According to Josephus (*Antiquities of the Jews* 18.84) military service was incompatible with the observance of the Jewish law.

19. The adjective *eusebēs* occurs only three times in the New Testament (Acts 10:2, 7; 2 Peter 2:9). Luke uses the adjective *eulabēs* to describe a "pious" Jew (Luke 2:25; Acts 2:5) and a Christian (Acts 8:2; 22:12). Wilcox ("God-Fearers," 104) points out that "the term εὐσεβής is applied by Josephus almost exclusively to Jewish saints and heroes." For a detailed analysis of the adjective *eusebēs*, see Foerster, "εὐσεβής," 175–85; Lieu, "Race of the God-fearers," 493–97; Lukasz, *Evangelizzazione e conflitto*, 53–54.

20. Haenchen (*Acts*, 351) says "Luke has the devout Cornelius to speak and think 'biblically.'"

Peter and Cornelius

by Cornelius himself who repeats exactly what the angel had said (10:31). Cornelius indicates to Peter—and obviously to the reader as well—that he was praying in his house at the ninth hour when the angel appeared to him (10:30). In addition to Cornelius' fervent prayer life, this Gentile centurion "gives alms generously to the people." Cornelius' charity—particularly to the *laos* (that is, "Israel")—is mentioned by the reliable narrator (10:2), accentuated by the angel (10:4) and repeated by Cornelius himself (10:31). Obviously Luke goes out of his way to show that this Gentile centurion is a generous benefactor of Israel.[21]

It is noteworthy that the mention of praying and alms-giving together is not arbitrary.[22] Alms-giving and prayer were two important characteristics of a pious Jew (Tob 12:8; Sir 7:10). Consequently, by highlighting Cornelius' piety Luke clearly wants to show the reader that this Gentile centurion is unlike impious pagans. Cornelius not only is no threat but on the contrary sympathizes with the Jewish nation.[23]

Cornelius is also characterized as a "God-fearing man" (*phoboumenos ton theon*). This religious quality is first mentioned by the reliable narrator (10:2) and then confirmed by Cornelius' messengers (10:22). Peter too makes explicit reference to Cornelius' God-fearing quality in his speech (10:35). Furthermore, the narrator also informs the reader—from an "inside view"—that Cornelius was "seized with fear" (10:4) when he saw the angel coming to him.

According to the biblical tradition, fearing God is a sign of reverence and obedience to God's will. Both the Torah and Wisdom literature frequently extol the children of Israel to fear God.[24] Hence Cornelius definitely

---

21. In the Greco-Roman world benefactors were recognized as persons of exceptional merit. Caesar Augustus and Nero were known as great benefactors. See Danker, *Luke*, 28–46.

22. These two themes are very dear to Luke: "alms-giving" (Luke 11:41; 12:43; Acts 9:36; 24:17) and "prayer."

There is a variant reading in 10:30 claiming that Cornelius was also "fasting." Although this variant reading (*nesteuōn kai* before *proseuchomenos*) is well attested with many respectable witnesses (P^{50} A^c $D(*)$ E Ψ 33^{vid} M it sy sa mae), it is probably an interpolation by later scribes, who wanted to augment the virtues of Cornelius or who felt that fasting was necessary before baptism (Acts 9:9 and *Didache* 7:4). According to Metzger (*Textual Commentary*, 330–31) the best attested witnesses seem to be those without *nesteuōn kai* (P^{74} a A* B C 81 323 945 1739 *pc* vg bo).

23. The reader is reminded of the centurion from Capernaum (Luke 7:1–10) who built a synagogue and was loved by the Jewish nation.

24. See Deut 6:2, 13, 24; 10:12, 20; Pss 15:4; 22:24; 25:12; 33:8; Prov 3:7; 12:2; 24:21;

possesses the characteristics of a "God-fearer." Without going into a long discussion about the historical existence of "God-fearers"[25] (which is not the aim of this investigation), it is enough to point out that according to Luke[26] Cornelius is probably one of those Gentile "faith-seekers" or "synagogue-adherents" who was attracted to Judaism and yet had not become a full convert or a proselyte (who bore the full yoke of the Mosaic Law).

There is no question about the authenticity of Cornelius' religious piety in the narrative. Tannehill says, "The emphasis on Cornelius' piety is a noteworthy feature of the narrative rhetoric of this episode."[27] Perhaps Luke so strongly emphasizes Cornelius' piety in order to counter the common perception of Jews that Gentiles were impious and godless.[28] Luke demonstrates that a Gentile could be as pious as a Jew.[29]

Cornelius is also described as "righteous" (*dikaios*). Although this direct characterization is made from the evaluative point of view of Cornelius'

Qoh 5:6; Sir 1:13, 14, 16; 2:7, 8, 15–17. See also Lukasz, *Evangelizzazione e conflitto*, 55; Jolley, "Fear," 457.

25. The existence of the "God-fearers" was called into question by Kraabel who claims that Luke invented this class of people for a theological purpose. Kraabel says that the archeological and literary evidence is "far from convincing proof for the existence of such a class of Gentiles as traditionally defined by the assumptions of the secondary literature" ("Disappearance," 121; *idem*, "Greek, Jews, and Lutherans," 147–57). For a similar view see Gager, "Jews, Gentiles, and Synagogues," 91–99.

However, many challenge Kraabel's conclusions and advocate the historical existence of "God-fearers." See Finn, "God-Fearers Reconsidered," 75–84; Overman, "God-Fearers," 17–26; Murphy-O'Connor, "Lots of God-Fearers?" 418–24.

For a literary and theological treatment of the subject, see Lieu, "Race of the God-Fearers," 483–501; Levinskaya, "God-Fearers," 17–126.

For a concise treatment of "God-fearers," see the following recent commentaries: Barrett, *Acts*, 1:499–501; Witherington, *Acts*, 341–44.

26. The references to "God-fearers"—other than Matthew 23:15—are found exclusively in Acts. Besides the occurrences in the P-C episode, "God-fearers" (as *hoi phoboumenoi ton theon* or *hoi sebomenoi ton theon*) are mentioned another seven times in the Acts of the Apostles (13:16; 13:26; 13:43; 13:50; 16:14; 17:4; 17:17).

For a discussion on how "God-fearers" could have been (and actually were) either the backbone of the Gentile Christian communities or the greatest impediment to the spread of the Christian mission in the Acts of the Apostles, see Levinskaya, "God-Fearers," 117–26. Furthermore, Witherington concludes that "Luke's obvious interest in folk like a Cornelius or a Titus might be because he himself, and/or Theophilus, had been a 'God-fearer' before becoming a Christian" (*Acts*, 344).

27. Tannehill, *Narrative Unity*, 2:133. See also Wilson, *Gentiles and Gentile Mission*, 176.

28. Barbi, "Cornelio," 279.

29. Wilcox, "God-Fearers," 118.

messengers (10:22), Cornelius' righteousness is unquestionable. Peter—a reliable character-narrator—commends Cornelius' deeds of "righteousness" (*dikaiosunē*) when he says, "in every nation the one who fears God and does righteousness is acceptable to him" (10:35). What the angel says to Cornelius ("Your prayers and your alms have ascended as a memorial before God," 10:4, 31) implies that he is a righteous person, for God only listens to those who are just and righteous—for example, Zechariah and Elizabeth (1:6) and Simeon (2:25).

In the Old Testament the Messiah is called righteous because his whole nature and all his actions are in conformity with the divine will.[30] In the Greco-Roman world as well as in the LXX the one who observed the law and fulfilled his civic duty was considered righteous and virtuous. He was the one who "fulfills his duties towards God and the theocratic society, meeting God's claim in this relationship. It is as he satisfies the demand of God that he has right on his side and therefore a righteous cause before God."[31]

Being righteous, Cornelius was acceptable to God, and thus he received the "gift" of the Holy Spirit and *glossolalia* (10:45–46). Furthermore God offered him salvation and redemption—"the repentance unto life" (11:18). Like a good Jew, Cornelius was awaiting the salvation of God. When the angel commanded him to send for Peter so that he and his household would be saved (11:14), Cornelius dispatched his servants without delay. We are also told that Cornelius was anxiously waiting (10:24) for Peter to arrive and to deliver the word commanded by the Lord (10:33). It is no surprise therefore that God granted Cornelius and his household "the repentance unto life" (11:18).

Reader's Perception

What is the reader's evaluative point of view or perception of Cornelius? The answer depends upon who the reader is. If the reader is a Gentile Christian, then he/she would identify with Cornelius and empathize with him.[32] For

---

30. Jer 23:5, 6; 33:15; Zech 9:9; Wis 2:18; 17:25, 28, 31, 42; 18:8. See Schrenk, "δίκαιος," 186–87.

31. Schrenk, "δίκαιος," 185.

32. The reader is more likely to empathize with characters who share a common evaluative point of view and common character traits. There are two types of empathy: *realistic empathy* (characters who are similar to the reader) and *idealistic empathy* (characters who represent what the reader would like to be). See Powell, *What is Narrative Criticism?*, 56; Marguerat and Bourquin, *How to Read*, 65.

example, Theophilus—who is a Gentile and the narratee of Acts—would certainly identify with Cornelius and empathize with his situation.[33]

On the other hand, if the reader is a Jewish Christian, he/she would probably only sympathize with Cornelius.[34] The reader would feel sympathy because of his religious and moral character. Though a Gentile, Cornelius lives almost like a Jew. Besides practicing the three cardinal virtues—piety, justice, and goodness (or charity),[35] this uncircumcised centurion is also a responsible patron.[36] Like a good *"paterfamilias"*[37] he fulfils the moral and religious obligations of educating his entire household to conform to a monotheistic and quasi-Judaic way of life. We are told that Cornelius is "devout and God-fearing *along with all his household*" (10:2; emphasis mine). Hence, Tannehill is correct in pointing out the "Jewishness" of this non-Jew. Luke even compares Cornelius' piety to that of faithful Jews like Mary and Ananias.[38] Needless to say, Cornelius' Jewishness would be appealing to a Jewish-Christian reader and to the implied reader as well. Thus, the reader—implied or real—would certainly sympathize with Cornelius and his situation.

Reliability

Cornelius receives an exceptionally favorable portrayal in the P-C episode. It seems that the narrator goes out of his way—even sometimes to the point of being redundant—to impress upon the reader the fact that Cornelius is not just any Gentile. He is religiously and morally upright. He is charitable

---

33. Witherington, *Acts*, 64. If Luke (before becoming a Christian) had been a "God-fearer" like Cornelius and Theophilus—as Witherington has suggested (*Acts*, 344)—then we can understand why Luke esteems Cornelius so highly.

Although Theophilus is probably a historical person and is the overt narratee of Luke-Acts, he simply symbolizes a wider audience.

34. Sympathy is related to empathy but sympathy has a less intense identification with another. Powell, *What is Narrative Criticism?*, 57; Marguerat and Bourquin, *How to Read*, 68.

35. Plato's fourth cardinal virtue is *sōphrōn* ("temperament or self-control"). See Schrenk, "δίκαιος," 182, n. 2.

36. According to Malina ("Patronage," 151), the word "patron" comes from the Greek and Latin word for father, *pater*. Furthermore, the title "father" in the Bible refers to the role and status of a patron when it is applied to someone who lacks the genetic qualifications. For a discussion on the patron-client relations in the social world of Luke-Acts, see Moxnes, "Patron-Client Relations," 241–68.

37. Lukasz, *Evangelizzazione e conflitto*, 58.

38. Tannehill, *Narrative Unity*, 2:133.

and sympathetic to the Jewish nation. His obedience to the command of the angel shows that he is a man of faith. Although he is a Roman centurion possessing a high social status, he is nevertheless humble and respectful.[39] Furthermore, he is open and receptive to the Gospel of Jesus Christ. This characterization not only makes Cornelius different from the stereotyped Gentiles—impious and idolatrous—but ironically makes him resemble a faithful Jew whom the implied author wants his reader to imitate.

The question that needs to be asked is: How reliable is Luke's characterization of Cornelius? Since the presentation of Cornelius is done primarily through direct characterization or "telling"—namely by the reliable narrator (Luke) and by the angel (the representative of God)—the characterization of Cornelius is indeed reliable. Furthermore, since the information comes directly from a reliable source and a divine figure, it impresses upon the implied reader the feeling of sympathy for or even empathy with Cornelius. Needless to say, if God accepts this Gentile by pouring out upon him the gift of the Holy Spirit, how can the church possibly turn him away?

Peter

Peter is the hero or the protagonist of the story. His actions and speech are indispensable to the plot of Acts 10:1—11:18. Being a fully developed character, he embodies both positive and negative traits—manifesting conflicting as well as contradictory tendencies. Similar to "real people," Peter grows, develops, and changes his mind as the story unfolds; furthermore, his behavior is often unpredictable. With such a dynamic personality Peter is undoubtedly a "round" character.

CHARACTERIZATION

The presentation of Peter—unlike that of Cornelius—is not so much an overt characterization as a collection of clues given in the text. This technique is called "showing" or indirect characterization. Indirect characterization can be displayed through: speech, action, external appearance, environment, and comparison and contrast.[40] Through careful detective

---

39. When Cornelius finally meets Peter face to face, the centurion falls down at the apostle's feet to reverence him (10:26).

40. Gowler (*Host, Guest, Enemy and Friend*, 72–73) clarifies these five features as follows:
    a) *Speech*. Everything the narrator and characters say, including reported internal speech (i.e., thoughts), must be taken into account in characterization. The form,

The Characters

work, which includes evaluating all the data inferred from the text, we are able to reconstruct the implied author's portrait of Peter. Before presenting the character traits exemplified in the text, let us first examine Peter's name.

There are four instances in Acts—noticeably all in the P-C episode—in which the phrase "Simon who is called Peter" is used:

- by the angel (10:5)
- by Cornelius' messengers (10:18)
- by Cornelius, who repeats the words of the angel (10:32)
- by Peter, who repeats Cornelius' words uttered by the angel (11:13)

Besides these four identifications of Peter, whose original name is Simon, the narrator in Acts prefers to call him simply "Rock"—a name which was given to him by Jesus in Luke 6:14.[41] The name Rock is more personal and endearing. It could symbolize solidity, resistance to change, and even stubbornness, since Peter the Rock three times resists the angel's command, "Rise, Rock; slaughter and eat!" Ironically, however, Rock's character is not subject to petrification, since he changes and develops as the story progresses. Like Cornelius, Rock too experiences conversion.

Peter possesses multiple traits—many of which are conflicting and even contradictory. Whether he wants to or not, Peter actually triggers a series of conflicts: with God (10:14–16), with the Gentile Cornelius (10:28), and with the leaders in Jerusalem (11:1–18). Furthermore, Peter's behavior

---

style, or content of the characters' speech, for example, can tell us much about their social standing, relationships with other characters, and other aspects of characterization.

b) *Action.* The actions of characters—although they are less explicit and more ambiguous—can also help to define characters more clearly. These references may be either acts of commission, acts of omission, or contemplated acts.

c) *External Appearance.* A character's external appearance—physical features, clothing, movements, gestures, and so on—also needs to be processed.

d) *Environment.* A character's environment, when described, can be of great importance in characterization. The environment includes the physical surroundings and even social relationships, such as one's family or social class.

e) *Comparison/Contrast.* Characterization may also be reinforced by comparing or contrasting one or more characters with another. These comparisons or contrasts may be made explicitly or implicitly.

41. Luke uses "Simon" eleven times in the Gospel. With the exception of Luke 5:8 all occurrences come before 6:14. The name "Cephas" does not appear at all in Luke-Acts. It is noteworthy that Paul refers to "Peter" in Gal 2:7–8 while using "Cephas" in Gal 1:18; 2:9, 11, 14 and in 1 Cor 1:12; 3:22; 9:5; 15:5. See Brown et al., eds., *Peter*, 9, n. 18, and 111, n. 244.

Peter and Cornelius

is often inconsistent. On the one hand he says that he is a strict observer of the dietary laws and never eats "anything profane and unclean" (10:14). On the other hand, Peter resides with a tanner whose trade and life-style are commonly considered to be unclean. Moreover, Peter hosts Gentiles in a Jewish home (10:23a), enters a Gentile house (10:25, 28), and then eats with them without qualms (10:48; 11:3). Clearly Peter's words are not consistent with his actions.

Peter also exhibits other intriguing human traits. The narrator overtly tells the reader that Peter is extremely confused by the heavenly vision (10:17). He is very slow to understand its meaning (10:19). Moreover, Peter hesitates to obey the angel's command to go immediately to Caesarea (10:20, 23a) and vacillates about entering a Gentile home (10:28). Interestingly however Peter's character changes after the outpouring of the Spirit upon the Gentiles. He is no longer hesitant and indecisive in his actions but rather bold and courageous. Having witnessed the Spirit descending upon Cornelius and his household, in the same way that he himself had experienced, Peter without question and without hesitation orders the Gentiles to be baptized immediately (10:47). Furthermore Peter graciously accepts Cornelius' hospitality and dines with the Gentiles without qualms (10:48; 11:3). As if strengthened by the Spirit himself, the apostle fearlessly goes up to Jerusalem[42] to give another testimony of his apostleship—a personal

---

42. Acts 11:2 contains the longest expansion of the Western text found in the P-C episode. It differs tremendously from the Alexandrian witnesses. Codex D (supported by p w^{syh*} mae) reads: "After some time Peter, therefore, wanted to journey to Jerusalem, and after having called the brothers and having strengthened them, [he departed] carrying out many discourses throughout the country and teaching them; he also went to meet them and reported to them the grace of God. But the brethren of the circumcision disputed with him . . ."

The Western text of this verse has been thoroughly studied by exegetes. After having critically analyzed the vocabulary and style, Boismard ("Texts of Acts," 147–57) concludes that the Western text is not only authentically Lukan but also the first addition of Luke's. In a more recent study, Geer ("Presence and Significance," 59–76) revisited the issue of Lukanisms in the Western text of Acts and criticized Boismard's conclusion as only plausible and not at all convincing.

Metzger (*Textual Commentary*, 337–38), who favors the Alexandrian text, might be correct in saying that the reason for the expansion of the Western text is "to avoid putting Peter in a bad light." In order to alleviate the negative impression of the Alexandrian text that Peter had to interrupt his missionary activities to go to Jerusalem in order to justify himself and his actions, the Western reviser edited the original text to explain that Peter was not summoned to Jerusalem but desired to go there. But before Peter goes up to Jerusalem to report on his missionary work, he went about not only preaching and teaching but also strengthening the brethren throughout the region. Based on the weight of its

witness which changes the course of Jewish-Gentile relations and of the Gentile mission.

Peter gives many important speeches in Acts.[43] His first sermon at Pentecost, for example, converted three thousand people (2:14-41). Even though Peter's last missionary speech in Acts 10:34-43 does not have such massive effect (only Cornelius and his household are converted),[44] it is nevertheless unlike many of the other speeches that Peter has given. The address contains more information about the ministry of Jesus than Peter's previous speeches. In fact the address is the most concise summary of the "apostolic *kerygma* in a nutshell."[45] It is also a "classic proclamation of the gospel to Gentile sympathizers."[46]

Since the focus of our analysis is on the characterization of Peter,[47] we need to ask: What does this speech tell us about his character? What one says and how one says it can reveal a lot about the nature of the speaker. Bar-Efrat keenly notes:

> Speech is also an important way of charactering individuals indirectly. Traits of both the speaker and the interlocutor are expressed through speech, or to be more precise, all speech reflects and exposes the speaker, while it sometimes also brings to light qualities of the person being addressed (or reveals the speaker's opinion of that person).[48]

Needless to say, the reader can learn much about Peter's theology and Christology through his speeches (Acts 10:34-43 and 11:4-17). First and foremost, Peter perceives God as "impartial" (*prosōpolēmptēs*),[49] showing

---

witnesses (P[45,74] ℵ A B 6 81 *pc*), the Alexandrian text is the preferred reading.

43. Acts 2:14-36; 3:12-26; 4:8-12; 5:29-32; 10:34-43. See Tannehill, "Functions," 400-414.

44. Interestingly, Matson (*Household Conversion Narratives*, 86-134) shows that this is still a mass conversion.

45. Bruce, *Acts*, 261.

46. Fitzmyer, *Acts*, 460.

47. To avoid repeating what others have already said, I am refraining from doing an exegetical analysis of Peter's speech. For such an analysis, see any major commentary, particularly Witherington, *Acts*, 355-59; Fitzmyer, *Acts*, 457-69; Johnson, *Acts*, 189-96; Barrett, *Acts*, 1:519-28. See also Soards, *Speeches*, 70-77; Tassin, "Conversion," 465-75.

48. Bar-Efrat, *Narrative Art*, 64-65.

49. The Greek phrase comes from the Hebrew idiom, which literally means "to lift up the face" (more idiomatically "to show favoritism"). Lev 19:15 forbids favoritism based upon appearances, particularly toward those who are weak. Deut 10:17 attributes

no favoritism toward anyone or toward any nation in particular. As long as a person fears the Lord and does righteousness, he/she is acceptable to God. Hence God is fair and just, inclusive and universal. Peter's frequent usage of words like "all," "anyone," and "everyone" clearly accentuates the universal nature of God.[50]

Secondly, Peter makes it theologically clear that God is the "main actor"[51] of all human events. God "sends out the message" (v. 36), "anoints Jesus of Nazareth" (v. 38), "raises him up on the third day" (v. 40), "allows him to show himself" (v. 40), and "chooses beforehand" those who are to be his witnesses (v. 41). Consequently, God has complete power and control over all human events and is actively involved in the salvation of humankind. Interestingly, Peter uses this theology to convince his opponents in Jerusalem to accept the Gentile mission. In his defense (Acts 11:4–17) Peter makes it clear to the Jerusalem assembly that the whole Cornelius episode was initiated and directed by God. According to Peter, it was God who showed him the "vision of the cloth" and told him "to slaughter and eat." It was God who told him to go to Caesarea without discrimination. Furthermore it was God who had commanded Cornelius to summon him to his house. And more importantly it was God who poured out the same gift of the Holy Spirit upon the Gentiles. Peter painstakingly points out (to the point of being redundant) that God was in full control and was the initiator of the whole affair. Peter, on the other hand, was just an "instrument" responding to the divine promptings.

Peter's personal testimony about Jesus (both in 10:34–43 and in 11:16–17) reveals his Christology. First of all, Peter testifies that Jesus of Nazareth is the "Christ" and "Lord of all" (v. 36). God has anointed him "with the Holy Spirit and power" (v. 38). Jesus is "the one appointed by God as judge of the living and the dead" (v. 42). Secondly, Jesus' ministry and mission were to preach "the good news of peace"[52] (v. 36), to do good, to

---

impartiality to God, "who has no favorites, accepts no bribes; who executes justice for the orphan and the widow, and befriends the alien, feeding and clothing him." New Testament authors too highlight God's impartiality as a central theological axiom (Rom 2:11; Col 3:25; Eph 6:9; 1 Pet 1:17; Jas 2:1, 9). For a detailed study, see Bassler, "Luke and Paul," 546–52. See also Johnson, *Acts*, 191; Barrett, *Acts*, 1:519; Templeton, "Reflecting on Acts," 97–105; Dupont, *Nouvelles études*, 320–23.

50. Matera, "Acts," 64.

51. Johnson, *Acts*, 193.

52. For a detailed discussion on "peace" as an underlying theme of Peter's whole speech, see O'Toole, "Εἰρήνη," 461–76.

heal and to cast out demons (v. 38). Although they killed Jesus by hanging him on a tree, God raised him up on the third day (v 40), after which he appeared to many, who ate and drank with him (v. 41). In a nutshell, Peter proclaims: Jesus of Nazareth is the Universal Savior and Messiah! He is the prophetic fulfillment of all the prophets of old had foretold (v. 43); therefore anyone who believes in him is saved through his name (v. 43; similarly in 11:17). Consequently, Peter's only qualification for salvation is "faith"—not the observance of the law nor the obligation of becoming a Jew!

In general, the content and the form of the speeches reveal that Peter is a theologian. His image of God—perhaps new to some—is solidly grounded in Scripture. Although his interpretation of the Christ event is theologically consistent with the author's Gospel narrative,[53] Peter's message of salvation through faith alone is radically new and definitely controversial. Though his style of Greek—particularly in 10:36–38—is "miserable"[54] (perhaps because it is meant to be delivered orally), the content of Peter's speech is nevertheless informative and appealing to his audience.[55] The form or style of the speeches shows that Peter is knowledgeable of Greek rhetoric, which he uses "to persuade the audience to come to a decision about Jesus Christ."[56]

In addition, Peter also appeals to his own experience and uses the first person plural to strengthen the credibility of his argument (notice the "we" and "us" in 10:39, 41, 42 and in 11:12, 15, 17). Peter explicitly claims that he too is one of the witnesses who saw all that Jesus did in the country of the Jews and in Jerusalem (10:39) and that he is one of the few chosen by God to eat and drink with the Risen Lord after he rose from the dead (10:41). And in his defense at Jerusalem Peter points out that he was not the only one who entered the Gentile's house, since six brothers accompanied him. Furthermore, Peter's usage of the first person plural demonstrates that God gave the Gentiles "the same gift as he had given us" (11:17). Consequently

---

53. Johnson, *Acts*, 195.

54. Fitzmyer, *Acts*, 460. As for whether the speech is a Lukan composition or not, Fitzmyer says, "The syntax of these verses, coupled with allusions to Isa 52:7 and 61:1, points much more to an echo of primitive kerygmatic preaching, undoubtedly derived from Palestinian tradition, than to a wholly Lucan composition."

55. Kurz (*Reading Luke-Acts*, 125) suggests that there is historical reliability in the ancient rhetorical practice of *prosopopoeia*, which creates speeches suited to particular speakers, occasions, and audiences.

56. Witherington, *Acts*, 355. Witherington also suggests that the speech in Acts 10:34–43 could be either forensic or deliberative rhetoric. According to Soards, the speech in 11:5–17 is a kind of "*judicial* rhetoric, offering a defense through *narration* that transfers the responsibility for Peter's action to God (metastasis)" (*Speeches*, 77).

Peter and Cornelius

Peter's personal testimony and inclusive language add credibility to his speech and prove irrefutable in his argument.

As the apostle whose name appears first on the list of the Twelve (Luke 6:14) and who was the first to see the Risen Lord (Luke 24:34),[57] Peter is rightfully a leader and spokesperson of the Jerusalem church. First of all, Peter is indirectly characterized as a spiritual leader. He is a leader who prays (Acts 10:9) and constantly directs his mind toward God to discover God's will and purpose (10:17, 19). Peter receives heavenly visions (10:10–20). He blindly—although at times hesitantly—collaborates with the "divine promptings,"[58] for without Peter's cooperation the vision would be ineffective. Interestingly, Peter shares his vision with others (first with Cornelius and then with the assembly in Jerusalem). More importantly, each time he narrates his story he discovers new meaning and significance in the vision. In other words, as a spiritual leader Peter involves others—even the whole community—in discerning the will of God.[59]

Besides being a spiritual leader, Peter is also the spokesperson of the Jerusalem church.[60] Although a leader supposedly carries a certain aura of authority and power, Peter nevertheless is humble and friendly. Peter humbly admits to Cornelius—and to the reader—that he is just "a mortal" (10:26). Moreover, although he is a Jew and a leader of a community, he associates with the servants and soldiers of a Gentile centurion and entertains them as guests (10:23a). Furthermore, when challenged (11:2–3), Peter does not impose his authority so that others accept his position nor does he appeal to Scripture. Rather he relates his personal experience, narrating the story in the order that he perceives (11:4–17). As Johnson rightly says,

---

57. Luke 24:34 hints that Peter is the first of the apostles to have seen the Risen Lord.

58. Tannehill (*Narrative Unity*, 2:128–29) highlights the significance of "divine promptings" in the P-C episode and how they require human response.

59. Johnson's discussion on discernment is enlightening: "Discernment enables humans to perceive their characteristically ambiguous experience as revelatory and to articulate such experience in a narrative of faith. Discernment enables others to hear such narratives as the articulation of faith and as having revelatory experience. Discernment enables communities to listen to such gathering narratives for the word of God that they might express. Discernment enables communities, finally, to decide for God" (*Scripture and Discernment*, 109).

60. Up to this point of the narrative Peter is the leader of the Jerusalem church. It is noteworthy that James has not yet been mentioned in the narrative. The leadership however passes over to James when Peter leaves Jerusalem in Acts 12:17. For a discussion on the relationship of Peter and the Jerusalem church, see Donfried, "Peter," 253–54.

"This and this alone moves the others to accept and ratify his decision."[61] In this respect, Peter is not only humble but also clever and wise.

Peter is also indirectly characterized as a missionary.[62] Prior to the P-C episode, Peter was "preaching the good news" in many Samaritan towns and villages (8:25). In Acts 9:32 he travels throughout Judea strengthening different members of the Christian community. At Lydda the apostle heals Aeneas (9:32–35), and in Joppa he restores Tabitha to life (9:36–43). In the P-C episode Peter travels to pagan territory (Caesarea, the farthest corner of the Jewish homeland), enters a Gentile house, preaches the Good News to Gentiles, and partakes in table fellowship with them. Since Cornelius and his household are presented in the narrative of Acts as the first Gentile converts,[63] Peter naturally becomes the inaugurator of the Gentile mission.[64] For Luke it seems fitting that the Gentile mission is initiated by none other than Peter—an apostle and a pillar of the church.

---

61. Johnson, *Scripture and Discernment*, 97.

62. It is noteworthy that after the experience at Caesarea—perhaps even because of his meeting and dining with Cornelius—Peter seems to disassociate himself from church administration to become a full-time missionary. Thus by Acts 15 Peter no longer appears as the decisive leader of the church but as a missionary. Oscar Cullmann comments, "It is quite remarkable that the apostle who later is regarded as the personification of organized church government in reality exercised such a function for only a short time at the beginning, and then exchanged it for missionary work" (*Peter*, 41).

63. One may ask about the case of the Ethiopian eunuch in Acts 8:26–40. Is he a Gentile? Or perhaps a diaspora Jew? Fitzmyer (*Acts*, 410) claims that he is a Jew or possibly a Jewish proselyte who comes from a distant land. Tannehill (*Narrative Unity*, 2:109–10) suggests that he is a Gentile. Since the facts presented by Luke are not absolutely clear, some pay less attention to whether he is a Jew or Gentile. However, Luke does not portray the eunuch's conversion as the turning point of the narrative but rather presents Cornelius as the first Gentile convert. After Cornelius the Gentile mission changed. Hence Johnson may be right when he says, "If the eunuch were a Gentile, then this story and not the conversion of Cornelius would mark the real start of the Gentile mission. The reader sensitive to the literary contours of Luke-Acts recognizes, of course, that the main issue is whether Luke meant the reader to see this as the start of the Gentile mission, and the answer to that is easy. The enormous effort Luke put into the Cornelius sequence (chapter 10–15) would make no sense at all if Cornelius did not represent a fundamental new step" (*Acts*, 159). For a similar view, see also Gaventa, *From Darkness to Light*, 123–24.

64. See Fitzmyer, *Acts*, 470; Witherington, *Acts*, 364, n. 149; Brown et al., eds., *Peter*, 43. Although Peter is credited as the "inaugurator" of the Gentile mission, he is nevertheless only an "instrument" used to carry out the will of God. As noted before, for Luke *God is the real initiator of the Gentile mission*.

Peter and Cornelius

Reader's Perception

Since Peter is a fully developed character whose personality is complex and dynamic, it is difficult to pinpoint exactly how a reader would identify with him. If the reader were a Jewish Christian, he/she would strongly identify with Peter's resistance to eat unclean food and to enter a Gentile home but might not identify with his theology—particularly with the idea that faith is the only qualification for salvation. As a matter of fact, some Jewish Christians—the more conservative ones—felt disdain or antipathy toward Peter because he had entered a Gentile home and ate with them (11:2–3). The narrative reveals that only after Peter had shown them that he was carrying out God's will did they give up their opposition (11:18). Hence, the evaluative point of view of the opponents in the narrative could represent the normal perception of a Jewish-Christian reader, particularly one with a more conservative stance.

On the other hand, if the reader were a Gentile Christian, he/she would sympathize or perhaps even empathize with Peter. Since Peter felt sympathetic with the Gentile Cornelius and his household—entering the centurion home, eating with them, baptizing them and then defending their case before the Jerusalem church—a Gentile reader would probably identify with Peter's behavior and character.

Reliability

The presentation of Peter's character is primarily done through the literary technique of "showing" rather than "telling." Unlike Cornelius, whose character traits are overtly revealed by the reliable narrator or by the divine figure, the character traits of Peter have to be inferred from the text itself, particularly from his speech and action. Although indirect characterization requires more work as well as good detective skills on the part of the reader in order to piece together a portrait of the character from scattered and often fragmented clues, the "showing" technique is more interesting and convincing than "telling."

Although Peter's behavior and actions are conflicting, inconsistent, and unpredictable, our analysis has revealed that Peter nevertheless grows and develops into a more consistent and wholesome character as the story progresses. As a preacher and a theologian Peter is coherent with the Gospel narrative and is faithful to Jesus' teaching. Peter's world view and value judgments are compatible with those of the implied author. Moreover, Peter's leadership and missionary qualities are idealized by the implied author, who wants his reader to imitate them. Since Peter is a reliable character, his speech is credible and his actions are authentic. Hence the implied reader of Luke-Acts—who is probably a Gentile Christian—would most likely feel empathetic (or at least sympathetic) with Peter.

THE MINOR CHARACTERS

There are two "character groups" that function as minor characters in the P-C episode. These character groups are Cornelius' messengers and the circumcised Christians. Although their role and function are limited and their character traits are few, they nevertheless play an active role in the plot of the story.[65] In the following analysis, we will examine these two character groups using the same approach which we have used in the previous section to reconstruct their portraits and character traits in order to establish their role and function in the story.

Cornelius' Messengers

The two house servants and the devout soldier may be treated collectively as a character group. For convenience sake, we shall name this character group "Cornelius' messengers." Although they are "agents" or "functionaries,"[66] they nevertheless play a decisive role in the narrative. They set the story in motion by carrying out the command dictated by the angel to Cornelius— "Send men to Joppa and summon a certain Simon" (10:5). Furthermore, their role is not just to relay a message to Peter or to persuade him to come to Caesarea but more importantly to enhance the image and quality of Cornelius.

CHARACTERIZATION

Despite being a minor character group, Cornelius' messengers possess some personality traits. Their characterization involves both "telling" and

---

65. In contrast, there are two other character groups that have no bearing on the resolution of the plot: the relatives and friends (10:24b, 27, 44), and the apostles and brothers (11:1). Since these minor characters are simply "crowds" or "walk-ons," they are completely passive; furthermore, since their roles are insignificant to the plot, it is not necessary to examine their characterization.

66. Many minor characters are "agents" or "functionaries" because their primary function is to help move the plot along. In other words they are merely instruments at the service of the plot. See Ska, *"Our Fathers,"* 87; Marguerat and Bourquin, *How to Read*, 60; Booth, *Rhetoric*, 344.

Peter and Cornelius

"showing." Since their presentation is brief and opaque, the reader knows little about these characters' thoughts and emotions. Furthermore, since these minor characters are static (consistent and unchanging), their actions and reactions are predictable. Hence they can be considered as "flat" characters.[67]

The reliable narrator tells the reader (direct characterization) that the soldier is "devout" (*eusebēs*), just like his master Cornelius. If this soldier is pious, perhaps he too is a God-fearer. But is he the only one who is pious among the three messengers? What about the two house servants? Although the narrator does not explicitly characterize them as "devout," the reader can presume that they too are pious since they are collectively treated as one character group. In other words, if one is devout, the others likely possess the same trait. Furthermore, since their mission (to fetch a Jewish-Christian leader named "Simon who is called Peter") requires diplomacy and sensitivity, these messengers must be knowledgeable about the Jewish religion and about etiquette. Otherwise Cornelius would not have entrusted this important task to these messengers. Moreover, their descriptions of Cornelius (a just man, a God-fearer, and well spoken of by the entire nation of the Jews) and of the angel (holy) reveal that they are quite familiar with the religious concept of piety.

The reader is told that these messengers are Cornelius' "personal attendants" (10:7). Obviously these are Cornelius' most trusted servants with whom he can share his vision and to whom he can entrust an important responsibility. Their actions show that they are obedient, and the fact that they accomplished their mission demonstrates that they are highly dependable. Their characterization of Cornelius (10:22) reveals that they know their patron well and are very loyal to him; furthermore they respect and

---

67. See Ska, *"Our Fathers"*, 83–84; Powell, *What is Narrative Criticism?*, 54; Gunn and Fewell, *Narrative*, 75; Berlin, *Poetics and Interpretation*, 23.

The Characters

honor him.[68] Thus, Cornelius' messengers are characterized (directly and indirectly) as model servants.[69]

Reader's Perception

Usually minor characters do not play a decisive role in the story. They make their appearance, speak their lines or perform their functions, and then disappear. In the case of Cornelius' messengers, their presence—though brief—is nonetheless significant to the plot of the story. Besides being "agents" or "functionaries" of Cornelius, they are also his "foils"—their presence in the narrative is to enhance his qualities. By being "devout" and "model servants" they give their master (Cornelius) public honor and praise[70] for being a good and responsible *paterfamilias*. Since Cornelius'

---

68. The relationship between masters and slaves were notorious in Greco-Roman times. The abuse of slaves was not uncommon. In legal terms the Romans (in the New Testament time) classified slaves as *instrumentum vocale* ("speaking tools"), just above the household's livestock in status. Furthermore, Jeffers says, "the head of the household, the *paterfamilias* in Roman terms, held great power over the slave. His power to execute slaves without just cause had diminished by the New Testament era, but he could do just about anything else" (*Greco-Roman World*, 229). For a discussion on slavery in the Greco-Roman world and New Testament, see Osiek and Balch, *Families*, 74–82, 174–92.

Mistreatment normally caused slaves to fear their master and to respond unenthusiastically to their work. Thus the attitude displayed by Cornelius' messengers reveals that Cornelius must have been a very good and respected master.

69. Servants/slaves are told in the New Testament to obey their masters "not just only when being watched, as currying favor, but in simplicity of heart, fearing the Lord" (Col 3:22). Similarly the author of the letter to the Ephesians writes, "Slaves, be obedient to your human masters with fear and trembling, in sincerity of heart, as to Christ" (Eph 6:5). Timothy too reminds slaves to respect their Christian masters and not take advantage of them (1 Tim 6:1–2). As for masters, they are to treat their slaves with justice and fairness (Col 4:1) and not to bully them (Eph 6:9).

70. First-century Mediterraneans were group-oriented people. They had a "dyadic" personality which means that they perceived themselves through the eyes of others. Recognition from others in the group was extremely important. For an in-depth study, see Moxnes, "Honor and Shame," 167–76. In his investigation, Moxnes shows that honor and shame provide a relevant framework for New Testament interpretation. See also Peristiany, ed., *Honour and Shame*; Gilmore, ed., *Honor and Shame and Unity*.

Honor is simply defined as "a claim to worth along with the social acknowledgment of worth" (Malina, *New Testament World*, 31). In other words, honor is how one sees one's status or one's positive worth plus the recognition of one's value in the eyes of his or her social group. It is closely connected with "saving face" and respect. Hence honor ultimately depends upon recognition from the group or from important people in society, who are known as "significant others" (Moxnes, "Honor and Shame," 168).

How others perceive one makes a world of a difference. Consequently, honor functions

messengers are "foils" whose service is to enhance the qualities of Cornelius, their favorable description of their master makes the reader even more sympathetic with Cornelius as a character. Furthermore, Luke encourages the reader—especially if he is a patron—to imitate Cornelius by treating servants or slaves with dignity, respect, justice and fairness. Likewise, if the reader is a Christian servant, he/she is encouraged to obey and honor human masters not just externally but with "sincerity of heart as to Christ" (Col 3:22; Eph 6:5–7).

Reliability

There is no reason to question the narrator's characterization of Cornelius' messengers. Since Luke is a reliable narrator, his direct report of their character traits must be genuine. Furthermore, his overt description is coherent with the messengers' speech and actions.

The messengers' characterization of Cornelius too is quite reliable. What they say about him is perfectly compatible with the narrator's report and with Cornelius' actions and speech. The positive description of their master and patron not only adds qualities to Cornelius' character but also strengthens his image and increases his honor as a character and as a worthy candidate. Consequently the ideal reader is impressed not only with Cornelius' messengers but even more so with Cornelius himself.

Circumcised Christians

The circumcised Christians may be treated collectively as one character group. They are the "brothers from Joppa" (10:23b) who accompany Peter and who are later identified by the narrator as the "circumcised believers" (10:44). Through Peter's testimony the reader also finds out that there were exactly six of them (11:12) who had entered Cornelius' house and had witnessed the event that took place in Caesarea. Obviously these six circumcised brothers serve as "witnesses" for Peter's defense in Jerusalem. The other circumcised Christians—appearing much later in the narrative (11:2)—function as "antagonists" confronting and challenging the actions of Peter, the protagonist. Even though there are two groups of circumcised

---

as a system of social rating and indicates a person's social standing and rightful place in society. For example, as a father is the head of the family, he gains honor and is publicly acclaimed when his children obey him. If his children disobey him, he would be dishonored, for his claim to worth is denied either by his family or village. He would definitely suffer shame that is a loss of honor, reputation, and respect in the eyes of others.

The Characters

Christians (one supports Peter and the other opposes him), for convenience sake we will group them together as one collective minor character.

CHARACTERIZATION

The presentation of the circumcised Christians is done primarily through indirect characterization. Besides the descriptions of "brothers" and "circumcised believers" there is no other direct characterization of this character group. Consequently the reader has to work hard to reconstruct the portrait of these characters, since their speech is brief and their actions are limited. Being typical minor characters, the circumcised Christians can be characterized as "stock" characters possessing a single trait and performing a perfunctory role in the story.[71] They either support Peter or oppose him.

The narrator characterizes two distinct groups existing among the circumcised Christians. The first group supports Peter. They are directly characterized as "brothers" (*adelphoi*, 10:23; 11:12) and "believers" (*pistoi*, 10:45). They accompany Peter from Joppa to Caesarea. They enter the Gentile home and probably together with Peter share the Eucharistic meal with Cornelius' household. More importantly, they witness the sudden outpouring of the gift of the Holy Spirit. The narrator provides the reader with an interior view (zero focalization) of their reaction, telling us that they "were amazed" (10:45) and that they "heard them speaking in tongues and praising God" (10:46). Furthermore, since it was not Peter who performed the ritual of baptism,[72] it is probably correct to assume that it was these circumcised brothers/believers who baptized Cornelius and his household. From the narrator's characterization and from their speech and actions, it is evident that this group of circumcised Christians supports Peter, accepts his theology and world view, and is therefore open to the idea that Gentile converts can be admitted into the church without first becoming Jews—that is, undergoing circumcision and observing the whole Jewish law.

It is noteworthy that the narrator characterizes this second group simply as "those who were circumcised" (*hoi ek peritomēs*, 11:2).[73] They are not "brothers" nor are they qualified as "believers." Who then are these circumcised men? They are most likely Jewish Christians who espouse cir-

71. Powell, *What is Narrative Criticism?*, 55; Berlin, *Poetics and Interpretation*, 32.
72. Haenchen, *Acts*, 354; Conzelmann, *Acts*, 84.
73. While the NASB correctly translates phrase as "those who were circumcised," the NIV and NRSV say they are "circumcised believers." In contrast the RSV identifies this group as the "circumcised party."

cumcision and strict observance of the Law. Hence when Peter returns to Jerusalem they confront him with two issues: entering a Gentile home and eating with them (11:3). For them Peter has violated the purity code and has even colluded in idolatry.[74] It is interesting that only Peter is explicitly challenged. Perhaps he as leader of the church should know better than to give bad example by breaking the Law. These conservative Jewish Christians thus confront Peter and oppose him face to face.

However, after hearing Peter's personal testimony, these opponents came to realize that Peter is not the one to blame, since he was simply following the directive of the Spirit. Since God initiated the event and since the Gentiles had received the same "gift" of the Holy Spirit as they had received, it became obvious that continued resistance to Peter was direct opposition to God, and this they simply could not do. So they became silent and then began to glorify God, saying "God has granted even to the Gentiles the repentance unto life" (11:18). With these words uttered by Peter's opponents, the P-C episode ends with a resounding effect. Peter has won his case; therefore his reputation is restored. The dissension in the community is peacefully resolved. More importantly, since the Gentile-Jewish table fellowship has been validated, the Gentile mission can now move forward. Thus the narrative ends as if the agitators are silenced for good. Unfortunately the issue is only temporary resolved until Acts 15, when the conflict reaches its climax.

Reader's Perception

Since the circumcised Christians are essentially "stock" characters who possess a single trait and who perform a perfunctory role in the story, the reader cannot relate to them as people.[75] However their presence provokes responses from Peter, the protagonist. As the servants are "foils" to Cornelius, the circumcised Christians too are "foils" to enhance the character traits of Peter. The presence of the "supporters" reveals that Peter has a group of "brothers" and "believers" who accompany him and assist him in his mission. However, while they share the apostle's world view and universal mission, they are completely passive in the defense of the Gentile

---

74. Johnson writes, "The sting in the charge, of course, is found in the ancient symbolism of table-fellowship: to eat with someone is to share spiritually with them as well; by implication to eat with Gentiles is to collude in idolatry" (*Acts*, 197).

75. Berlin, *Poetics and Interpretation*, 32.

mission. In the moment of crisis they fall silent and abandon Peter, who has to defend the Gentile mission all by himself.

The opponents too serve to enhance the image of Peter, a pillar of the Jerusalem church. Their opposition gives Peter the opportunity to show his leadership skills and to express his view concerning the issue of Gentile admission and integration. The confrontation reveals that Peter is a person who is open to the will of the Spirit and to the concerns of the community. Furthermore, this leading apostle boldly inaugurates the Gentile mission and publicly defends its cause.

Ironically the presence of the circumcised Christians—both the supporters and opponents—helps the reader to sympathize with Peter even more. Furthermore, the reader learns that not all Jewish Christians oppose the Gentile mission but only some. Even so, the whole event impresses upon the reader that conflict in community can be resolved peacefully through proper dialogue in an appropriate forum.

Reliability

The question is not whether the presentation of the circumcised Christians is consistent and coherent in the narrative (which they are), but rather how reliable are the character traits of Peter which are revealed through the characterization of these minor characters? By means of comparison and contrast we have shown that the circumcised Christians are "foils" to enhance Peter's status and honor. Consequently the characterization of Peter—as leader, missionary, and stout defender of the Gentiles—is a consistent portrait of the apostle. Moreover, the characterization is coherent with Peter's role and function throughout the whole book of Acts. The positive—perhaps even repetitious—characterization of Peter serves to impress upon the reader a lasting image about this honorable apostle and pillar of the Jerusalem church who after this episode quickly fades from the pages of Acts.

CONCLUSION

Luke uses both techniques—"telling" and "showing"—to characterize his main characters in the story of Acts 10:1—11:18. In the case of Cornelius Luke favors a direct method of characterization by using various voices—the reliable narrator, the angel, the messengers, and Cornelius himself—to accentuate the objectivity and reliability of his characterization. The analysis of the character of Cornelius reveals that this Roman centurion is unlike other stereotypical Gentiles. Cornelius is a pious God-fearer who is religiously and morally upright. He is a generous benefactor of the Jewish people and obedient to the divine command. Despite being a Gentile, Cornelius acts and lives somewhat like a faithful Jew. Furthermore, the characterization of Cornelius' messengers as "foils" enhances the image and quality of Cornelius. By being devout and model servants, these messengers render Cornelius (their master) public honor and praise, for he is a good patron and a responsible *paterfamilias*. Such positive characterization of Cornelius—even to the point of exaggeration—impresses upon the reader a feeling of empathy for this Gentile character who deserves to be admitted to and integrated into the Christian community.

The presentation of Peter—unlike that of Cornelius—is seldom direct or explicit but usually indirect through the clues given in the text. Although the reader has to work hard at gathering the data, the outcome is more satisfying and convincing. At any rate Luke's characterization of Peter reveals that he is a multi-facetted character. He first appears hesitant, inconsistent, and unpredictable. But as the story proceeds he gradually matures and develops into a strong-willed and self-assertive character. Through Peter's speeches the reader learns that he is a theologian as well as an eloquent and persuasive speaker skilled in Greek rhetoric. His actions too demonstrate that he is a spiritual and wise leader who involves others in the discernment of God's will without imposing his authority upon them.

If that is not enough to convince the reader to sympathize with Peter, the characterization of the circumcised Christians—both his supporters and his opponents—enhances the image and portrait of the apostle. Their presence as "foils" confirms that Peter is not only a stout defender of the Gentile mission but more significantly its inaugurator. Who could better evoke the sympathies of the implied reader in order to accept this historical move? Certainly no one was more suitable than Peter—an apostle and a pillar of the Jerusalem church.

6

The Theological Significance

WE HAVE BEEN ANALYZING the two basic components of *story* and *discourse* of Acts 10:1—11:18. The analysis of these two essential elements of a narrative has yielded important insights. But it is not enough to simply examine the *story* or "what" (which consists of settings, plot, and characters) and the *discourse* or "how" of Acts 10:1—11:18. We need to examine also the theological implications behind the Lukan narrative.

This chapter focuses on the theological significance of Acts 10:1—11:18. First, we will examine Luke's portrait of God in the P-C episode. Second, we will discuss how Luke justifies the Gentile mission as a fulfillment of God's salvific plan. Third, we will explore the effect of Acts 10:1—11:18 upon the reader. This theological exposition is based upon the results and insights which have been established in our narrative analysis of discourse, settings, plot, and characterization.

THE ROLE OF GOD IN THE GENTILE MISSION

Direct references to God in Acts 10:1—11:18 are abundant. The term God (*theos*) appears twenty-two times in this episode: 10:2 (*bis*), 3, 4, 15, 22, 28, 31, 33, 34, 38 (*bis*), 40, 41, 42, 46; 11:1, 9, 17 (*bis*), 18 (*bis*). There are also four other indirect references to God represented by the Greek third person masculine pronoun: him (*auton*) (10:35 [bis]) and he (*autos*) (10:36; 11:17). Appearing twenty-six times in sixty-six verses, God is clearly the central focus of this narrative.[1] In approximately every three verses the word God (*theos*) appears while in the preceding unit (Acts 9:32–42) there are no references to God, and in the following unit (Acts 11:19-29) God

---

1. Mowery ("Lord, God, and Father," 90–91) points out that God is the numerically dominant title in Acts. It occurs 159 times.

is mentioned only once (11:23). Thus, the story of Peter and Cornelius in Acts 10:1—11:18 is highly theocentric, while its surrounding units are not.

From the very beginning to the end of the story (as we have demonstrated throughout this investigation, especially in the chapter on plot), God is the primary actor and initiator. The Spirit of God commanded Peter to go with the messengers to Caesarea "without hesitation because I [Spirit] *have sent* them" (10:19–20; 11:9). In Peter's vision the voice declared three times, "What God *has made clean*, you must not continue to call unclean" (10:15; 11:9). Peter's understanding of the vision was attributed to God's action: "God *has shown* me not to call any person profane or unclean" (10:28). Peter later recognized that "God *shows* no favoritism" (10:35).

Divine initiative is especially accentuated in Peter's speech concerning the life and ministry of Jesus. Peter made a series of faith proclamations: "God *sent* the message to the children of Israel, preaching the good news of peace through Jesus Christ" (10:36); "God *anointed* Jesus from Nazareth with the Holy Spirit and power" (10:38); "God *raised* him on the third day and *allowed* him to show himself" (10:40); Jesus is "the one *appointed* by God as judge of the living and the dead" (10:42); and God *was present* "with him" (10:38). Furthermore, in the analysis of the characterization, Peter painstakingly points out in his speech that God is in full control and is the initiator of the whole affair. Peter, on the other hand, is just an "instrument" responding to the divine promptings.

Moreover, Luke shows the reader that the Gentile mission was first and foremost initiated by God. In the defense speech Peter attests: "God *gave* them [the Gentiles] the same gift as he *had given* us" (11:17). His opponents publicly admit: "God *has granted* even to the Gentiles the repentance unto life" (11:18).

In short, both the key terms and the actions of God highlight the theocentric motif of God's guidance in Acts 10:1—11:18. God is evidently the primary actor throughout the P-C episode. God guided Peter to the house of the Gentile Cornelius and helped the apostle to understand the meaning of his vision. God was directly involved in the life, ministry, death and resurrection of Jesus. Even the final judgment falls within the divine providence. The mission to the Gentiles too is presented as an activity initiated by God.

Luke's portrait of God is greatly influenced by the Hebrew Scriptures.[2] For Luke, God is a sovereign who controls events both in heaven and on

---

2. Rosner, "Acts and Biblical History," 78–80; O'Toole, *Unity*, 23–32; Marshall, *Luke*,

The Theological Significance

earth. God determines what will happen, as well as when, where, and how events will occur. Since God is completely in charge, everything happens according to the will and plan of God.[3] Certain key terms that emphasize the foreknowledge, will, plan, or purpose of God make this apparent. These terms include compound verbs formed by the prefix "before" (*pro-*) and the verbs: "to do" (*poieō*), "to fulfill" (*plēroō*), "to determine" (*horizō*), "to set" (*tithēmi*), "to stand or set up" (*histēmi*), "to appoint" (*tassō*), and "to be destined" (*mellō*).[4] Three other words or expressions also denote God's sovereignty: "it is necessary" (*dei*),[5] "the plan of God" (*hē boulē tou theou*),[6] and "will" (*thelēma*).[7]

Key events in Acts are narrated as the action of God.[8] They take place under the guidance of God: the day of Pentecost (2:17–21), the Samaritan mission (8:1–40), Paul's conversion on the road to Damascus (9:1–19), the apostolic council in Jerusalem (15:1–35), and the mission of Paul and Barnabas to the Gentiles (13:1—14:28). Likewise, Luke painstakingly shows that God always intended and directly authorized the Gentile mission and their integration into the church in the P-C episode. It has been demonstrated in the analysis of the temporal settings that divine revelations or visions are

---

103–15; Sweetland, "Luke the Christian," 52. The theme of divine control or guidance of history is also a widespread belief among Greco-Romans. Providence was a central theme in Hellenistic historiography, where it often had an apologetic or religious application. See Squires, *Plan of God*, 37–52.

3. The plan of God as a central theme in Luke-Acts has been noted by many scholars. See Bovon, *Luc le théologien*, 11–84; Conzelmann, *Die Mitte der Zeit*, 141–44; Marshall, *Luke*, 103–15; Fitzmyer, *Luke I-IX*, 179–81; Sweetland, "Luke the Christian," 49–51; Powell, *What Are They Saying About Acts?*, 39–40; Soards, *Speeches*, 184–85.

For a more comprehensive discussion, see Squires, *Plan of God*. Squires points out that, while many scholars recognize the plan of God as the central theme of Luke-Acts, they nevertheless only treat it superficially. For an excellent survey of the literature on this theme, see pages 3–10 of his book.

4. For the references to these terms in Luke-Acts, see O'Toole, *Unity*, 23–28; Squires, *Plan of God*, 1–3; Rosner, "Acts and Biblical History," 79; Fitzmyer, *Luke I-IX*, 179–80.

5. Luke's frequent usage of the term "it is necessary" (*dei*) is noteworthy. *Dei* occurs eighteen times in Luke and twenty-four times in Acts (forty-two times of its one hundred and two appearances in the New Testament). See Squires, *Plan of God*, 2, n. 6.

6. The term *boulē*, used in reference to the plan of God occurs once in Luke (7:30) and five times in Acts (2:23; 4:28; 5:38; 13:36; 20:27). The only other references in the New Testament are at 1 Cor 4:5, Eph 1:11, and Heb 6:17.

7. *Thelēma* appears in Luke 11:2; 22:42; Acts 13:22; 18:21; 21:14; 22:14.

8. See Squires, *Plan of God*, 37–77.

Peter and Cornelius

connected with prayer.[9] It is through prayer that Cornelius experiences the presence of the angel of God; likewise, it is through prayer that Peter discovers the salvific will and plan of God which is now offered to the Gentiles.

The analysis of the spatial and social-cultural settings of Acts 10:1—11:18 reveals that crossing boundaries between the sacred and the profane are fluid, whether the movements be horizontal (Jewish homeland to Gentile territory), vertical (heaven and earth), or exterior to interior (entering unclean Gentile home). God has completely torn down the wall of separation between the clean and the unclean, between the Jews and the Gentiles. Hence Peter—who is completely being guided by God—may enter the home of the Gentiles and participate in table fellowship with them.

In addition, four important verbs highlight the theme of God's sovereignty in Acts 10:1—11:18: God sent (*apostellō*) the message to the children of Israel (10:36), anointed (*chriō*) and appointed (*horizō*) Jesus of Nazareth (10:38, 42), and chose him in advance (*procheirotoveō*, 10:41). Consequently, the P-C episode is narrated as an event completely within the sovereignty of God. It is God who directs the whole affair of the Gentile mission and their integration.

GENTILE MISSION AS FULFILLMENT OF GOD'S PLAN

For Luke, God's purpose and plan is particularly realized in terms of fulfillment of prophecy.[10] This is an important theme in Luke-Acts. In the preface of the Gospel, Luke describes the aim of his work—"to set down an orderly account of the events that have been fulfilled among us" (Luke 1:1; NRSV). Towards the end of the Gospel, the risen Jesus reiterates the theme of fulfilled prophecy by saying, "everything written about me in the law of Moses and the prophets and the psalms must be fulfilled" (24:44). Likewise the opening verses of Acts indicate both the promises and ongoing fulfillment of Scripture concerning the gift of the Holy Spirit, which will be poured upon Jews as well as Gentiles (Acts 1:5, 8; 16–20; 2:16–21). At the end of Acts Paul quotes Isaiah 6:9-10 to show that the Gentile mission and salvation are fulfilling Sacred Scripture (Acts 28:25–28). Thus, John T. Squires rightly observes, "The beginning and ending of each volume point

---

9. See chapter 3.

10. Fitzmyer, *Luke I–IX*, 180. See particularly Peterson, "Motif of Fulfilment and Purpose," 83–104.

The Theological Significance

to the importance of fulfilled prophecies in Luke's literary and theological purposes."[11]

One of the major theological and apologetic concerns of Luke is to show that the mission to the Gentiles is intended by God and consequently fulfills the words of the prophets.[12] How then does Luke demonstrate that the Gentile mission in Acts 10:1—11:18 is a prophecy-fulfillment which is in accordance with the salvific will and plan of God? The whole event is realized in or legitimated by: a) visions and heavenly beings; b) the Holy Spirit; c) Jesus; and d) the Sacred Scriptures.[13]

Visions and Angels

Visions (Acts 2:17, 19; 10:3; 10:11–19; 11:5–10; 16:9–10) and angels (Acts 5:19; 8:26; 10:3, 7, 22; 11:13; 12:7–15, 23; 27:23–24) play an important role in revealing as well as executing God's plan in Luke's second volume.[14] In the P-C episode, both Cornelius (10:3–7) and Peter (10:11–20) saw visions[15] and were guided by an angelic messenger or a spirit[16] to begin the Gentile mission. It is noteworthy that visions and angels appear in almost every scene of Acts 10:1—11:18.[17]

There is a fourfold reporting of Cornelius' vision. It is significant that these four versions of the same event are narrated from four different points of view: first, by the narrator to the reader (10:1–8); then by the messengers to Peter (10:22); later Cornelius himself tells Peter about it (10:30–33); and finally Peter tells the Jerusalem church (11:13–14). It has

---

11. Squires, *Plan of God*, 137.

12. Squires (*Plan of God*, 121–54) rightfully points out that the two most important events fulfilling prophecy in Luke's two volumes are the passion of Jesus and the mission to the Gentiles.

13. According to Talbert (*Reading Luke*, 234–40), fulfilled prophecy in Lukan narrative comes from three types of sources: 1) the Jewish Scriptures; 2) a living prophet; 3) a heavenly being. It is noticeable that our text consists of not three but four types of sources, and furthermore the order is different from Talbert.

14. References to visions and angels are frequent, particularly in the infancy narratives of the Gospel of Luke. See O'Toole, *Unity*, 30–31.

15. The word "vision" (*horama*) appears in 10:3, 5, 17, 19, and the word "trance" (*ekstasis*) occurs in 10:10; 11:5.

16. In Cornelius' vision, it is an "angel" (10:3; 11:13) or "a man in dazzling clothes" (10:30) who appears and speaks. In Peter's vision, however, it is either a heavenly "voice" (10:13, 15; 11:7, 9) or the "spirit" (11:12) who speaks.

17. This has been demonstrated in chapter 2.

been pointed out that there is a steady progression in what the reader (or hearer) learns from each of these four accounts. Furthermore, the fourfold account of Cornelius' vision—particularly from the point of view of different character-narrators—not only creates suspense and interest but more importantly enhances the role of God's action and initiative in the entire P-C episode.

Unlike Cornelius' vision, which is told and retold four times, Peter's vision is narrated only twice: first, by the narrator to the reader (10:9–16), and secondly, by Peter himself to the assembly in Jerusalem (11:5–10). While the variation in details between the two versions is minimal and appears relatively insignificant, the difference in point of view adds vividness and color to the repetition and more importantly reinforces the divine guidance through the perspective of Peter, the reliable character-narrator.

In short, the visions of Cornelius and Peter are told and retold repeatedly from different points of view. While each version adds new information in order to maintain the reader's interest, the variation in perspectives reinforces the function and purpose of Luke's repetitive rhetorical techniques. Luke assures the reader that the whole ordeal of going to the Gentile home and eating with them is completely guided by God. Moreover, the divine plan for the salvation of the Gentiles is being realized through the guidance of visions and angelic messengers.[18]

The Holy Spirit

No one can deny the important role of the Holy Spirit in Luke-Acts. The frequent references to the Holy Spirit[19] in these two volumes and the enormous amount of scholarly investigation[20] of this theme prove its sig-

18. For the role of visions and angels in God's salvific plan, see Rosner, "Acts and Biblical History," 79; O'Toole, *Unity*, 30, 40, and 106; Talbert, *Reading Luke*, 234–40.

19. References to the Holy Spirit occur at least seventeen times in Luke (1:15, 35, 41, 67; 2:25, 26, 27; 3:16, 22; 4:1 [*bis*], 14, 18; 10:21; 11:13; 12:10, 12), and fifty-seven times in Acts (1:2, 5, 8, 16; 2:4 [*bis*], 17, 18, 33, 38; 4:8, 25, 31; 5:3, 9, 32; 6:3, 5, 10; 7:51, 55; 8:15, 17, 18, 19, 29, 39; 9:17, 31; 10:19, 38, 44, 45, 47; 11:12, 15, 16, 24, 28; 13:2, 4, 9, 52; 15:8, 28; 16:6, 7; 19:2 [*bis*], 6, 21; 20:22, 23, 28; 21:4, 11; 28:25). The Spirit is mentioned only six times in Mark, twelve times in Matthew, and about fifteen times in the Gospel of John. For a complete listing, see Fitzmyer, *Luke I–IX*, 227.

20. Baer, *Der Heilige Geist*; Lampe, "Holy Spirit," 159–200; Prats, *L'Esprit force*; Shepherd, *Narrative Function*; Bruce, "Holy Spirit," 166–83; Lincoln, "Theology and History," 204–9; Turner, "'Spirit of Prophecy,'" 327–48; Rasco, "Spirito e istituzione," 301–22.

For a complete bibliography and review of this research see Bovon, *Luc le théologien*, 211–54; Powell, *What Are They Saying About Acts?*, 50–56; Shepherd, *Narrative Function*, 3–11.

The Theological Significance

nificance for understanding Lukan theology. Due to the scope of the presentation our examination focuses primarily on the role of the Holy Spirit in Acts 10:1—11:18. More specifically, the analysis concentrates on how the Holy Spirit functions within God's salvific plan for the Gentile mission. We begin by examining the terminology of the Holy Spirit in the P-C episode.

The term "Spirit" or "Holy Spirit" appears eight times in the P-C episode:

- the Spirit (*to pneuma*, 10:19; 11:12)
- the Holy Spirit (*to pneuma to hagion,* 10:44, 47; 11:15)
- Holy Spirit (*pneuma hagiō*, 10:38; 11:16)
- The gift of the Holy Spirit (*he dōrea tou hagiou pneumatos*, 10:45)

The frequent occurrence of these terms shows that the Holy Spirit plays a crucial role in the narrative.[21] Furthermore, the manifestation of the Spirit among the Gentiles in the P-C episode is elaborately portrayed.[22] First and foremost, the event is narrated twice. The actual outpouring of the Spirit takes place in Acts 10:44–48, which Peter later recounts in 11:15–17. Secondly, since there are two accounts of the same event, the descriptions of the Spirit's manifestation are more elaborate. The event is perceived and interpreted by various characters (the narrator, Peter, and the circumcised believers).

In the P-C episode the Spirit is manifested to the Gentiles in six different ways.[23] First, the narrator recounts that "the Holy Spirit *fell upon* (*epipiptō*) all those who were listening to the word" (10:44). Likewise in his defense Peter declared that "the Holy Spirit *fell upon* (*epipiptō*) them just as it had upon us at the beginning" (11:15). Second, the circumcised believers saw that "the gift of the Holy Spirit *had been poured out* (*ekcheō*) even on the Gentiles (10:45).[24] Third, Peter said that the Gentiles are those "who

---

21. It is interesting to note that the P-C episode has only two fewer occurrences than Acts 1 and 2 combined.

22. Other important texts are: Acts 2:1–4 (Pentecost); 4:31 (the community at prayer); 8:14–17 (the Samaritan mission); 19:1–6 (John's disciples). For a comparison of and contrasts between these principal texts, see Richard, "Pentecost," 135–43.

23. In addition to these six manifestations, the narrator says that Jesus was *anointed* (*chriō*) with the Holy Spirit and power (10:38). Perhaps Luke is making a thematic link with Luke 4:16–21, which in turns alludes to Isaiah 61:1. See Dupont, *Nouvelles études*, 327–28.

24. Richard ("Pentecost," 138) correctly points out that the verb "pour out" (*ekcheō*) is rare in Luke. It occurs here and at Pentecost. Luke's usage here definitely alludes to Joel's

have *received (lambanō)* the Holy Spirit just as we have" (10:47). Fourth, Peter recalled Jesus' words saying, "you *will be baptized (baptizō)* by the Holy Spirit" (11:16).[25] Fifth, the circumcised believers witnessed the Gentiles "*speaking in tongues (laleō glōssais)*" (10:46). Sixth, Peter testified that "God *gave (didōmi)* them the same *gift (dōrea)* as he had given us" (11:17).[26]

Obviously Luke uses various terms and different characters (although Peter is the most important and most frequent witness) to describe the manifestation of the Spirit to the Gentiles. The language is rich in imagery. Furthermore, the different speakers create a powerful effect upon the reader (or hearer). The perspectives give the impression that this event was real and reliable because it was witnessed by many people. Moreover, the double versions and the repetitious descriptions of the same event impress upon the reader (or hearer) that the Gentiles have indeed received the same gift of the Holy Spirit. Luke goes out of his way to make sure that no reader misses this crucial aspect of the story.

The manifestation of the Spirit to the Gentiles does not follow a fixed pattern. In the P-C episode the outpouring is not a result of baptism (2:38), of prayer (4:31), or of the laying on of hands (8:17). Rather it is a result of Peter's preaching or *kerygma*.[27] The narrator clearly points out that "while Peter was still speaking these things, the Holy Spirit fell upon all those who were listening to the word" (10:44). Through preaching the Gentiles were able to hear the word which led them to believe. Thus it is through faith that the Gentiles were granted the gift of the Holy Spirit.

There are three principal missions of the early church which Luke attributed to the working of the Holy Spirit.[28] These missionary beginnings are: the mission to the Jews (2:1–42), to the Samaritans (8:4–25), and to the Gentiles (10:1—11:18). On all three occasions the Spirit functions as the authenticator of Christian missionary activity. Throughout the P-C episode the Holy Spirit plays a major role in launching and authenticating the Gentile mission. In chapter 3 we have demonstrated that it was the Spirit who guided Peter to Caesarea. The same Spirit directed him to enter Cornelius' house and to participate in table fellowship with uncircumcised Gentiles.

---

citation: "I will pour out my Spirit upon all flesh" (Acts 2:17, 18; Joel 3:1–5).

25. The "baptism with the Spirit," first mentioned by John (Luke 3:16) and promised by Jesus (Acts 1:5), is now fulfilled according to Peter (11:16).

26. Luke also refers to the Spirit as a gift (*dōrea*) in 2:38; 8:18; 10:45.

27. Richard, "Pentecost," 139, 145.

28. Ibid., 143.

The Theological Significance

We have also shown in chapter 4 that the coming of the Spirit—particularly the granting of the gift of *glossolalia*—irrefutably legitimated the Gentile mission as an activity of the Spirit. Peter indicates several times in his defense that the Gentiles' reception of the gift of the Holy Spirit is equal to that of the first believers in Jerusalem (11:15, 17; again 15:8-9). The divine initiative and the equality of the gift of the Holy Spirit convinced the Jerusalem community to accept unconditionally both the expansion of the Gentile mission and Jewish-Gentile table fellowship.

Consequently, the Spirit plays an important role in the implementation and authorization of the Gentile mission in the P-C episode. The Spirit is portrayed as its driving force (10:38, 44; 11:16) and its legitimator (10:45-46; 11:17). Nevertheless, like the angels, the Holy Spirit serves as God's agent to implement and execute God's salvific will and plan for the inclusion of the Gentiles. For Luke, God is the director of the whole affair. God is the one who gives the gift of the Holy Spirit (11:17) and is also the one who grants salvation to the Gentiles (11:18).

Luke often portrays the Holy Spirit as the biblical Spirit of prophecy.[29] Furthermore, the Spirit is the fulfillment of the promises made by the Father (Luke 24:49; Acts 1:4; 2:39), by John the Baptist (Luke 3:16; Acts 1:5) and by Jesus (1:8). Similar to the Jewish Pentecost (Acts 2:1-4), the outpouring of the Holy Spirit upon the Gentiles in the P-C episode also fulfills the Old Testament prophecy of Joel. Luke says that "the gift of the Holy Spirit *had been poured out* even on the Gentiles" (10:45). The verb "to pour out" (*ekcheō*) is rarely used by Luke. It appears once in our passage and twice in Peter's Pentecostal address. In that address Peter says:

> This is what was spoken through the prophet Joel: "In the last days it will be, God declares, that I *will pour out* my Spirit upon all flesh, and your sons and your daughters shall prophesy, and your young men shall see visions, and your old men shall dream dreams. Even upon my slaves, both men and women, in those days I *will pour out* my Spirit; and they shall prophesy" (Acts 2:16-18; NRSV; emphasis mine).

This citation of Joel 3:1-2 authenticates the Jewish Pentecost as a prophecy-fulfillment. Since the Gentiles received exactly the same gift as those first followers had received at the beginning, Luke clearly links the Gentile

---

29. For a comprehensive survey of scholarly research on this theme, see Shepherd, *Narrative Function*, 11-22. For a more concise presentation, see Powell, *What Are They Saying About Acts?*, 50-56; Turner, "'Spirit of Prophecy,'" 327-48.

Pentecost with the Jewish Pentecost. Thus, if the Jewish Pentecost fulfills the prophecy of Joel, then the Gentile Pentecost fulfills the same prophecy.

The outpouring of the Spirit upon the Gentiles in the P-C episode is also a fulfillment of the promises made by John the Baptist and by Jesus. In his defense speech, Peter recalls the word of the Lord, who said: "John baptized with water, but you will be baptized by the Holy Spirit" (11:16). This is an exact citation of Jesus' direct speech in Acts 1:5, which in turn fulfills the promise made by John the Baptist. John says, "I baptize you with water; but he who is mightier than I is coming . . . he will baptize you with the Holy Spirit and with fire" (Luke 3:16). By showing that the Gentile Pentecost fulfills the Baptist's promise, Peter also demonstrates that it is the Spirit of Jesus which was poured out on the Gentiles. Furthermore, the outpouring of the Spirit of Jesus on the Gentile believers fulfills the promise made by God the Father (Luke 24:49; Acts 1:4; 2:39). At the end of his speech, Peter concludes: "If God gave them the same gift as he had given us, when we believed in the Lord Jesus Christ, who was I to be able to hinder God?" (11:17).

Jesus

Salvation is a central Lukan theme.[30] In fact, the words "salvation" and "savior" are found only in Luke-Acts.[31] For Luke, the plan of God is a plan of salvation. God wills and directs salvation history.[32] God has brought salvation to Israel in the past and continues to bring salvation in the present through Jesus.[33] Thus, according to Luke, Jesus Christ is *the* agent of God's salvation. Joseph A. Fitzmyer writes:

---

30. Marshall, *Luke*, 77–102; Green, "'Salvation,'" 83–106. For a survey of research on Lukan theology, see especially Bovon, *Luc le théologien*, 119–210, 255–307; Richard, "Luke," 3–15.

31. The terms occur eight times in Luke (1:47, 69, 71, 77; 2:11, 30; 3:6; 19:9) and nine times in the book of Acts (4:12, 5:31; 7:25; 13:23, 26, 47; 16:17; 27:34; 28:28). For a complete list of terms related to the theme of salvation, see Green, "'Salvation,'" 86.

32. The most influential work on this theme is that of Conzelmann, *Die Mitte der Zeit*. He proposes that salvation history is divided into three distinct periods: Israel (from creation to the imprisonment of John the Baptist); Jesus (from his baptism to his ascension); and Church (from Jesus' ascension to his parousia). For a concise summary and criticism of Conzelmann's work, see Fitzmyer, *Luke I–IX*, 181–92.

33. Bovon, "Le Dieu de Luc," 279–300; Sweetland, "Luke the Christian," 52–54; Kee, *Good News*, 6–27; Soards, *Speeches*, 186–89.

The Theological Significance

> The key figure in Lucan salvation-history is Jesus Christ himself, for he is the one in whom God's activity in human history is now manifested. He is not only the one who proclaims salvation; he becomes himself the object of the proclamation.[34]

In the Acts of the Apostles salvation is always offered "in the name of Jesus" (Acts 2:21, 38; 3:16; 4:7–18; 8:12; 10:43). Apostles and Christians heal (3:6; 4:30), teach (5:28, 40), baptize (8:16; 10:48; 19:5), exorcise demons (16:18; 19:13), preach (9:27–28), witness (9:15), and serve (15:26) in Jesus' name. They also call upon (9:14, 21; 22:16), suffer for (5:41; 9:16; 21:13; 26:9) and honor (19:17) the name of Jesus.[35]

Luke's salvation, which is exclusively found in Jesus' name (4:12), is not limited to Israel but includes Gentiles as well. Jesus says, "repentance and forgiveness of sins should be preached in his name to all nations, beginning from Jerusalem" (Luke 24:47). Just before Jesus ascends to heaven, he commissions his disciples, "you shall be my witnesses in Jerusalem and in all Judea and Samaria and to the ends of the earth" (Acts 1:8). Consequently, according to Luke's geographical plan of salvation, Acts 10:1—11:18 fulfills the third part of Luke programmatic purpose and structure—namely "to the ends of the earth" (Acts 1:8). A close examination of the P-C episode will reveal that for Luke Jesus is also the Savior of the Gentiles.

In the Greco-Roman world of the first century CE, the title "savior" (*sōtēr*) was specifically used only of people who had exceptional merit and honor. It was often applied to gods, philosophers, physicians, kings, and emperors.[36] These saviors were also often called "benefactors" (*euergetēs*).[37] Augustus Caesar was acclaimed "Savior" because he had brought peace to whole the world.[38] The famous Priene inscription from the Provincial Assembly of Asia (today's western Turkey), which is dated around 9 BCE, gives an historical account of Augustus being honored and worshiped as divine and the savior who fulfilled humanity's hope and aspiration:

---

34. Fitzmyer, *Luke I–IX*, 192.
35. Buckwalter, "Divine Savior," 118–19.
36. Fitzmyer, *Luke I–IX*, 204.
37. Danker (*Luke*, 28) points out that the verb *sōzō* and *euergeteō* were used interchangeably. Danker defines *euergeteō* as "to render exceptional service, especially to a community" (*BDAG*, 405). Green notices that the noun "salvation" was a semantic cousin of "benefaction" ("'Salvation,'" 87). Talbert ("Concept of Immortals," 420–25) suggests that Greco-Roman immortals (exemplary rulers and philosophers) were also considered benefactors. They attained immortality because of their benefactions to humanity.
38. Nguyen, "Evangelizing Empire," 100.

Peter and Cornelius

> Since the providence that has divinely ordered our existence has applied her energy and zeal and has brought to life the most perfect good in Augustus, whom she filled with virtues for the benefit of mankind, bestowing him upon us and our descendants as *savior*—he who put an end to war and will order peace, Caesar, who by his epiphany exceeded the hopes of those who prophesied good tidings [*euangelia*] . . . .; and since the birthday of the god first brought to the world the good tidings [*euangelia*] residing in him. . . . For that reason, with good fortune and safety, the Greeks of Asia have decided that the New Year in all the cities should begin on 23rd September, the birthday of Augustus (OGIS 458).[39]

Interestingly, Augustus was depicted in poetry and inscribed in stone tablets as Son of God and Savior of the world. Moreover, his reign or victory was announced as "gospels" or "good news."[40] Similarly, the emperor Nero was pronounced "Savior and Benefactor of the world."[41]

In the P-C episode Jesus is addressed by various titles: "Lord" (10:36; 11:16, 17), "Jesus Christ" (10:36, 48, 17), and simply "Jesus from Narazeth" (10:38).[42] One particular title—which occurs exclusively in Luke-Acts—merits our attention.[43] In his sermon Peter depicts Jesus as "Benefactor" (10:38), a title which is significant and very familiar to the Gentile Cornelius. According to Frederick W. Danker, the Greek participle *euergetōn* in 10:38 functions as a substantive which should be translated as followed: "Benefactor that he was, he went about healing all who were being tyrannized by the Devil."[44]

Besides the title, Peter's sermon contains many traditional elements that depict Jesus as Benefactor.[45] These include Jesus as the bearer of the

---

39. Quoted from Crossan, *God and Empire*, 148. For a full text of this Priene inscription and explanations, see Craig Evans' article entitled, "Mark's Incipit and the Priene Calendar Inscription: From Jewish Gospel to Greco-Roman Gospel," found on http://www.craigaevans.com/Priene%20art.pdf, accessed on March 7, 2009.

40. For further in-depth study on the impact of Roman Empire on the New Testament, see Nguyen, "Evangelizing Empire," 99–105 and "Roman Empire and New Testament," 84–86.

41. For a detailed description of the inscriptions of Augustus and Nero, see Danker, *Luke*, 29–30; for other important inscriptions, see Danker, *Benefactor*, 26–48.

42. For a discussion on these titles, see Fitzmyer, *Luke I–IX*, 197–219; Jones, "Title *Christos*," 69–76.

43. Two other occurrences are found in Luke 22:25 and Acts 4:9.

44. Danker, *Luke*, 32, n. 6.

45. See Danker, *Luke*, and Talbert, "Concept of Immortals," 419–36.

The Theological Significance

good news of peace (10:36) and Jesus as a servant who went about doing good and healing all who were in need (10:38). Jesus' words and deeds are noticeably compatible with the Greek concept of Benefactor. Similar to many saviors or benefactors, Jesus was unjustly put to death (10:39). However after three days God raised him up and allowed him to show himself to his followers (10:40), while anyone who believes in him receives forgiveness of sins through his name (10:43).[46] Evidently Luke depicts Jesus as the Savior/Benefactor who exhibits exceptional merit and who confers God's beneficence and salvation. Luke's audience—whether Cornelius or Theophilus—would certainly understand such a familiar presentation because it is steeped in the imagery of Hellenistic benefactors and in the Mediterranean culture and milieu.[47]

As Benefactor Jesus is "Lord of all" (10:36). He healed all (10:38) and offers salvation to anyone who believes in his name (10:43). Jesus' arrival brings "good news of peace" for the whole world (10:36).[48] The impact of Jesus is universal for he is Savior not only of the Jews but also of the Gentiles. Although the Gentile mission does not actually begin until Acts 10:1—11:18, the theme of universal salvation has already been introduced by Luke (Luke 1:48b, 79; 2:14, 30–32; 3:6; 4:25–30; 7:1–10; 24:47; Acts 1:8; 3:25; 9:15).[49] The numerous promises of universal salvation—particularly of the Gentiles—are fulfilled in the story of Peter and Cornelius. Gentiles are included among the people of God. Since Jesus is "Lord of all," salvation applies not only to the Jews but to the Gentiles as well. God has always designed it to be so.[50] Thus Peter rightly recognizes that the acceptance and integration of Gentiles is not a scandal but a fulfillment of God's plan and purpose which neither he nor anyone else can hinder (10:47; 11:17).

In summary, according to Luke the plan of God is the plan of salvation to all people, including the Gentiles. The acceptance of Gentiles is

---

46. For a discussion of the lives of benefactors and virtuous people who became immortals, see Talbert, "Concept of Immortals," 417–36.

47. Ibid., 432–36.

48. Various scholars correctly point out the close connection between "peace" (*eirēnē*) and "salvation" (*sōtērion*) in Luke-Acts. Furthermore, the peace (*eirēnē*) which Jesus brings upon earth is universalistic and not restricted nationally, politically, socially, or economically. See Swartley, "Politics or Peace," 18–37.

49. See O'Toole, "Why Did Luke Write Acts?," 72–73; Navone, "Three Aspects," 130–32.

50. For a discussion on Gentile mission fulfilling the promise that God made long ago, see Bock, "Scripture and Realization," 57–62.

not a scandal but a fulfillment of God's plan and purpose. This promise is now realized in Jesus. Jesus is the agent of God's salvation and beneficence. Those who believe in him will be saved. Salvation is no longer a matter of inheritance but is a gift for those who respond positively to the good news of Jesus Christ.[51] Nevertheless, for Luke salvation ultimately comes from God. God is the true Savior and the Great Benefactor of all. Green poignantly says, "Though Jesus is the agent of salvation, God's redemptive plan was operative prior to Jesus' birth and subsequent to his ascension (cf., 13:16–41); before Luke's soteriology is christocentric, it is theocentric."[52]

Sacred Scriptures

Luke uses the Old Testament extensively in his two-volume work to demonstrate that events are being fulfilled according to God's providential and salvific plan.[53] Joseph A. Fitzmyer points out that, besides the thirty-seven direct citations, there are many allusions to the Old Testament throughout the Acts of the Apostles.[54] In the P-C episode biblical allusions and echoes are abundant, reflecting the importance of this passage for Luke.[55] There are two clear Old Testament allusions in the P-C episode. The angel's message to Cornelius in 10:4 alludes to various Old Testament passages dealing with sacrifices and the criteria for God's acceptance of one's prayers and offerings (Lev 2:2, 9, 16; 5:12; Ps 111:6; Tob 12:12).[56] Sirach 35:5–6 states, "The offering of the upright graces the altar, and its savour rises before the Most High. The sacrifice of the upright is acceptable, its memorial will not be forgotten"

---

51. Ibid., 57.

52. Green, "Salvation," 98.

53. For the pattern of fulfillment in the Gospel of Luke, see Peterson, "Motif of Fulfilment," 87–94. Peterson notices that the terms and theme of fulfillment are extensively used in the infancy narratives (Luke 1:20, 23, 45, 57; 2:6, 21, 22, 39, 43), where Luke introduces some of the main themes of his Gospel. For a survey of this theme, see Bovon, *Luc le théologien*, 85–117.

54. For the list of the citations found in Acts, see Fitzmyer, *Acts*, 90; Witherington, *Acts*, 123–24. For Luke's skillful use of Old Testament citations placed on the lips of his characters to express the author's point of view and ideology, see Arnold, "Luke's Characterizing Use," 300–323.

55. According to Handy, ("Gentile Pentecost," 40–61), in the P-C episode there are two definite biblical allusions, at least seven probable echoes, and several more possible echoes or overtones. On the contrary, Tyson ("Gentile Mission," 629) says that apart from the reference in Acts 10:43, Scripture plays no role in the story of Cornelius in providing a justification for the Gentile mission.

56. For further references and explanation, see Johnson, *Acts*, 183.

The Theological Significance

(NJB). In the P-C episode the angel tells Cornelius that his prayers and alms have ascended as a memorial before God (10:4). The allusion implies that, although a Gentile, Cornelius' prayers and alms have been accepted as if they were a sacrifice made by a righteous Jew. Clearly God makes no ethnic distinctions when it comes to prayers.

The second biblical allusion occurs in 10:34. Peter sets the tone of his sermon by saying, "In truth I realize that God shows no partiality." God's impartiality—which occasionally implies the willingness to listen to the poor, the widows, and foreigners—is accentuated in various biblical passages (Deut 10:17–19; 2 Chr 19:7; Sir 35:15–16). These biblical passages highlight the covenant that God made with Abraham and David and portray God as merciful, inclusive, and impartial.[57] As we have shown in chapter 3, the Lukan purity arrangements are not based on the Old Testament notion of "holiness" (belonging to the covenant of Moses) but on "mercy" (belonging to the covenant of Abraham and David). This confirms the words of the voice made from heaven, "What God has made clean, you must not call unclean" (10:15; 11:9). At the Jerusalem Council Peter—referring back to the Cornelius episode—again says, "God made no distinction between us and them, but cleansed their hearts by faith" (Acts 15:9). Clearly God has not only annulled the distinction between clean and unclean foods but also between clean and unclean persons. Thus for Luke the biblical allusions to the covenant of mercy, which God made with Abraham and David, justify the Gentile mission and legitimate the social intercourse of Jewish-Gentile table fellowship.[58]

Besides the two definite Old Testament allusions, Acts 10:1—11:18 has five major biblical echoes and two possible hints. The five biblical echoes[59] are briefly listed here according to their degree of significance:

---

57. Biblical literature distinguishes two types of covenant, the covenant with Moses (which emphasizes the Law and holiness), and that with Abraham and David (which emphasizes God's mercy). Luke-Acts favors the Abrahamic-Davidic type of covenant. See Neyrey, "Symbolic Universe," 296–97; Bock, "Scripture and Realisation," 49–52.

58. For an opposing view, see Tyson, "Gentile Mission," 619–31. According to Tyson, Luke omitted quotations and allusions to Scripture in the Cornelius episode precisely because he was aware of the difficulty that Scripture has concerning the issue of annulling dietary regulations; thus, Luke appeals to a higher authority than Scripture can provide, namely God.

59. For a detailed examination of some of these biblical echoes, see Handy, "Gentile Pentecost," 42–61.

- The references to "making a distinction" between clean and unclean (Acts 10:20; 11:2, 12; 15:9) echo Leviticus 10:10; 11:46–47; 20:25.
- Peter's protest against the divine command to eat non-kosher food in 10:14 and 11:8 echoes a similar protest in Ezekiel 4:14.
- The descent of the Spirit is described in terms of "being poured out" (Acts 10:45), which echoes Acts 2:17–18, which in turns alludes to Joel 3:1–2.
- The story of the gentile Cornelius echoes Luke 4:27, which in turns alludes to the Old Testament story of the pagan general Naaman in 2 Kings 5.
- The P-C episode echoes the mission of the seventy-two (Luke 10:1–12), which in turns alludes to the table of seventy-two nations in Genesis 10.

In addition, Luke makes two possible biblical hints in the P-C episode. First, the reluctance of Peter to preach to the Gentiles may hint at the story of Jonah.[60] Second, the references to "fearing God" (Acts 10:2, 34) might indirectly refer to the wisdom motif concerning "the fear of the Lord is the beginning of knowledge" (Prov 1:7; 9:10). Although these are possible hints, the strong biblical allusions and echoes illustrate that Luke made good use of the Sacred Scripture to justify and legitimate the mission to the Gentiles. Furthermore, since the mission to the Gentiles is part of God's design, it naturally fulfills the biblical promises.[61]

THE EFFECT OF ACTS 10:1—11:18 UPON THE READER

The reception of the Spirit by Cornelius and his household was the decisive indication and legitimation that salvation was also destined for the Gentiles. Moreover, the elaborate descriptions of the manifestation of the Holy Spirit as well as the strong emphasis on prophecy-fulfillment in the P-C episode reassure the reader that it is God's will and purpose that Gentiles be fully admitted and completely integrated into the church as equal members. However, two questions need to be addressed: First, what is the practical effect of the reception of the Spirit? Second, how should one respond to God's salvific activity now made available to the Gentiles? This section

---

60. See Wall, "Peter, 'Son of Jonah,'" 70–90. According to Handy ("Gentile Pentecost," 41), the hint is weak because it is really only an overtone.

61. See Bock, "Scripture and Realisation," 41–62.

The Theological Significance

focuses on these two questions. According to Luke God's salvific activity, which is now available to the Gentiles, provokes different responses and reactions from the reader. There are three responses in the P-C episode that Luke would like the reader to imitate. The first is reflected in the character and role of Peter the apostle. The second is exemplified in the characterization of Cornelius whose attitude and openness to the Christian message are paradigmatic for Gentile converts. Finally, the third response comes from the Jerusalem community.

Peter

In the P-C episode, Peter is depicted as a model apostle and believer.[62] As one who is filled with the Holy Spirit, he courageously inaugurates the Gentile mission, faithfully gives witness to Jesus as the resurrected Christ, and proclaims the message of salvation to the Gentiles. Consequently Peter is portrayed as a paradigm for Christians to imitate since he responds appropriately to the continual salvific activity of God.

ENGAGING IN MISSION

In the first half of the book of Acts, Peter is portrayed as a missionary. Prior to Acts 10:1—11:18 Peter had already engaged in missionary activity: in many Samaritan towns and villages (8:25); throughout Judea (9:32); in Lydda (9:32–35); and in Joppa (9:36–43). In the P-C episode Peter is clearly depicted as a missionary who has been summoned (*metapempomai*) by God to journey to Caesarea (10:5, 22, 29, 33). Moreover, Peter entered into a Gentile home, preached the good news of salvation to them, and then unconventionally partook in table fellowship with the uncircumcised. As one who has been filled with the Spirit (Acts 2:4) and who has been commanded by the Lord to preach to the people (10:42), Peter courageously inaugurated the Gentile mission, which according to Luke forms part of God's salvific activity.

As a missionary Peter faithfully gives witness to Jesus as the resurrected Christ (10:40–41) and as the "Lord of all" (Acts 10:36).[63] Bearing witness is an important theme in the book of Acts.[64] In the opening verses of Acts,

---

62. For a full characterization of Peter, see chapter 5.

63. One of the primary functions and roles of an apostle is to give witness to Jesus' resurrection. See Clark, "Role of Apostles," 169–90.

64. Various scholars have already pointed out the important theme of "witness" in Luke's theology, particularly in the book of Acts. For a concise discussion on this theme,

Peter and Cornelius

Jesus promised his disciples the gift of the Holy Spirit to help them bear witness to his name "in Jerusalem and in all Judea and Samaria and to the end of the earth" (1:8). Prior to Acts 10:1—11:18 Peter, who is filled with the Spirit, frequently offered testimony to Jesus as the resurrected Christ: to Jews in Jerusalem (Acts 2:14–41); to the Israelites at Solomon's portico (3:12–26); to the religious leaders in Jerusalem (4:8–12); and to the Sanhedrin (5:29–32). In the P-C episode Peter claimed that he had been chosen by God to be a witness (*martus*) of Jesus Christ (10:39, 41). Furthermore, Peter was directly commanded by the Lord "to testify (*diamarturomai*) that he [Jesus] is the one appointed by God as judge of the living and the dead" (10:42). Peter pointed out that it was to Jesus that "all the prophets bear witness (*martureō*)" (10:43). Besides the evident terminology of "witness," Peter's defense in Acts 11:5–17 is also a testimony of divine initiative and of God's salvific plan to incorporate the Gentiles into the church.

Preaching the Word

It has been noted that in the beginning Peter (as well as the reader) did not fully understand why he was summoned to the Gentile home.[65] Cornelius' messengers only said that the angel had instructed the centurion to summon Peter to his house in order "*to hear* words (*rēmata*) from you" (10:22). The message became clearer when Cornelius said to Peter, "Now then we are all present before God *to hear* all that you have been commanded by the Lord" (10:33). Only in retrospect did Peter completely understand why he was summoned, namely, to preach the message of salvation (11:14). Cornelius was ready to hear the message, but how could he hear it if there was no one to preach? Indeed, salvation begins with the preaching of the word (cf. Rom 10:14–15).

For Luke the proclamation of the good news of Jesus is a major factor in the expansion of the Christian community.[66] The primary role of the apostles and of other believers is to preach the word—so much so that

---

see Soards, *Speeches*, 192–200; Bolt, "Mission and Witness," 191–214. Both of these studies have a fine bibliography.

65. We have discussed in chapter 5 that the content of the message has been concealed by the narrator. The information is only revealed gradually bit by bit throughout the narrative (10:22, 33; 11:14) in order to add suspense and interest to the story.

66. Kee, *Good News*, 72.

in the Acts of the Apostles speeches occupy a significant portion of the narrative.[67]

It is noteworthy that Peter gives many significant speeches in the first half of Acts. Prior to Acts 10:1—11:18 Peter delivers five important speeches (Acts 1:15–22; 2:14–41; 3:12–26; 4:8–12; 5:29–31).[68] In our passage Peter gives two more: "the sermon" (10:34–43) and "the defense" (11:5–17). Despite the minor discrepancy between 10:44 and 11:15,[69] Luke takes pains to show in both speeches that the salvation to the Gentiles is accomplished by Jesus' death and resurrection. Their awareness or acceptance of it occurs because of the preaching. Whether this occurred at the end or during the course of Peter's speech makes little difference. The outpouring of the gift of the Holy Spirit upon the Gentiles in an identical fashion to that of the first believers in Jerusalem (11:17) proves that the Gentiles can also respond to God's grace through the preaching of the *kerygma*.

In summary, through the characterization of Peter, Luke invites the reader to engage actively in the mission of the church, to give faithful witness to Jesus the risen Christ, and to preach boldly the word, just as Peter did. Engaging in mission, bearing witness to Jesus, and preaching the word are proper responses of Christian discipleship. Believers are given the gift of the Holy Spirit to participate in such missionary and prophetic activities of the church. These are essential tasks for the followers of Jesus.

Cornelius

Similar to that of Peter, Luke's favorable presentation of Cornelius also provides the reader a model of what it means to respond appropriately to the Christian message. Although he was a Gentile, Cornelius heard the Christian message and responded to it. Furthermore through the preaching of the *kerygma* Cornelius believed in Jesus and accepted baptism.

---

67. It has been estimated that the speeches in Acts occupy about one-third of the book. See Soards, *Speeches in Acts*, 1; Witherington, *Acts*, 116–17.

68. For a complete list of the major speeches made by different personages, see Witherington, *Acts*, 118.

69. The discrepancy between 10:44 and 11:15 has been sufficient dealt with in chapters 2 and 4.

Peter and Cornelius

HEARING AND REPENTING

For conversion to take place, one must be open to hear God's word.[70] Throughout Acts,[71] Luke consistently shows that salvation is offered to those who are willing to hear the word preached to them (Acts 2:37; 4:4; 8:6; 13:44, 48; 18:8; 19:5, 10).[72] Apart from hearing the word salvation is not really possible (7:57; 17:32).[73] Although a Gentile, Cornelius is depicted like a pious Jew who longs to hear God's word. The reader is told twice (by Cornelius' messengers and by Cornelius himself) about his desire "to hear" all that Peter has to say (10:22) and all that has been commanded by the Lord (10:33). The narrator also recounts that Cornelius was anxiously awaiting the arrival of Peter (10:24b). When Peter arrived, Cornelius told the apostle what the angel had told him, "Cornelius, your prayer has been heard . . ." (10:31). It is not certain what that prayer entailed; however from the context of the dialogue it is very possible that Cornelius' prayer had to do with his desire to hear the message of salvation. Being a God-fearer and a faith seeker, he would certainly want to be enlightened by the truth. Thus the angel's command to summon a certain Peter from Joppa to speak words by which he and his household will be saved was exactly what Cornelius needed and longed for.

Cornelius' receptivity of God's word led him to repentance and conversion—although little is said specifically about conversion. Luke tells us that, "the Holy Spirit fell upon those who were listening to the word" (10:44) and that "the Gentiles had also accepted the word of God" (11:1). It is the Jerusalem community which confirms that "God has granted even

---

70. The case of Paul is an apparent exception since he receives a direct revelation of Jesus Christ (Acts 9:3–6).

71. The theme of receptivity to God's word is highlighted in Luke's gospel. Luke even claims that hearing God's word and putting it into practice is better than being Jesus' mother or brother (Luke 8:19–21). See also the following passages which deal with the importance of hearing Jesus or God's word: the parable of the sower (8:4–15); the transfiguration (9:28–36); the privileges of discipleship (10:23–24); Mary and Martha (10:38–42); true blessedness is hearing God's word (11:27–28); the simile of salt (14:34–35).

72. Kittel, "ἀκούω," *TDNT* 1:216–221; Marshall, *Luke*, 192.

73. Marshall, *Luke*, 192. Marshall points out that throughout Acts people can do nothing to save themselves. Salvation is completely dependent upon the grace of God. It is God who takes the initiative in granting repentance to individuals like the Ethiopian eunuch, Paul, and Cornelius. While salvation seems to be completely dependent upon divine grace, Luke nevertheless stresses the importance of human cooperation. Luke shows that those who are pious and just attain salvation (Acts 8:27; 10:2–4, 22). Piety and good works are signs of the attitude needed for divine grace to take effect (188–92).

The Theological Significance

to the Gentiles the repentance (*metanoia*) unto life" (11:18). According to Luke, therefore, Cornelius' receptivity of God's word led him to repentance (*metanoia*).[74] His response is paradigmatic, not only for God-fearers or Gentile converts but for all believers.

Responding in Faith

Before hearing the *kerygma*, Cornelius seems more like a believing Jew than a typical Gentile. A believing Jew might be expected to pray to God constantly (10:2, 30), see visions and angels (10:3, 22, 30; 11:13), respond positively to the divine commands (10:4, 8, 22, 33; 11:13), and receive favors from God (10:4, 31). Interestingly, Peter evaluates the Gentile's attitude and faith positively when he says, "in every nation the one who fears him [God] and does righteousness is acceptable to him" (10:35).

While these signs of religions are well and good, Peter nevertheless points out that the fundamental response that really counts is faith in Jesus Christ. Peter declares, "everyone who believes in him [Jesus] receives forgiveness of sins through his name" (10:43). It is precisely at this juncture that the Holy Spirit interrupts Peter's speech and falls "upon all those who were listening to the word" (10:44). The surprising manifestation of the Spirit, especially the gift of *glossolalia* (10:46), confirms Cornelius' faith and his acceptance by God.

From this moment on Cornelius is no longer like a believing Jew but rather an authentic and legitimate Christian who believes in Jesus as the Christ and as Lord of all. Through the example of Cornelius' conversion—from a God-fearer to a believing Christian—Luke invites the reader to imitate Cornelius by responding appropriately to the Christian message. For Luke the fundamental response to the Christian *kerygma* is undoubtedly faith in Jesus Christ.

Baptism in the name of Jesus is also an important response to the proclamation of the Christ-event.[75] In Acts people who were converted were baptized in the name of Jesus Christ (Acts 2:38, 41; 8:12–13; 9:18; 19:5). For Luke baptism was a clear indication of faith.[76] Like other believers, Cornelius and his household were also baptized. Having witnessed the

---

74. According to Fitzmyer (*Luke I–IX*, 237), *metanoia* means "repentance" which literally denotes a change of mind. In the New Testament it always has a religious sense of turning from sin.

75. Fitzmyer, *Luke I–IX*, 239–41.

76. Marshall, *Luke*, 195–96.

Peter and Cornelius

pouring of the Holy Spirit upon the Gentiles and having heard them speaking in tongues, Peter was completely convinced of their faith. Therefore he "ordered them to be baptized in the name of Jesus Christ" (10:48).[77] For Luke baptism was indispensable for it was an outward sign of faith and a clear indication of membership in the Christian community. The reception of baptism is therefore a fundamental response of every Christian.

In summary, Cornelius responded very positively to the Christian message. Although he was a Gentile, the centurion heard the Christian message and converted. Furthermore, through the preaching of the *kerygma* Cornelius believed in Jesus and accepted baptism without objection. Thus the three positive responses of Cornelius provide the reader with an example of what it means to respond to God's salvific activity.

The Community

The issue of the Gentile mission was not an unimportant matter for the early church. As we have noted, Peter's inauguration of the Gentile mission is a prophecy-fulfillment of God's promise. The question remains: How should the community react to this new development? Luke presents two reactions which serve as models for the Christian community living in the new era.

COMMUNAL DISCERNMENT

Acts 11:2 indicates that the Christian community in Jerusalem was not in perfect harmony about the issue of Gentile membership in the church. There was clearly dissension over the issue of Peter having gone to the home of the uncircumcised and having participated in table fellowship with them (11:2–3).[78] This issue was no small matter. How then was the conflict resolved? How should the community react to this new development?

Instead of imposing his authority as leader over the Jerusalem church, Peter humbly and cleverly led the community into a process of communal discernment by means of personal testimony or "story-telling."[79] Through his narrative Peter was able to persuade the Jerusalem community (including his opponents) to recognize that the missionary outreach to the Gen-

---

77. We have already noted the unusual order of receiving the Spirit before baptism.

78. The spatial, temporal, and social-cultural dynamics of the P-C episode have been thoroughly addressed in chapter 3.

79. For an analysis of the narrative layers of Peter's testimony see chapter 2.

The Theological Significance

tiles came from divine initiative. Furthermore, Peter demonstrated that it was God's will that the Gentiles be included in the Christian community. This was clearly manifested through their baptism of the Holy Spirit.

Luke shows the reader that conflict and opposition must not be avoided but rather confronted in community. Through personal testimony and genuine dialogue, a crisis can be resolved in a peaceful way. Furthermore, decision-making in the church through communal discernment is essential for a community which must continually confront new issues and challenges.[80]

Joy and Celebration

The second correct communal reaction is joy and celebration. According to Luke,[81] joy not only accompanies the progress of the church's mission (Acts 5:41; 11:23; 12:14; 15:3, 31) but is also the consequence of individual as well as collective conversion (Acts 2:46; 8:8, 39; 13:48, 52; 16:34).[82]

In the P-C episode joy is expressed in various ways and by different characters. The Gentile converts express joy by "speaking in tongues and praising God" (10:46). The circumcised believers express it through their amazement that "the gift of the Holy Spirit had been poured out even on the Gentiles" (10:45). Peter demonstrates his joy (even though joy is not mentioned explicitly) by ordering the Gentiles to be baptized immediately in the name of Jesus Christ (10:48), since the celebration of baptism is an appropriate ritual to welcome joyfully the new uncircumcised members into the Christian community (cf. Acts 16:33–34). Even the opponents (as well as the whole Jerusalem community) glorify God saying, "God had granted even to the Gentiles the repentance unto life" (11:18).

CONCLUSION

The chapter has demonstrated that the Gentile mission in Acts 10:1—11:18 is fully initiated and completely guided by God and hence fulfills God's salvific will and plan. God is not only the actor and initiator but also the director of the whole event. Luke reassures the reader—especially through the repetitive techniques of recounting visions—that the entire event of

---

80. For an analysis on decision-making as a theological process, see Johnson, *Scripture and Discernment*, 89–105.

81. The theme of joy is particularly emphasized in the Third Gospel. See O'Toole, *Unity*, 225–60.

82. Marshall, *Luke*, 202.

entering a Gentile home and eating with the uncircumcised is completely guided by God through divine visions and angels. The Holy Spirit too serves as God's representative to implement and to legitimate God's salvific will and plan for the inclusion of the Gentiles. Luke shows that the outpouring of the Spirit of prophecy upon the Gentiles not only fulfills the promises made by Joel and John the Baptist, but also those made by Jesus himself and by the Father. As God's anointed Messiah, Jesus becomes the "Lord of all." Moreover as universal Savior and Benefactor Jesus has the power to confer God's beneficence and salvation to anyone who calls upon his name. Jesus' salvation of all people, including Gentiles, fulfills the promise made by God long ago. The abundant biblical allusions and echoes also indicate that the Gentile mission fits within God's great design and naturally fulfills scriptural promises.

God's salvific will and plan for the Gentiles provokes different responses from the reader. Since Peter is a model of Christian response, the reader is invited to imitate him by engaging in mission, by witnessing faithfully to Jesus, and by preaching God's word to all people. Cornelius too is a model of Christian response. The reader is invited to imitate him in three ways: by hearing the Christian message and being converted; by believing in Jesus; and by becoming a member of the church.

The mission to the Gentiles and the issue of Jewish-Gentile table fellowship gave rise to conflicts and opposition in the early Christian community. However such crises should not impede the Christian community from coming together for dialogue. For communal discernment in the spirit of Jesus is always appropriate for a church that continually faces new issues and challenges. And since the whole event of Acts 10:1—11:18 is a fulfillment of God's salvific will and plan, the most appropriate reaction of the Christian community is naturally one of joy and celebration.

Conclusion

EVERY NARRATIVE IS COMPOSED of two essential aspects: the *story* and the *discourse*. According to Seymour Chatman, the *story* is the "what" of the narrative and therefore consists of events, characters, and settings; the *discourse* is the "how" of the narrative. The *discourse* focuses on the particular way in which a given story is told—the arrangement of the events, the type of narrator, the point of view, the style and the rhetorical devices. For the purpose of our analysis we have isolated these narrative features and have examined them separately; however, it is good to realize that the *story* and the *discourse*, the "what" and the "how," are intricately connected and cannot be completely separated in any narrative. In order to fully discover the integral impact of Acts 10:1—11:18, we need to piece the P-C episode back together—story and discourse, form and content, theology and technique—and interpret it in the light of the whole narrative. In this way we will discover the intention and message of the implied author and the anticipated or ideal response of the reader.

THE "IDEAL" READER'S READING

First, we need to clarify a very important question: Which reader are we referring to? The reader in whom we are interested is not the flesh-and-blood person who actually engages in the act of reading, but rather the *implied reader* who is presupposed by the narrative itself.[1] When speaking about the role of the implied author and the implied reader, Wayne Booth says,

---

1. We have already noted earlier that in order to understand the implications of the many narrative gaps and biblical allusions or echoes, the intended reader of Luke-Acts must have had a good knowledge of Christian doctrine and catechesis as well as familiarity with the Greek Old Testament. He or she must have been a Christian (from either a Jewish or a God-fearer background); otherwise the reader could not fully understand the indirect allusions nor supply the necessary connections in order to fill in the gaps.

Peter and Cornelius

> The author creates, in short, an image of himself and another image of his reader; he makes his reader, as he makes his second self, and the most successful reading is one in which the created selves, author and reader, can find complete agreement.[2]

The goal of narrative criticism is to uncover the meaning or image intended by the implied author, the meaning that the implied reader is expected to grasp or the image that the implied reader is expected to become.

The analysis of the *story* and *discourse* of Acts 10:1—11:18 reveals that the implied author uses different narrative features and rhetorical techniques to communicate with the reader and to convince the reader to accept the author's point of view—namely his attitudes, values, beliefs, and world view. The four ways in which the implied author guides the implied reader are: the voice of the narrator, the arrangement of the plot, the ideological point of view of the implied author, and the evaluative point of view of God.

The Voice of the Narrator

An important device which the implied author uses to guide the implied reader is the voice of the narrator. The analysis of the discourse of Acts 10:1—11:18 (chapter 2) demonstrates that the narrator of the P-C narrative (who is *extradiegetic/heterodiegetic*) is omniscient and completely reliable. Employing a mixture of the modes of discourse, the narrator can either tell (*diegesis*) what happens as an objective observer or he can show (*mimesis*) the actions as they appear. Furthermore, he is capable of reporting from any perspective—from an external focalization which allows the reader to observe from the outside or from an internal focalization which allows the reader to enter into the narrative and experience what the characters themselves see, hear, feel and even think. The narrator can even set aside his privilege of omniscience to become a neutral observer and to allow a reliable character-narrator—like Peter—to convince the reader to adopt the implied author's value judgment in ways which an omniscient narrator could not employ without being intrusive. An authoritative and unobtrusive narrator, whose perspective parallels that of the implied author, presents a point of view that is completely trustworthy and therefore should be accepted by the reader—just as it was accepted by Peter and eventually by the Jerusalem church.

---

2. Booth, *Rhetoric of Fiction*, 138.

Conclusion

The Plot

The second way by which the implied author guides the reader in interpreting and understanding the story according to the author's design is the arrangement of the events (plot). The analysis of the events of Acts 10:1—11:18 (chapter 4) reveals that the story embodies the *quinary* (five-stage) plot structure: exposition, complication, climax, resolution, and final situation.

In the *exposition* (10:1–8) the narrator introduces Cornelius; however, by using "delayed exposition" the narrator continues to add new information about his traits, status, and religious piety throughout the narrative (10:22, 33; 11:14). While the delaying technique makes Cornelius a more attractive and worthy candidate for admission and fellowship, it also creates greater interest and adds suspense to the plot of the story. Next comes the *complication* or crisis (10:9–43). At this stage of the plot, the protagonist Peter experiences three conflicts: with the Spirit (that is, with God), with himself, and with Cornelius and his household. Following the conflict is the *climax* (10:44–46) which is the heart of the story. The effect of the Holy Spirit, in particularly the *glossolalia*, was so strong and so obvious that neither Peter nor the circumcised believers could doubt or deny it. Having personally witnessed the outpouring of the Spirit upon the Gentiles, Peter is personally transformed. In the fourth stage of the P-C episodic plot, the *resolution* (10:47–48), Peter finally and completely accepts these Gentiles by baptizing them and by participating in table fellowship with them.

Though the P-C episode comes to a moment of rest in 10:48, the episodic plot of the story is not over yet. When Peter goes up to Jerusalem the story resumes, and a *second complication* (11:1–14) is introduced—namely, the conflict with the Jerusalem church. Peter had to defend his actions by recounting the event once again, which adds not only interest and tension to the story but also a *second climax* (11:15) and a *second resolution* (11:16–17) to the P-C episodic plot. Peter's testimony of God's initiative convinced the leaders of the Jerusalem church. Their silence, followed by their praise of God—which is the *final situation* (11:18) of the *quinary* scheme—brings closure and rest to the narrative.

Interestingly, the issue of Jewish-Gentile table fellowship is not completely resolved but only suspended until Acts 15. At the Jerusalem Council Peter made explicit references to the P-C episode in his speech. He also claimed that God's initiative in pouring out the same gift of the Holy Spirit upon the Gentiles in Caesarea provided an irrefutable test case of God's approval and acceptance of Gentiles.

As we have clearly demonstrated, the P-C narrative is not just a number of random events that have been thrown together; rather the events are arranged or "plotted" in a logical sequence of cause and effect. Furthermore, the plots are organized in a meaningful way not only to arouse the reader's interest and emotional involvement but also—and more importantly—to communicate the essential message of the story and to persuade the reader to accept the author's standards of judgment—namely to accept Gentiles unconditionally into the church as equal members without imposing upon them circumcision and the observance of the Mosaic law.

The Implied Author's Ideological Point of View

The third way by which the implied author influences the reader's comprehension of the P-C episode is guiding the reader to suspend his or her own judgment in the act of reading in order to adopt the ideological point of view of the implied author. This is done through the arrangement of the settings and the characterizations.

THE SETTINGS

The analysis of the spatial settings—namely the geopolitical space (Joppa, Caesarea, and Jerusalem), topographical space (heaven and earth), and architectural space (house)—reveals that *crossing the boundaries between the sacred and the profane is no longer considered an act of defilement*. Movements are fluid whether they are horizontal (Jewish homeland to Gentile territory), vertical (heaven and earth), or exterior to interior (entering an unclean Gentile home). Since sacred space is no longer confined to fixed geopolitical, topographical, or architectural parameters, movement across traditional boundaries is permissible.

The analysis of the temporal settings (durative and locative time) reveals that divine revelations or visions are connected with *prayer*. It is through prayer that Cornelius experiences the vision of the angel; likewise, it is through prayer that Peter discovers the divine plan of God's salvation which is now offered to Gentiles.

The narrative settings of the P-C episode also focus on the key social-cultural issue of *purity and impurity*. In Israel clean and unclean, holy and profane determined whether things, persons, and places were acceptable and appropriate. However, according to the implied author of Luke-Acts, purity arrangements based on the Old Testament notion of "holiness" no longer determine who belongs to God's people. The new criterion of membership is not God's holiness but God's mercy, which is inclusive and impartial. Furthermore, the only boundary that separates the members of God's covenant, whether they are Jews or Gentiles, is faith in Jesus.

In short, the spatial, temporal, and social-cultural settings of Acts 10:1—11:18 (chapter 3) reveal that, according to the ideological point of view of the implied author, God has completely torn down the wall of separation between the clean and unclean, between insiders (chosen Israelites) and outsiders (non-Jews). Furthermore, since the Christian community is now based on faith in Jesus Christ, the reader should accept the Gentile mission and more importantly be willing to sit down at the same table with non-Jews in order to share common Eucharistic meals.

The Characterizations

The manner in which the implied author presents the two main characters (Cornelius and Peter) and the two minor characters (Cornelius' messengers and the circumcised Christians) influences the reader's judgment of these characters in the story (see chapter 5). The presentation of Cornelius—primarily through direct characterization or "telling"—reveals to the reader that this Roman centurion is unlike other stereotypical Gentiles. Cornelius is a pious God-fearer who is religiously and morally upright and who immediately obeys the divine command. He is also a generous benefactor of the Jewish people. Despite being a Gentile, this centurion thinks, acts, and lives almost like a faithful Jew. Furthermore, the presentation of Cornelius' messengers—who function as "foils" in the story—enhances even more the image of this Gentile centurion. By being devout and model servants, these messengers render Cornelius (their master) public honor and praise, for they demonstrate that he is a good patron and a responsible *paterfamilias*. Such a favorable portrayal of Cornelius rouses within the reader a feeling of empathy for this Gentile character, who deserves to be admitted to and integrated into the Christian community.

Peter's character is primarily revealed by the literary technique of "showing" (rather than "telling"). The implied author's indirect characterization of Peter reveals that he is a "round" character who possesses multiple traits—many of which are conflicting and even contradictory. He first appears hesitant, inconsistent, and unpredictable. But as the story proceeds he gradually matures and develops into a strong-willed and self-assertive character who single-handedly defends the legitimation of the Gentile mission and their integration into the church. While Peter's speeches (10:34–43; 11:4–17) show that he is a theologian as well as an eloquent and persuasive speaker skilled in Greek rhetoric, his actions demonstrate that he is a spiritual and wise leader. Peter is a leader who prays (10:9) and constantly directs his mind toward God to discover God's will and purpose (10:17, 19). Furthermore, when he is challenged by others as to why he goes to the Gentiles and eats with them (11:2–3), Peter neither imposes his authority nor appeals to Scripture to defend his actions. Rather he relates his personal experience, narrating the story in the order that he perceives (11:4–17), as a way to involve others—even the whole community—in discerning the will of God. Just as the servants are "foils" to Cornelius, the circumcised Christians too are "foils" to enhance the character traits of Peter. Their presence as "foils"—both as supporters and opponents of Peter—confirms that Peter is the leading apostle who boldly inaugurates the Gentile mission and publicly defends its cause.

In short, although Peter's behavior and actions are at first conflicting, inconsistent, and unpredictable, this apostle nevertheless grows and develops into a more consistent and wholesome character as the story progresses. The implied author's characterization of Peter gives the reader the impression that this protagonist is a real person whose speech is credible and whose actions are authentic. Furthermore, since his speech and actions are coherent with the gospel and are faithful to Jesus' teaching, Peter's world view and value judgments are compatible with those of the implied author. Hence in the act of reading, the implied reader should feel empathetic (or at least sympathetic) with this leading apostle. Moreover, the reader ought to imitate Peter's speech and action—namely defending the Gentile mission and participating in Jewish-Gentile table fellowship.

God's Evaluative Point of View

The fourth way in which the implied author of the P-C episode effectively guides the reader to accept his evaluative point of view as standard of judgment is making God's evaluative point of view his own. The right way of thinking and judging undoubtedly coincides with God's point of view. The analysis of the theological significance of Acts 10:1—11:18 (chapter 6) shows that God is evidently the primary actor and initiator throughout the story. Furthermore, according to the implied author the Gentile mission

Conclusion

is a prophecy-fulfillment which is in accordance with the salvific will and plan of God. The whole event is legitimated by: 1) visions and angels; 2) the Holy Spirit; 3) Jesus; and 4) the Sacred Scriptures.

Visions and Angels

Visions and angels play an important role in revealing as well as executing God's plan in the P-C story. While the vision of Peter is narrated only twice—first, by the narrator to the reader (10:9–16), and secondly, by Peter to the assembly in Jerusalem (11:5–10)—the vision of Cornelius is told and retold four times. In fact, the vision of Cornelius is recounted from four different points of view: by the narrator to the reader (10:1–8); by the messengers to Peter (10:22); by Cornelius to Peter (10:30–33); and by Peter to the Jerusalem church (11:13–14). While each version adds new information in order to maintain the reader's interest, the variation in perspectives reinforces the function and purpose of the implied author's repetitive rhetorical techniques. The author assures the reader that the action of going to the Gentile home and eating with them is completely guided by God. Moreover, the divine plan for the salvation of the Gentiles is being realized through the guidance of visions and angelic messengers.

The Holy Spirit

The Holy Spirit too plays an important role in the implementation and authorization of the Gentile mission in the P-C episode. As God's agent, the Spirit is portrayed as the driving force (10:38, 44; 11:16) and the legitimator (10:45–46; 11:17) of the Gentile mission and integration. According to the implied author, it was the Spirit who guided Peter to Caesarea and directed him to enter Cornelius' house and to participate in table fellowship with uncircumcised Gentiles. Moreover, the coming of the Spirit—particularly the granting of the gift of *glossolalia*—irrefutably legitimated the Gentile mission as an activity of the Spirit. Peter indicates numerous times in his defense that the Gentiles' reception of the gift of the Holy Spirit is equal to that of the first believers in Jerusalem (11:15, 17; again 15:8–9). The divine initiative and the equality of the gift of the Holy Spirit convinced the Jerusalem community to accept unconditionally both the expansion of the Gentile mission and Jewish-Gentile table fellowship.

It is noticeable that the manifestation of the Spirit among the Gentiles in the P-C episode is elaborately portrayed. First and foremost, the event is narrated twice. The actual outpouring of the Spirit takes place in Acts 10:44–48, which Peter later recounts in 11:15–17. Secondly, since there are two accounts of the same event, the descriptions of the Spirit's manifestation are more elaborate. The event is perceived and interpreted by various characters (the narrator, Peter, and the circumcised believers). The different speakers create a powerful effect upon the reader. Their perspectives give the impression that this event was real and reliable because it was witnessed by many people. Moreover, the two versions and the repetitious descriptions of the same event impress upon the reader that the Gentiles have indeed received the same gift of the Holy Spirit. Obviously the implied author goes out of his way to make sure that the reader does not miss this crucial aspect of the story.

Jesus

According to the implied author, God has brought salvation to Israel in the past and continues to bring salvation in the present through Jesus. Jesus is portrayed as the Savior/Benefactor who exhibits exceptional merit and who confers God's beneficence and salvation. Similar to many saviors or benefactors, Jesus was unjustly put to death (10:39). However after three days God raised him up and allowed him to show himself to his followers (10:40), while anyone who believes in him receives forgiveness of sins through his name (10:43). As *the* agent of God's salvation Jesus is not only the Savior (10:36) and Benefactor (10:38) of the Jews but also of the Gentiles. Since Jesus is the agent of God's salvation and beneficence, whoever believes in him will be saved. Consequently, salvation is no longer a matter of inheritance but is a gift for those who respond positively to the good news of Jesus Christ.

The Sacred Scriptures

There are two clear Old Testament allusions in the P-C episode. The angel's message to Cornelius in 10:4 alludes to various Old Testament passages dealing with sacrifices and the criteria for God's acceptance of one's prayers and offerings (Lev 2:2, 9, 16; 5:12; Ps 111:6; Tob 12:12; Sir 35:5–6). The allusion implies that, although a Gentile, Cornelius' prayers and alms have been accepted as if they were a sacrifice made by a righteous Jew. Clearly God makes no ethnic distinctions when it comes to prayers. The second allusion in 10:34 alludes to various biblical passages dealing with God's impartiality

(Deut 10:17–19; 2 Chr 19:7; Sir 35:15–16). These biblical passages highlight the covenants that God made with Abraham and David and portray God as merciful, inclusive, and impartial. Besides these two definite Old Testament allusions, Acts 10:1—11:18 also contains numerous biblical echoes and hints. These abundant biblical allusions and echoes illustrate that the implied author made good use of sacred Scripture to justify and legitimate the mission to the Gentiles. Since that mission is part of God's design, it naturally fulfills the biblical promises.

In summary, the implied author cleverly guides the reader with the help of God's reliable agents—angels, visions, Jesus, and the Holy Spirit—to align with God's point of view in order to legitimate the Gentile mission and integration into the church without restrictions. Furthermore through numerous biblical allusions and echoes the implied author influences the reader to adopt these scriptural references as the word of God. Since this is God's evaluative point of view, the reader must accept it as the normative interpretation of the P-C episode.

THE RESPONSE OF THE READER

The narrative techniques of Acts 10:1—11:18 provoke different personal responses in the reader. The first is reflected in the character and role of Peter, who is depicted as a model apostle and believer. Filled with the Holy Spirit, he courageously inaugurates the Gentile mission, faithfully gives witness to Jesus as the resurrected Christ, and proclaims the message of salvation to the Gentiles. Consequently Peter is portrayed as a paradigm for Christians to imitate, since he responds appropriately to the continual salvific activity of God. The reader is invited to imitate him by engaging in mission, by witnessing faithfully to Jesus, and by preaching God's word to all people without distinction.

Luke's favorable presentation of Cornelius provides the reader with a model of someone who responds appropriately to the Christian message. Although he was a Gentile, Cornelius not only heard the Christian message but also responded positively to it. Through Peter's preaching of the *kerygma* Cornelius believed in Jesus and accepted baptism. Since he is a model of Christian response, the reader is invited to imitate this Gentile centurion in three ways: by hearing the Christian message and being converted; by believing in Jesus Christ; and by becoming a member of the church.

Acts 10:1—11:18 also has communal implications. The problems of the church today are not the mission to the Gentiles and the Jewish-Gentile table fellowship, yet they do concern the relationships among Christians from different nations, cultures, and political-social-economic backgrounds. The Christian community of today is challenged to cherish the richness and the diversity of God's people. Moreover, cultural and ethnic differences should not impede the Christian community from coming together for dialogue and for liturgical celebration.

A PORTRAIT OF THE IMPLIED AUTHOR

While the reading of P-C episode from the implied reader's point of view helps to identify the intention and message of the implied author, it does not however tell us who he really is. Who then is the implied author of Acts 10:1—11:18? And what does this portrait invite the reader to become?

First and foremost, the implied author of Acts 10:1—11:18 is neither a systematic theologian nor a modern-day historian. The narrative analysis of our story reveals that he is a "pastoral theologian" who works with diverse traditions to put together in story form (or biblical history) an answer for the issues concerning the faith of the community. As the Christian movement grew and as Gentiles—especially God-fearers like Cornelius—were converted to Christianity, the author had to search for continuity amidst discontinuity to resolve the burning issue of the mission to the Gentiles and their integration into the church.

How then does the implied author go about guiding and persuading his reader (hearer) to accept the Gentile mission and integration? Instead of composing a long theological treatise, the implied author, who is paradigmatic of a pastoral theologian, employs the art of storytelling. The analysis of the *story* and *discourse* has demonstrated that the author of our narrative is a master storyteller. Well educated in Greek and rhetoric, as well as being gifted in storytelling, the author creatively and effectively guides the reader not only to conform to his evaluative world view but also to align with the standard of God's judgment.

Strengthening faith and rediscovering gospel values through storytelling is indeed an effective way of doing theology. This method of teaching is certainly not a new phenomenon. Many of the biblical writers wrote stories and taught by means of them. Jesus of Nazareth was known for his stories. Our Christian heritage is built upon stories. Indeed stories usually touch us at our deepest levels and convince us of truth. Thus the image of the implied author of the P-C episode, who is a master storyteller, invites us to engage in biblical storytelling as an effective way of teaching and preaching.

Conclusion

In a sophisticated and technological world, where effective communication depends upon creativity and imagination, the best way to reveal the hidden truth of the gospel message and to change the heart and soul of our listeners is through the art of storytelling.

APPENDIX A

Table of Narrative Codes

Characters:	C	Cornelius
	P	Peter
	A	Angel
	M	Messengers of Cornelius
	HS	Holy Spirit
	B	Brothers from Joppa
	RF	Relatives and friends
	AB	Apostles and brothers
	CC	Circumcised Christians
	( )	character is passive in the narrative
Locale:	*ls*	local setting
	lc	local connective (with link to preceding narrative)
	lchg	local change (an explicit shift in locale)
Time:	*ts*	temporal setting
	tc	temporal connective (with link to preceding narrative)
	tchg	temporal change (an explicit shift in time)
Other devices:	*com*	commentary of narrator
	constop	conversation stopper
	dep	departure (often makes conclusion of scene)
	desc	description
	dis	dismissal
	elip	ellipsis
	intr	intrusion

Appendix A

postpone	postponement
recap	recapitulation
rep	report
repet	repetitive narration
retro	retrospective
termf	terminal function

Appendix B

Glossary[1]

Agent (functionary): a simple character, playing a minor (or single) role in the development of the plot.

Architectural space: the artificially enclosed space or human-made structure, such as, house, synagogue, temple, door, roof, or housetop.

Characterization: the set of techniques resulting in the constitution of character. Characterization can be either direct or indirect.

Closure of the text: the totality of narrative indicators which fix a beginning and an end to the narrative, thus delimiting a space where meaning is produced.

Defocalizing process: reverses the focalizing process by dispersing the characters, expanding the space, lengthening the time frame, or introducing a terminal function.

Direct characterization: the literary technique of presenting the character through the mode of telling or *diegesis* which is recounted by the narrator, by the character himself or herself, or by another character.

Discourse time: the material time necessary to tell the narrative which are measured in words, sentences, lines, paragraphs, etc.

Ellipsis: a temporal gap or an extreme pace of the narration, which passes over a period of the story in silence.

---

1. The following definitions are largely citations of or adaptations from Funk, *Poetics*; Marguerat and Bourquin, *How to Read*; Prince, *Dictionary of Narratology*.

Appendix B

External focalization: a narrative mode coinciding with what the readers could observe themselves, but generally superior to what the character in the story knows.

Extradiegetic narrator: the primary narrator who is external to the story.

Flat character: a character endowed with one or very few traits and highly predictable in behavior.

Focalizing process: the narrator focuses the narrative by bringing a set of characters together in a specific time and particular place.

Foil: a simple character whose role is to enhance the quality of another character in the story.

Geopolitical space: the area of the earth (*geo-*), which is defined by human-made boundaries of civic or governmental units (*-political*). These spatial areas are named village, city, country, and region.

Heterodiegetic narrator: a narrator who does not participate in the narrative or is absent from the story that he or she narrates.

Homodiegetic narrator: a narrator who is present or makes himself or herself explicitly known in the story that he or she relates.

Implied author: not the flesh-and-blood figure but rather the image or persona of the author's second self which can be reconstructed from the text.

Implied reader: not the flesh-and-blood figure but rather the image or the ideal reader who shares the same perspective and values of the implied author and in whom the author invites to perform in the act of reading.

Indirect characterization: the literary technique of presenting the character through the mode of showing or *mimesis* which is deducible from the character's actions, reactions, thoughts, or emotions.

Internal focalization: a narrative mode by which the narrator associates the readers with the inner feelings of a character.

Intradiegetic narrator: the secondary narrator who is internal to the story.

Glossary

Iterative narration: a mentioning once something that has happened several times in the story.

Macro-narrative: the maximal narrative unit conceived as a whole by the narrator. Examples are a Gospel or the Acts of the Apostles.

Micro-narrative: a minimal narrative entity presenting a narrative episode the unity of which can be identified the indicators of closure.

Narratee: the one whom the narrator addresses (either explicitly or inexplicitly) in the text.

Narrator: a literary device which the author uses to tell the story and to tell it in a certain fashion.

Plot: the arrangement of the events in a certain causal order which make up the story.

Point of view: the position or perspective from which an event or a story is told.

Quinary scheme: a structural model dividing up the plot of the narrative into five successive moments: initial situation (or exposition), complication, transformation action (or climax), denouement (or resolution), and final situation.

Real author: the historical figure, whether an individual or a group, who is actually responsible for writing the story and who exists outside of the narrative or text.

Real reader: the one who actually engages in the act of reading or listening whether or not he or she is explicitly addressed by the real author.

Round character: a complex, multidimensional, unpredictable character, who is capable of demonstrating surprising behavior.

Showing (mimesis): a mode of presentation in which the narrator shows events rather than describing them.

Stock character: a conventional character who possesses a single trait and performs a perfunctory role in the story.

Appendix B

Story time: the duration of the actions and events in the story which are measured in seconds, minutes, hours, days, etc.

Telling (diegesis): a mode of exposition in which the narrator reports what has transpired without permitting the reader to witness events directly or immediately. In *diegesis* the narrator recounts rather than enacts, tells rather than shows.

Topographical space: that which is part of, or relating to, the physical features of the earth, for example, roads, rivers, lakes, seas, wilderness, mountains, and the earth.

Walk-on: a simple character, playing a passive or quasi-passive (background) role in the narrative.

Zero focalization: a narrative mode in which the narrator uses his privilege or omniscience to communicate crucial information to the reader and says more than the characters in the story know.

Bibliography

Abrams, Meyer H. *A Glossary of Literary Terms*. 4th ed. Forth Worth: Holt, Rinehart and Winston, 1981.
Aland, K. and B. Aland. *The Text of the New Testament*. 2nd ed. Translated by E. F. Rhodes. Grand Rapids: Eerdmans, 1989.
Aletti, J.-N. "L'approccio narrativo applicato alla Bibbia: stato della questione e proposte." *RivB* 39 (1991) 257–76.
———. *L'art de raconter Jésus Christ*. Paris: Seuil, 1989.
———. *Quand Luc raconte: Le récit comme théologie*. Paris: Cerf, 1998.
Alter, Robert. *The Art of Biblical Narrative*. New York: Basic Books, 1981.
———. *The World of Biblical Literature*. New York: Basic Books, 1992.
Alter, Robert, and F. Kermode, eds. *The Literary Guide to the Bible*. Cambridge, MA: Belknap, 1987.
Amit, Yaira. *Reading Biblical Narratives: Literary Criticism and the Hebrew Bible*. Minneapolis: Augsburg Fortress, 2001.
Aristotle. *Poetics*. Translated by Ingram Bywater. New York: Oxford University Press, 1954.
Arnold, B. T. "Luke's Characterization Use of the Old Testament in the Book of Acts." In *History, Literature, and Society in the Book of Acts*, edited by Ben Witherington III, 300–323. New York: Cambridge University Press, 1996.
Aune, David E. *The New Testament in Its Literary Environment*. Philadelphia: Westminster, 1987.
Baer, Heinrich von. *Der Heilege Geist in den Lukas-schriften*. Struttgart: W. Kohlhammer, 1926.
Bal, Mieke. *Narratology: Introduction to the Theory of Narrative*. Translated by Christine van Boheemen. Toronto: University of Toronto Press, 1985.
Barbi, Augusto. "Cornelio (At 10,1—11,18): Percorsi per una piena integrazione dei pagani nella chiesa." *Richerche Storico Bibliche* 8 (1996) 277–95.
Bar-Efrat, Shimon. *Narrative Art in the Bible*. Sheffield, UK: Sheffield Academic Press, 1989.
———. "Some Observations on the Analysis of Structure in Biblical Narrative." *VT* 30 (1980) 154–73.
Barrett, Charles K. *A Critical and Exegetical Commentary on the Acts of the Apostles*. 2 vols. Edinburgh: T & T Clark, 1994.
Barthes, R. "L'analyse structurale du récit à propos d'Actes X-XI." *RSR* 58 (1970) 17–37.

Bibliography

Bassler, Jouette M. *Divine Impartiality: Paul and a Theological Axiom*. SBLDS 59. Chico, CA: Scholars, 1982.

———. "Luke and Paul on Impartiality." *Bib* 66 (1985) 546–52.

Bauckham, R. "James and the Gentiles (Acts 15:13–21)." In *History, Literature, and Society in the Book of Acts*, edited by Ben Witherington III, 154–84. New York: Cambridge University Press, 1996.

Bauer, Walter, et al. *A Greek-English Lexicon of the New Testament and Other Early Christian Literature*. 3rd ed. Chicago: University of Chicago Press, 2000.

Berlin, Adele. *Poetics and Interpretation of Biblical Narrative*. Sheffield, UK: Almond, 1983.

Betori, G. "Alla ricerca di un'articolazione per il libro degli Atti." *RivB* 37 (1989) 187–205.

———. "La strutturazione del libro degli Atti: una proposta." *RivB* 42 (1994) 3–34.

Bock, D. "Scripture and the Realisation of God's Promises." In *Witness to the Gospel: The Theology of Acts*, edited by I. Howard Marshall and David Peterson, 41–62. Grand Rapids: Eerdmans, 1998.

Boismard, Marie-Emile. "The Texts of Acts: A Problem of Literary Criticism?" In *New Testament Textual Criticism: Its Significance for Exegesis. Essays in Honour of Bruce M. Metzger*, edited by Eldon J. Epp and Gordon P. Fee, 147–57. Oxford: Clarendon, 1981.

Boismard, Marie-Emile, and A. Lamouille. *Les Actes des deux Apôtres: I. Introduction—Textes; II. Le sens des récits; III. Analyses litteraires*. Ebib. 12–14. Paris: Libraire Lecoffre, 1990.

———. *Le Texte Occidental de Actes des Apôtres; Reconstruction et rehabilitation*. 2 vols. Paris: Editions Recherche sur les Civilisations, 1984.

Bolt, Peter G. "Mission and Witness." In *Witness to the Gospel: The Theology of Acts*, edited by I. Howard Marshall and David Peterson, 191–214. Grand Rapids: Eerdmans, 1998.

Booth, Roger P. *Jesus and the Laws of Purity: Tradition History and Legal History in Mark 7*. Sheffield, UK: JSOT, 1986.

Booth, Wayne C. *The Rhetoric of Fiction*. 2nd ed. Chicago: University of Chicago Press, 1983.

Bottini, Giovanni C. *Introduzione all'opera di Luca: Aspetti teologici*. Jerusalem: Franciscan Printing, 1992.

Bovon, François. *De Vocatione Gentium: Histoire de l'interprétation d'Actes 10,1—11,18 dans les six premiers siècles*. Beiträge zur Geschichte der Biblischer Exegese 8. Tübingen: Mohr/Siebeck, 1967.

———. "Le Dieu de Luc." *RSR* 69 (1981) 279–300.

———. *Luc le théologien: Vingt-cinq ans de recherches (1950-1975)*. 2nd ed. Geneva: Labor et Fides, 1988.

———. *Luke the Theologian : Fifty-Five Years of Research (1950-2005)*. 2nd rev. ed. Waco, TX : Baylor University Press, 2006.

———. "Tradition e rèdaction en Actes 10,1—11,18." *Theologische Zeitschrift* 26 (1970) 22–45.

Bovon, François, A. G. Brock, and C. R. Matthews, eds. *The Apocryphal Acts of the Apostles*. Cambridge, MA: Harvard University Center for the Study of World Religions, 1999.

Brandt, P.-Y., and A. Lukinovich. "Οἶκος et οἰκία chez Marc comparé à Matthieu et Luc." *Biblica* 78 (1997) 525–553.

Brawley, Robert L. *Luke-Acts and the Jews: Conflict, Apology, and Conciliation*. Atlanta: Scholars, 1987.

Brooks, Peter. *Reading for the Plot: Design and Intention in Narrative.* New York: Knopf, 1984.
Brossier, F. "Corneille, le premier païen converti." *Le Monde de la Bible* 56 (1988) 34–35.
Brown, Raymond E., et al., eds. *Peter in the New Testament: A Collaborative Assessment by Protestant and Roman Catholic Scholars.* Minneapolis: Augsburg, 1973.
Bruce, Frederick F. *The Acts of the Apostles: The Greek Text with Introduction and Commentary.* 3rd rev. and enlarged ed. Grand Rapids: Eerdmans, 1990.
———. "The Holy Spirit in the Acts of the Apostles." *Int* 27 (1973) 166–83.
Buckwalter, H. Douglas. "The Divine Savior." In *Witness to the Gospel: The Theology of Acts,* edited by I. Howard Marshall and David Peterson, 107–23. Grand Rapids: Eerdmans, 1998.
Burnett, Fred W. "Characterization and Reader Construction of Character in the Gospels." *Semeia* 63 (1993) 3–28.
Cadbury, H. J. "Some Lukan Expression of Time (Lexical Notes on Luke-Acts VII)." *JBL* (1963) 272–78.
Cassidy, Richard J. *Society and Politics in the Acts of the Apostles.* Maryknoll, NY: Orbis, 1987.
Cassidy, Richard J., and Philip J. Scharper, eds. *Political Issues in Luke-Acts.* Maryknoll, NY: Orbis, 1983.
Catrice, P. "Réflexions missionaries sur la vision de Saint Pierre à Joppé: Du judéo-christianisme à l'église de tous les peuples." *BVC* 79 (1968) 20–39.
Chatman, Seymour. *Story and Discourse: Narrative Structure in Fiction and Film.* Ithaca, NY: Cornell University Press, 1978.
Clark, A. C. *The Acts of the Apostles.* Oxford: Clarendon, 1933.
———. *The Primitive Text of the Gospels and Acts.* Oxford: Clarendon, 1914.
———. "The Role of the Apostles." In *Witness to the Gospel: The Theology of Acts,* edited by I. Howard Marshall and David Peterson, 169–90. Grand Rapids: Eerdmans, 1998.
Cohen, Shaye J. D. *From the Maccabees to the Mishnah.* Louisville: Westminster John Knox, 1987.
Conzelmann, Hans. *Acts of the Apostles: A Commentary on the Acts of the Apostles.* Hermeneia. Philadelphia: Fortress, 1987.
———. *Die Mitte der Zeit: Studien zur Theologie des Lukas.* 6th ed. Tübingen: Mohr, 1977.
Cope, L., et al. "Narrative Outline of the Composition of Luke According to the Two Gospel Hypothesis." *SBLSP* (1994) 516–72.
Crampsey, J. A. "The Conversion of Cornelius (Acts 10:1—11:18): Societal Apologetic and Ecclesial Tension." PhD diss., Vanderbilt University, 1982.
Crane, R. S. "The Concept of Plot." In *The Theory of the Novel,* edited by P. Stevick, 141-45. New York: Free Press, 1967.
Crehan, J. "Peter according to the D-Text of Acts." *TS* 18 (1957) 596–603.
Crites, S. "The Narrative Quality of Experience." *JAAR* 39 (1971) 291–311.
Crossan, John D. *God and Empire: Jesus Against Rome, Then and Now.* New York: Harper, 2007.
Cullmann, Oscar. *Peter: Disciple, Apostle, Martyr.* Translated by F. V. Filson. New York: World, 1958.
Culpepper, R. Alan. *Anatomy of the Fourth Gospel: A Study in Literary Design.* Philadelphia: Fortress, 1983.
Danker, Frederick W. *Benefactor: Epigraphic Study of a Graeco-Roman and New Testament Semantic Field.* St. Louis, MO: Clayton, 1982.

Bibliography

———. *Luke*. Proclamation Commentaries. Philadelphia: Fortress, 1987.
Darr, John A. "Discerning the Lukan Voice: The Narrator as Character in Luke-Acts." *SBLSP* (1992) 255–65.
———. "Narrator as Character: Mapping a Reader Orientated Approach to Narrator in Luke-Acts." *Semeia* 63 (1993) 43–60.
———. *On Character Building: The Reader and the Rhetoric of Characterization in Luke-Acts*. Louisville: Westminster John Knox, 1992.
Darton, Michael. *Modern Concordance to the New Testament*. Garden City, NY: Doubleday, 1976.
Dawsey, James M. "The Literary Unity of Luke-Acts: Questions of Style—A Task for Literary Critics." *NTS* 35 (1989) 48–66.
———. *The Lukan Voice: Confusion and Irony in the Gospel of Luke*. Macon, GA: Mercer University Press, 1988.
———. "'What's in a Name? Characterization in Luke." *BTB* 16 (1986) 143–147.
Delebecque, É. "La montée de Pierre de Césarée à Jérusalem selon le *Codex Bezae* au chapître 11 des *Actes des Apôtres*." *ETL* 58 (1982) 106–10.
Derrett, J. D. M. "Clean and Unclean Animals (Acts 10,15; 11,9): Peter's Pronouncing Power Observed." *HeyJ* 29 (1988) 205–21.
———. "Luke's Perspective on Tribute to Caesar." In *Political Issues in Luke-Acts*, edited by Richard J. Cassidy and P. J. Scharper, 38-47. Maryknoll, NY: Orbis, 1983.
Dibelius, Martin. "Die Bekehrung des Cornelius." In *Aufsätze zur Apostelgeschichte*, 96–107. Göttingen: Vandenhoeck & Ruprecht, 1968.
———. "The Conversion of Cornelius." In *Studies in the Acts of the Apostles*, edited by Heinrich Greeven and Paul Schubert, 109–22. New York: Scribner's, 1956.
Dillon, R. J. "Previewing Luke's Project from His Prologue (Luke 1,1–4)." *CBQ* 43 (1981) 205–27.
Donfried, K. P. "Peter." In *ABD* 5:251–63.
Douglas, Mary. "Deciphering a Meal." In *Food and Culture: A Reader*, edited by Carole Counihan and Penny Van Esterik, 36–51. New York: Routledge, 1997.
———. "Food as a System of Communication." In *In the Active Voice*, 82–124. London: Routledge, 1982.
———. "Impurity of Land Animals." In *Purity and Holiness: The Heritage of Leviticus*, edited by M. J. H. M. Poorthuis and J. Schwartz, 33–45. Leiden: Brill, 2000.
———. *Purity and Danger: An Analysis of Concepts of Pollution and Taboo*. London: Routledge, 1966.
Dunn, J. D. G. *The Acts of the Apostles*. Epworth Commentary. London: Epworth, 1996.
Dupont, Jacques. *Les Actes des Apôtres*. 3rd ed. Paris: Cerf, 1964.
———. *Nouvelles études sur les Actes des Apôtres*. Paris: Cerf, 1984.
Eco, Umberto. *The Role of the Reader: Exploration in the Semiotics of Texts*. Bloomington, IN: Midland, 1979.
Egger, Wilhelm. *How to Read the New Testament: An Introduction to Linguistic and Historical-critical Methodology*. Peabody, MA: Hendrickson, 1996.
Elliott, J. K. "The Text of Acts in the Light of Two Recent Studies." *NTS* 34 (1988) 250–58.
Elliott, John H. "Household and Meals versus Temple Purity: Replication Patterns in Luke-Acts (Acts 10)." *BTB* 21 (1991) 102–108.
———, ed. *Social-Scientific Criticism of the New Testament and Its Social World*. Semeia 35. Decatur, GA: Scholars, 1986.

———. "Temple versus Household in Luke-Acts: A Contrast in Social Institutions." In *The Social World of Luke-Acts: Models for Interpretation*, edited by Jerome H. Neyrey, 211–40. Peabody, MA: Hendrickson, 1991.

———. *What is Social-Scientific Criticism?* Minneapolis: Fortress, 1993.

Epp, Eldon Jay. *The Theological Tendency of Codex Bezae Cantabrigiensi in Acts*. London: Cambridge University Press, 1966.

Epp, Eldon Jay, and Gordon D. Fee, eds. *New Testament Textual Criticism: Its Significance for Exegesis*. Oxford: Oxford University Press, 1981.

Erwin, E. "Between Text and Sermon: Acts 10:34–43." *Int* 49 (1995) 179–82.

Esler, Philip F. *Community and Gospel in Luke-Acts: The Social and Political Motivations of Lucan Theology*. Cambridge: Cambridge University Press, 1987.

———. "Glossolalia and the Admission of Gentiles into the Early Christian Community." *BTB* 22 (1992) 136–42.

Fianu, E. K. "A Narrative-Critical and Theological Study of Luke 24,13–35." STD diss., Pontificia Università Gregoriana, 1999.

Finn, T. M. "The God-Fearers Reconsidered." *CBQ* 47 (1985) 75–84.

Fitzmyer, Joseph A. *The Acts of the Apostles*. New York: Doubleday, 1998.

———. *Luke the Theologian: Aspects of His Teaching*. New York: Paulist, 1989.

———. "The Use of the Old Testament in Luke-Acts." *SBLSP* (1992) 524–38.

Foakes-Jackson, F. J., and K. Lake, eds. *The Beginnings of Christianity: Part I. The Acts of the Apostles*. 5 vols. Grand Rapids: Baker, 1979.

Foerster, W. "εὐσεβής." In *TDNT* 7:175–85.

Fokkelman, P. *Reading Biblical Narrative: An Introduction Guide*. Translated by I. Smit. Louisville: Westminster John Knox, 1999.

Fowler, Robert M. *Let the Reader Understand: Reader-Response Criticism and the Gospel of Mark*. Minneapolis: Fortress, 1991.

———. "Who is 'the Reader' in Reader Response Criticism?" *Semeia* 31 (1985) 5–23.

Freedman, David N., ed. *Eerdmans Dictionary of the Bible*. Grand Rapids: Eerdmans, 2000.

Frizzi, G. "La 'missione' in Luca-Atti: Semantica, critica e apologia lucana." *RivB* 32 (1984) 395–423.

———. "La soteriologia nell'opera lucana." *RivB* 23 (1975) 113–45.

Funk, Robert W. *The Poetics of Biblical Narrative*. Sonoma, CA: Polebridge, 1988.

Gaertner, D. "Tanning." In *EDB*, 1275.

Gager, J. G. "Jews, Gentiles, and Synagogues in the Book of Acts." *HTR* 79 (1986) 91–99.

Gasque, W. W. "A Fruitful Field: Recent Study Of The Acts Of The Apostles." *Int* 42 (1988) 117–31.

Gaster, T. H. "Earth." In *IDB* 2:2–3.

Gaventa, Beverly R. *From Darkness to Light: Aspects of Conversion in the New Testament*. Philadelphia: Fortress, 1986.

———. "Toward a Theology of Acts: Reading and Rereading." *Int* 42 (1988) 148–50.

Geer, T. C. "The Presence and Significance of Lucanisms in the 'Western' Text of Acts." *JSNT* 39 (1990) 57–76.

Genette, Gerard. *Figures of Literary Discourse*. Translated by Alan Sheridan. Ithaca, NY: Columbia University Press, 1982.

———. *Narrative Discourse: An Essay in Method*. Translated by Jane E. Lewin. Ithaca, NY: Cornell University Press, 1980.

———. *Nouveau discours du récit*. Paris: Seuil, 1983.

Bibliography

Gilmore, D. G., ed. *Honor and Shame and the Unity of the Mediterranean.* Washington, DC: American Anthropological Association, 1987.
Gold, V. R. "Joppa." In *IDB* 4:970–71.
Gonzales, Justo. *Acts: The Gospel of the Spirit.* Maryknoll, NY: Orbis, 2001.
Gowler, David B. "Characterization in Luke: A Socio-Narratological Approach." *BTB* 19 (1989) 54–62.
———. *Host, Guest, Enemy and Friends: Portraits of the Pharisees in Luke and Acts.* New York: Peter Lang, 1991.
Grant, R. M. "Dietary Laws among Pythagoreans, Jews and Christians." *HTR* 73 (1980) 299–310.
Green, Joel B. "'Salvation to the End of the Earth' (Acts 13:47): God as Savior in the Acts of the Apostles." In *Witness to the Gospel: The Theology of Acts,* edited by I. Howard Marshall and David Peterson, 83–106. Grand Rapids: Eerdmans, 1998.
Grilli, M. "Autore e lettore: il problema della comunicazione nell'ambito dell'esegesi biblica." *Greg* 74 (1993) 447–59.
Gunn, David M., and Danna N. Fewell. *Narrative in the Hebrew Bible.* New York: Oxford University Press, 1993.
Haacker, K. "Dibelius und Cornelius: Ein Beispiel formgeschichtlicher Überlieferungskritik." *BZ* 24 (1980) 234–51.
Haenchen, Ernst. *The Acts of the Apostles: A Commentary.* Translated by Bernard Noble and Gerald Shinn. Philadelphia: Westminster, 1971.
Haenchen, E., and P. Weigandt. "The Original Text of Acts?" *NTS* 14 (1967–68) 469–81.
Handy, D. A. "The Gentile Pentecost: A Literary Study of the Story of Peter and Cornelius (Acts 10:1—11:18)." PhD diss., Union Theological Seminary, Virginia, 1998.
Harrington, D. J. "Second Testament Exegesis and the Social Sciences: A Bibliography." *BTB* 18 (1988) 77–85.
Haulotte, E. "Fondation d'une communauté de type universel: Actes 10,1—11,18." *RSR* 58 (1970) 63–100.
Haya Prats, G. *L'Esprit force de l'Eglise: Sa nature et son activité d'après les Actes des Apôtres.* Paris: Cerf, 1975.
Hengel, M. *Acts and the History of Earliest Christianity.* London: SCM, 1979.
Hensell, E. "Heaven." In *CPDBT*, 424–27.
Hohlfeldger, R. L. "Caesarea." In *ABD* 1:798–802.
Holladay, J. S. "House, Israelite." In *ABD* 3:308–18.
Holum, K. G. "Caesarea." In *EDB*, 206–7.
Hoppe, L. J. "Earth." In *CPDBT*, 233–34.
House, C. "Defilement by Association: Some Insights from the Usage of koinós/koinóu in Acts 10 and 11." *AUSS* 21 (1983) 143–53.
Hull, R. F. "'Lucanisms' in the Western Text of Acts? A Reappraisal." *JBL* 107 (1988) 695–707.
Humphrey, E. M. "Collision of Modes? Vision and Determining Argument in Acts 10:1—11:18." *Semeia* 71 (1995) 65–84.
Iser, Wolfgang. *The Act of Reading: A Theory of Aesthetic Response.* Baltimore: Johns Hopkins University Press, 1978.
———. *The Implied Reader: Patterns of Communication in Prose Fiction from Bunyan to Beckett.* Baltimore: Johns Hopkins University Press, 1983.

———. "Interaction between Text and Reader." In *The Reader in the Text: Essays on Audience and Interpretation*, edited by Susan R. Suleiman and Inge C. Wimmers. Princeton: Princeton University Press, 1980.
———. *The Range of Interpretation*. New York: Columbia University Press, 2000.
Jeffers, James S. *The Greco-Roman World of the New Testament Era: Exploring the Background of Early Christianity*. Downers Grove, IL: InterVarsity, 1999.
Jeremias, Joachim. *Jerusalem in the Time of Jesus*. Philadelphia: Fortress, 1975.
Jervell, Jacob. *Luke and the People of God*. Minneapolis: Augsburg, 1972.
———. "Retrospect and Prospect in Luke-Acts Interpretation." *SBLSP* 30 (1991) 383-404.
———. *The Theology of the Acts of the Apostles*. Cambridge: Cambridge University Press, 1996.
Johnson, Luke T. *The Acts of the Apostles*. Collegeville, MN: Liturgical, 1992.
———. *Scripture and Discernment: Decision Making in the Church*. Nashville: Abingdon, 1996.
Jolley, M. A. "Fear." In *EDB*, 457.
Jones, D. J. "The Title *Christos* in Luke-Acts." *CBQ* 32 (1970) 69–76.
Joy, M., ed. *Paul Ricoeur and Narrative: Context and Contestation*. Calgary: University of Calgary Press, 1997.
Kaplan, J., and H. R. Kaplan. "Joppa." In *ABD* 3:946–49.
Karris, Robert J. *Luke: Artist and Theologian: Luke's Passion Account as Literature*. New York: Paulist, 1985.
———. "Missionary Communities: A New Paradigm for the Study of Luke-Acts." *CBQ* 41 (1979) 80–97.
———. *Prayer and the New Testament*. New York: Crossroad, 2000.
Kayama, H. "The Cornelius Story in the Japanese Cultural Context." In *Text and Experience: Towards a Cultural Exegesis of the Bible*, edited by D. Smith-Christopher, 180–94. Sheffield, UK: Sheffield Academic Press, 1995.
Kee, Howard C. *Good News to the End of the Earth: The Theology of Acts*. Philadelphia: Trinity, 1990.
Kelly, S. "The First Lukan Convert: The Ethiopian Eunuch or Cornelius?" *SBL Abstracts* (1995) 176.
Kiddle, M. "The Admission of the Gentiles in St. Luke's Gospel and Acts." *JTS* 36 (1935) 160–73.
Kieffer, R. "From Linguistic Methodology to the Discovery of a World of Metaphors." *Semeia* 81 (1998) 77–93.
Kilgallen, John J. "Clean, Acceptable, Saved: Acts 10." *ExpT* 109/10 (July 1998) 301–2.
———. "Did Peter Actually Fail to Get a Word in? (Acts 11,15)." *Bib* 71 (1990) 405–10.
King, P. J. "Jerusalem." In *ABD* 3:747–66.
Kingsbury, Jack D. *Conflict in Luke, Jesus, Authorities, Disciples*. Minneapolis: Fortress, 1991.
———, ed. *Gospel Interpretation: Narrative-Critical and Social-Scientific Approaches*. Harrisburg, PA: Trinity, 1997.
———. "The Plot of Luke's Story of Jesus." *Int* 48 (1994) 369–78.
Kirk-Duggan, C. A. "Heaven." In *EDB*, 563–64.
Kistemaker, S. J. *Exposition of the Acts of the Apostles*. New Testament Commentary. Grand Rapids: Baker, 1990.

Bibliography

Kliesch, K. "Der revolutionäre Schritt des Urchristentums: Petrus und die Heidenmission (Apg 10,1—11,18)." *BK* 55 (2000) 74-78.
Kort, Wesley A. *Narrative Elements and Religious Meanings*. Philadelphia: Fortress, 1975.
Kraabel, A. T. "The Disappearance of the 'God-Fearers.'" *Numen* 28 (1981) 113-26.
———. "Greeks, Jews, and Lutherans in the Middle Half of Acts." *HTR* 79 (1986) 147-57.
Kurz, William S. "Effects of Variant Narrators in Acts 10-11." *NTS* 43 (1997) 570-86.
———. "Narrative Approaches to Luke-Acts." *Bib* 68 (1987) 195-230.
———. *Reading Luke-Acts: Dynamics of Biblical Narrative*. Louisville: Westminster John Knox, 1993.
Lampe, G. W. H. "The Holy Spirit in the Writings of Luke." In *Studies in the Gospels: Essays in Memory of R. H. Lightfoot*, edited by D. E. Nineham, 159-200. Oxford: Blackwell, 1955.
Lee, David. *Luke's Stories of Jesus: Theological Reading of Gospel Narrative and the Legacy of Hans-Frei*. Sheffield, UK: Sheffield Academic Press, 1999.
Lenchak, Timothy. "Clean and Unclean." In *EDB*, 262-63.
Levinskaya, Irina. *The Book of Acts in Its First Century Setting*. Vol. 5: *Diaspora Setting*. Grand Rapids: Eerdmans, 1996.
Licht, Jacob. *Storytelling in the Bible*. Jerusalem: Magnes, 1978.
Liddell, H. G., and Robert Scott. *An Intermediate Greek-English Lexicon*. Oxford: Oxford University Press, 2001.
Lieu, J. M. "The Race of the God-Fearers." *JTS* 46 (1995) 483-501.
Lim, Y. C. "Acts 10: A Gentile Model for Pentecostal Experience." *Asian Journal of Pentecostal Studies* 1 (1998) 62-72.
Lincoln, A. T. "Theology and History in the Interpretation of Luke's Pentecost." *ExpT* 96 (1985) 204-9.
Longenecker, Richard N., ed. *God's Presence: Prayer in the New Testament*. Grand Rapids: Eerdmans, 2001.
Löning, K. "Die Korneliustradition." *Biblische Zeitschrift* 18 (1974) 1-19.
Lotz, D. "Peter's Wider Understanding of God's Will: Acts 10:34-48." *International Review of Missions* 77 (1988) 201-7.
Lowe, N. J. *The Classical Plot and the Invention of Western Narrative*. Cambridge: Cambridge University Press, 2000.
Lukasz, Czeslaw. *Evangelizzazione e conflitto: Indagine sulla coerenza letteraria e tematica della pericope di Cornelio (Atti 10,1—11,18)*. European University Studies 23/484. Frankfurt: Peter Lang, 1993.
Lundin, Roger, et al., eds. *The Promise of Hermeneutics*. Grand Rapids: Eerdmans, 1999.
Mackenzie, R. S. "The Western Text of Acts: Some Lucanisms in Selected Sermons." *JBL* 104 (1985) 637-50.
Malbon, E. S. "Disciples/Crowds/Whatever: Markan Characters and Readers." *NovT* 28 (1986) 104-30.
———. *Narrative Space and Mythic Meaning in Mark*. Sheffield, UK: JSOT, 1991.
Malina, B. J. "Christ and Time: Swiss or Mediterranean?" In *The Social World of Jesus and the Gospels*, 179-214. London: Routledge, 1996.
———. *The New Testament World: Insights from Cultural Anthropology*. 3rd ed., rev. and expanded. Louisville, KY: Westminster John Knox Press, 2001.
———. "Patronage." In *Handbook of Biblical Social Values*, edited by J. J. Pilch and B. J. Malina, 151-55. Peabody, MA: Hendrickson, 1998.

———. "Reading Theory Perspective: Reading Luke-Acts." In *The Social World of Luke-Acts: Models for Interpretation*, edited by Jerome H. Neyrey, 3–23. Peabody, MA: Hendrickson, 1991.

Maloney, L. M. *All That God Had Done With Them*. New York: Lang, 1991.

Marguerat, Daniel, and Yvan Bourquin. *How to Read Bible Stories: An Introduction to Narrative Criticism*. Translated by J. Bowden. London: SCM, 1999.

Marin, Louis. "Essai d'analyse structurale d'Actes 10,1—11,18." *Recherches de Science Religieuse* 58 (1970) 39–61.

Marshall, I. Howard. *The Acts of the Apostles*. Sheffield, UK: JSOT, 1992.

———. "How Does One Write on the Theology of Acts." In *Witness to the Gospel: The Theology of Acts*, edited by I. Howard Marshall and David Peterson, 3–16. Grand Rapids: Eerdmans, 1998.

———. *Luke: Historian and Theologian*. Grand Rapids: Zondervan, 1971.

Marshall, I. Howard, and David Peterson, eds. *Witness to the Gospel: The Theology of Acts*. Grand Rapids: Eerdmans, 1998.

Martin, Francis. *Narrative Parallels to the New Testament*. Atlanta: Scholars, 1988.

Martini, C. M. "La figura di Pietro secondo le varianti del codice D negli Atti degli Apostoli." In *San Pietro: Atti della XIX Settimana biblica*, 279–89. Brescia: Paideia, 1967.

Matera, F. J. "Acts 10,34–43." *Int* 41 (1987) 62–66.

Matson, David L. *Household Conversion Narratives in Acts: Pattern and Interpretation*. JSNT Supplement Series 123. Sheffield, UK: Sheffield Academic Press, 1996.

McConnel, Frank, ed. *The Bible and the Narrative Tradition*. New York: Oxford University Press, 1986.

McCracken, David. "Character in the Boundary: Bakhtin's Interdividuality in Biblical Narratives." *Semeia* 63 (1993) 29–42.

Merenlahti, Petri, and Raimo Hakola. "Reconceiving Narrative Criticism." In *Characterization in the Gospel: Reconceiving Narrative Criticism*, edited by David Rhoads and Kari Syreeni, 13–48. (JSNT Sup 184). Sheffield, England: Sheffield Academic Press, 1999.

Metzger, Bruce M. *A Textual Commentary on the Greek New Testament*. 2nd ed. Struttgart: Deutsche Biblegesellschaft, 2000.

Mitchell, W. J. T., ed. *On Narrative*. Chicago: University of Chicago Press, 1981.

Mlakuzhyil, George. *The Christocentric Structure of the Fourth Gospel*. Analecta Biblica 117. Rome: Editrice Pontificio Istituto Biblico, 1987.

Mowery, Robert L. "Lord, God, and Father: Theological Language in Luke-Acts." *Society of Biblical Literature Seminar Papers* 34 (1995) 82–101.

Moxnes, Halvor. "Honor and Shame." *BTB* 23 (1993) 167–76.

———. "Meals and the New Community in Luke." *Svensk Exegetisk Arsbok* 51–52 (1987) 158–67.

———. "Patronage-Client Relations and the New Community in Luke-Acts." In *The Social World of Luke-Acts: Models for Interpretation*, edited by Jerome H. Neyrey, 241–68. Peabody, MA: Hendrickson, 1991.

———. "The Social Context of Luke's Community." *Int* 48 (1994) 379–87.

Murphy-O'Connor, Jerome. "Lots of God-Fearers? *Theosebeis* in the Aphrodisias Inscription." *RB* 99 (1992) 418–24.

Navone, J. "Three Aspects of the Lucan Theology of History." *BTB* 3 (1973) 115–32.

Neirynck, F. "Actes 10,36a τὸν λόγον ὅν." *ETL* 60 (1984) 118–23.

Bibliography

Neufeld, D. "Jesus' Eating Transgressions and Social Impropriety in the Gospel of Mark: A Social Scientific Approach." *BTB* 30 (2000) 15–26.

Neusner, J. "History and Purity in First-Century Judaism." *HR* 18 (1978) 1–17.

———. "The Idea of Purity in Ancient Judaism." *JAAR* 43 (1975) 15–26.

Neyrey, Jerome H. "Ceremonies in Luke-Acts: The Case of Meals and Table Fellowship." In *The Social World of Luke-Acts: Models for Interpretation*, edited by Jerome H. Neyrey, 361–87. Peabody, MA: Hendrickson, 1991.

———. "Meals, Food, Table Fellowship." In *The Social Sciences and New Testament Interpretation*, edited by Richard Rohrbaugh, 160–82. Peabody, MA: Hendrickson, 1996.

———. "The Symbolic Universe of Luke-Acts: 'They Turn the World Upside Down.'" In *The Social World of Luke-Acts: Models for Interpretation*, edited by Jerome H. Neyrey, 271–304. Peabody, MA: Hendrickson, 1991.

Nguyen, vanThanh. "Dismantling Cultural Boundaries: Missiological Implications of Acts 10:1—11:18." *Missiology: An International Review* 40.4 (October 2012) 455–66.

———. "Evangelizing Empire: The Gospel and Mission of St. Paul." *SEDOS Bulletin* 41 (May–June 2009) 99–105.

———. "Luke's Point of View of the Gentile Mission: The Test Case of Acts 11:1–18." *Journal of Biblical and Pneumatological Research* 3 (Fall 2011) 85–98.

———. "The Roman Empire and the New Testament." *New Theology Review* 21/2 (May 2008) 84–86.

O'Toole, Robert F. "Εἰρήνη, an Underlying Theme in Acts 10,34–43." *Bib* 77 (1996) 461–76.

———. "Luke's Position on Politics and Society in Luke-Acts." In *Political Issues in Luke-Acts*, edited by R. J. Cassidy and P. J. Scharper, 1–17. Maryknoll, NY: Orbis, 1983.

———. *The Unity of Luke's Theology: An Analysis of Luke-Acts*. Good News Studies 9. Wilmington, DE: Michael Glazier, 1984.

———. "Why Did Luke Write Acts (Lk-Acts)?" *BTB* 7 (1977) 66–76.

Osiek, Carolyn, and David L. Balch. *Families in the New Testament World: Households and House Churches*. Louisville: Westminster John Knox, 1997.

Overman, J. A. "The God-Fearers: Some Neglected Features." *JSNT* 32 (1988) 17–26.

Parsons, Mikeal C. *Luke: Storyteller, Interpreter, Evangelist*. Peabody, MA: Hendrickson, 2007.

Parson, Mikeal C., and Richard I. Pervo. *Rethinking the Unity of Luke and Acts*. Minneapolis: Fortress, 1993.

Parsons, Mikeal C., and Jospeh B. Tyson, eds. *Cadbury, Knox, and Talbert: American Contributions to the Study of Acts*. Atlanta: Scholars, 1992.

Peristiany, J. G. *Honour and Shame: The Values of Mediterranean Society*. Chicago: University of Chicago Press, 1974.

Pervo, Richard I. *Profit with Delight: The Literary Genre of the Acts of the Apostles*. Philadelphia: Fortress, 1987.

Petersen, Norman R. *Literary Criticism for New Testament Critics*. Philadelphia: Fortress, 1978.

Peterson, David. "Luke's Theological Enterprise: Integration and Intent." In *Witness to the Gospel: The Theology of Acts*, edited by I. Howard Marshall and David Peterson, 521–44. Grand Rapids: Eerdmans, 1998.

———. "The Motif of Fulfilment and the Purpose of Luke-Acts." In *The Books of Acts in Its Ancient Literary Setting*, edited by Bruce W. Winter and Andrew D. Clarke, 1:83–104. Grand Rapids: Eerdmans, 1994.
Pilch, John J., and Bruce J. Malina, eds. *Handbook of Biblical Social Values*. Peabody, MA: Hendrickson, 1998.
Plümacher, E. "Acta Forschung 1974–82." *TRev* 49 (1984) 113–20.
Plunkett, M. A. "Ethnocentricity and Salvation History in the Cornelius Episode." *SBLSP* 24 (1985) 465–79.
Plymale, Steven F. *The Prayer Texts of Luke-Acts*. New York: Lang, 1991.
Pourthuis, Marcel, and Joshua Schwartz, eds. *Purity and Holiness: The Heritage of Leviticus*. Leiden: Brill, 2000.
Powell, Mark A. *The Bible and Modern Literary Criticism: A Critical Assessment and Annotated Bibliography*. New York: Greenwood, 1992.
———. "The Religious Leaders in Luke: A Literary-Critical Study." *JBL* 109 (1990) 93–110.
———. *What Are They Saying About Acts?* New York: Paulist, 1991.
———. *What Are They Saying About Luke?* New York: Paulist, 1989.
———. *What is Narrative Criticism? A New Approach to the Bible*. London: SPCK, 1993.
Prats, G. Haya. *L'Esprit force de l'Église: Sa nature et son activité d'après les Actes des Apôtre*. Paris: Cerf, 1975.
Prince, Gerald. "Aspects of a Grammar of Narrative." *Poetics Today* 1/3 (1980) 49–63.
———. *Dictionary of Narratology*. Rev. ed. Lincoln: University of Nebraska Press, 2003.
———. *A Grammar of Stories: An Introduction*. The Hague: Walter de Gruyter, 1973.
———. *Narratology: The Form and Functioning of Narrative*. Berlin: Mouton, 1982.
Rasco, E. "Spirito e istituzione nell'opera lucana." *RivB* 30 (1982) 301–22.
Ray, Jerry L. *Narrative Irony in Luke-Acts: The Paradoxical Interaction of Prophetic Fulfillment and Jewish Rejection*. Lewiston, NY: Mellen Biblical, 1996.
Resseguie, James L. *Narrative Criticism of the New Testament: An Introduction*. Grand Rapids: Baker, 2005.
Rhoads, David M. "Narrative Criticism and the Gospel of Mark." *JAAR* 50 (1982) 411–34.
Rhoads, David M., et al. *Mark as Story: An Introduction to the Narrative of a Gospel*. 2nd ed. Minneapolis: Fortress, 1999.
Rhoads, David, and Syreeni, Kari, eds. *Characterization in the Gospels: Reconceiving Narrative Criticism*. Sheffield, UK: Sheffield Academic, 1999.
Richard, Earl. "Pentecost as a Recurrent Theme in Luke-Acts." In *New Views on Luke and Acts*, edited by Earl Richard, 133–49. Collegeville, MN: Liturgical, 1990.
Ricoeur, Paul. "The Narrative Function." *Semeia* 13 (1978) 177–202.
———. *Time and Narrative*. Vol. 2. Translated by Kathleen McLaughlin and David Pellauer. Chicago: University of Chicago Press, 1990.
Riesenfeld, H. "The Text of Acts x36." In *Text and Interpretation: Studies in the New Testament Presented to Matthew Black*, edited by E. Best and R. M. Wilson, 191–94. Cambridge: Cambridge University Press, 1979.
Rimmon-Kenan, Shlomith. *Narrative Fiction: Contemporary Poetics*. London: Methuen, 1983.
Robbins, V. K. "The Social Location of the Implied Author of Luke-Acts." In *The Social World of Luke-Acts: Models for Interpretation*, edited by Jerome H. Neyrey, 305–32. Peabody, MA: Hendrickson, 1991.

Bibliography

Robinson, W. C. *Der Weg des Herrn: Studien zur Geschichte und Eschatologie im Lukas-Evangelium.* Hamburg: H. Reich, 1964.

Roemer, M. *Telling Stories: Postmodernism and the Invalidation of Traditional Narrative.* Maryland: Rowman & Littlefield, 1995.

Rohrbaugh, Richard, ed. *The Social Sciences and New Testament Interpretation.* Peabody, MA: Hendrickson, 1996.

Ropes, James H. "An Eclectic Study of the Text of Acts." In *Biblical and Patristic Studies in Memory of Robert Pierce Casey*, edited by J. N. Birdsall and R. W. Thomson, 64–77. Freidburg: Herder, 1963.

———. *The Text of Acts.* The Beginnings of Christianity. Vol. 3. London: MacMillan, 1922.

Rosner, Brian S. "Acts and Biblical History." In *The Books of Acts in Its Ancient Literary Setting*, 1:65–82. Grand Rapids: Eerdmans, 1994.

Schnackenburg, R. "The Petrine Office: Peter's Relationship to the Other Apostles." *Theology Digest* 20 (1972) 148–52.

Scholes, Robert, and R. Kellogg. *The Nature of Narrative.* New York: Oxford University Press, 1966.

Schrenk, G. "Δίκαιος." In *TDNT* 2:182–225.

Schweizer, E. "Πνεῦμα." In *TDNT* 6:332–452.

Scott, J. J. "The Cornelius Incident in the Light of Its Jewish Setting." *JETS* 34 (1991) 475–84.

Segal, A. F. "The Costs of Proselytism and Conversion." *SBLSP* (1988) 336–69.

Sellick, M. D. L. "The Cornelius Affair." *ExpT* 94 (1983) 245–47.

Sheeley, Steven M. *Narrative Asides in Luke-Acts.* Sheffield, UK: JSOT, 1992.

Shepherd, William H. *The Narrative Function of the Holy Spirit as a Character in Luke-Acts.* Atlanta: Scholars, 1994.

Ska, J. L. *"Our Fathers Have Told Us:" Introduction to the Analysis of Hebrew Narratives.* Subsidia Biblica 13. Rome: Editrice Pontificia Universita Gregoriana, 1990.

Soards, Marion L. *The Speeches in Acts: Their Content, Context, and Concerns.* Louisville: Westminister John Knox, 1994.

Speidel, M. P. "The Roman Army in Judea under the Procurator: The Italian and Augustan Cohort in the Acts of the Apostles." *Ancient Society* 13–14 (1982/1983) 233–40.

Spencer, F. S. "Acts and Modern Literary Approaches." In *The Books of Acts in Its Ancient Literary Setting*, edited by B. W. Winter and A. D. Clarke, 1:381–414. Grand Rapids: Eerdmans, 1993.

Squires, John T. *The Plan of God in Luke-Acts.* Cambridge: Cambridge University Press, 1993.

———. "The Plan of God in the Acts of the Apostles." In *Witness to the Gospel: The Theology of Acts*, edited by I. Howard Marshall and David Peterson, 19–39. Grand Rapids: Eerdmans, 1998.

Stenschken, C. "The Need for Salvation." In *Witness to the Gospel: The Theology of Acts*, edited by I. Howard Marshall and David Peterson, 125–44. Grand Rapids: Eerdmans, 1998.

Sternberg, Meir. *Expositional Modes and Temporal Ordering in Fiction.* Baltimore: Johns Hopkins University Press, 1978.

———. *The Poetics of Biblical Narrative: Ideological Literature and the Drama of Reading.* Bloomington: Indiana University Press, 1985.

Stibbe, Mark W. G. *John as Storyteller: Narrative Criticism and the Fourth Gospel.* Cambridge: Cambridge University Press, 1992.
Strange, W. A. *The Problem of the Text of Acts.* Cambridge: Cambridge University Press, 1992.
Strong, James. *The New Strong's Exhaustive Concordance of the Bible.* Nashville: T. Nelson, 1984.
Stuehrenberg, P. F. "Cornelius and the Jews: A Study in the Interpretation of Acts before the Reformation." PhD diss., University of Minnesota, 1988.
Stuhlmueller, C., et al., eds. *The Collegeville Pastoral Dictionary of Biblical Theology.* Collegeville, MN: Liturgical, 1996.
Swartley, W. M. "Politics or Peace (Eirēnē) in Luke's Gospel." In *Political Issues in Luke-Acts,* edited by Richard J. Cassidy and Philip J. Scharper, 18–37. Maryknoll, NY: Orbis, 1983.
Sweetland, Denis M. "Luke the Christian." In *New Views on Luke and Acts,* edited by Earl Richard, 48–63. Collegeville, MN: Liturgical, 1990.
Talbert, Charles H. "The Concept of Immortals in Mediterranean Antiquity." *JBL* 94 (1975) 419–36.
———. "The Fulfillment of Prophecy in Luke-Acts." In *Reading Luke: A Literary and Theological Commentary on the Third Gospel,* 234–40. New York: Crossroad, 1984.
———. *Literary Patterns, Theological Themes, and the Genre of Luke-Acts.* Cambridge, MA: Society of Biblical Literature, 1974.
———, ed. *Luke-Acts: New Perspective from the Society of Biblical Literature Seminar.* New York: Crossroad, 1984.
———. *Reading Acts: A Literary and Theological Commentary on Acts of the Apostles.* New York: Crossroad, 1997.
———. *Reading Luke: A Literary and Theological Commentary on the Third Gospel.* New York: Crossroad, 1984.
———. *Reading Luke-Acts in its Mediterranean Milieu.* Leiden: Brill, 2003.
Tannehill, Robert C. "The Functions of Peter's Mission Speeches in the Narrative of Acts." *NTS* 37 (1991) 400–414.
———. *The Narrative Unity of Luke-Acts: A Literary Interpretation.* 2 vols. Philadelphia: Fortress, 1986.
Tassin, C. "Conversion de Corneille et conversion de Pierre." *Spiritus* 141 (1995) 467–75.
Templeton, E. "Reflecting on Acts: Acts 10: 'God Shows No Partiality.'" *One in Christ* 28 (1992) 97–105.
Thompson, Richard P., and Thomas E. Phillips, eds. *Literary Studies in Luke-Acts: Essays in Honor of Joseph B. Tyson.* Macon, GA: Mercer University Press, 1998.
Tiede, D. L. "Acts 11,1–18." *Int* 42 (1988) 175–80.
Townsend, J. T. "The Speeches in Acts." *ATR* 42 (1960) 150–59.
Trainor, Michael F. *The Quest for Home: The Household in Mark's Community.* Collegeville, MN: Liturgical, 2001.
Trites, A. A. "The Prayer Motif in Luke-Acts." In *Perspectives on Luke-Acts,* edited by C. H. Talbert, 168–86. Danville, VA : Association of Baptist Professors of Religion, 1978.
Turner, M. "The 'Spirit of Prophecy' as the Power of Israel's Restoration and Witness." In *Witness to the Gospel: The Theology of Acts,* edited by I. Howard Marshall and David Peterson, 327–48. Grand Rapids: Eerdmans, 1998.
Tyson, J. B. *The Death of Jesus in Luke-Acts.* Columbia: University of South Carolina Press, 1986.

Bibliography

———. "The Emerging Church and the Problem of Authority in Acts." *Int* 42 (1988) 132–45.

———. "The Gentile Mission and the Authority of Scripture in Acts." *NTS* 33 (1987) 619–31.

———. *Images of Judaism in Luke-Acts*. Columbia: University of South Carolina Press, 1992.

———, ed. *Luke-Acts and the Jewish People: Eight Critical Perspectives*. Minneapolis: Augsburg, 1988.

Uspensky, Boris. *A Poetics of Composition: The Structure of the Artistic Text and Typology of a Compositional Form*. Translated by Valentina Zavarin and Susan Wittig. Berkeley: University of California Press, 1973.

Valentini, Alberto. *Il Magnificat: genere letterario, struttura, esegesi*. Bologna: Edizioni Dehoniane Bologna, 1987.

Wall, R. W. "Peter 'Son' of Jonah: The Conversion of Cornelius in the Context of Canon." *JSNT* 29 (1987) 79–90.

Walsh, Jerome T. *Style and Structure in Biblical Hebrew Narrative*. Collegeville, MN: Liturgical, 2001.

Walworth, A. J. "The Narrator of Acts." PhD diss., Southern Baptist Theological Seminary, 1984.

Watts, J. W. "Narrative Time in Luke's Gospel." *Paradigms* 1/2 (1985) 65–80.

Welch, John W., ed. *Chiasmus in Antiquity: Structures, Analyses, Exegesis*. Hildesheim: Gerstenberg, 1981.

Wenham, G. J. "The Theology of Unclean Food." *EQ* 53 (1981) 6–15.

Wight, Fred H. *Manners and Customs of Bible Lands*. Chicago: Moody, 1953.

Wikenhauser, A. "Doppelträume." *Bib* 29 (1948) 100–111.

Wilcox, M. "The God-Fearers in Acts—A Reconsideration." *JSNT* 13 (1981) 102–22.

Wilson, Stephen G. *The Gentiles and the Gentile Mission in Luke-Acts*. Cambridge: University Press, 1973.

Wilson, W. T. "Urban Legends: Acts 10:1—11:8 and the Strategies of Greco-Roman Foundation Narratives." *JBL* 120 (2001) 77–99.

Witherington, Ben, III. *The Acts of Apostles: A Socio-Rhetorical Commentary*. Grand Rapids: Eerdmans, 1998.

———, ed. *History, Literature, and Society in the Book of Acts*. New York: Cambridge University Press, 1996.

Witherup, Ronald D. "Cornelius Over and Over and Over Again: 'Functional Redundancy' in the Acts of the Apostles." *JSNT* 49 (1993) 45–66.

Yao, S. "Dismantling Social Barriers through Table Fellowship (Acts 2:42–47)." In *Mission in Acts: Ancient Narrative in Contemporary Context*, edited by Robert L. Gallagher and Paul Hertig, 29–36. Maryknoll, NY: Orbis, 2004.

Zerwick, Maximilian. *Biblical Greek*. Rome: Editrice Pontificio Istituto Biblico, 2001.

Index

Abrams, Meyer H., 15, 83, 85
Aletti, J.-N., 83
Alexandrian text, 39, 118–19
Alter, Robert, 85, 108
Amit, Yaira, 83, 85, 92
angel, 18–20, 22, 27, 30, 43, 56,
    63–64, 67–68, 73–74, 86, 89,
    110–12, 114, 116–18, 125–26,
    131, 136–38, 141, 146–47,
    150, 152–53, 156, 158, 160,
    163–65, 169
Apostolic (Jerusalem) Council, 77,
    80–82, 99–106, 135, 147, 159
Aristotle, 82–83, 107
Arnold, B. T., 146

Baer, Heinrich von, 138
Balch, David, 127
Barbi, Augusto, 110, 113
Bar-Efrat, Shimon, 69, 83, 85, 94–95,
    98, 108, 110, 119
Barrett, Charles K., 29, 31, 39, 41,
    50, 61, 89–90, 93, 98, 119–20
Bassler, Jouette M., 120
Bauckham, R., 103–4
Berlin, Adele, 21, 83, 87, 90, 109,
    126, 129–30
Betori, G., 99
Bock, D., 145, 147–48
Boismard, Marie-Emile, 118
Booth, Roger P., 14–15, 21, 39–40,
    75, 108, 125, 157–58

Bottini, Giovanni C., 59
Bovon, François, xiii, 110, 135, 138,
    142, 146
Bourquin, Yvan, 1–2, 4, 13–14, 17,
    46, 48, 55, 67, 69, 71, 83, 85,
    87, 90, 92, 98–99, 107–9,
    114–15, 125, 171
Brandt, P.-Y., 66
Brooks, Peter, 83
Brown, Raymond E., 117, 123
Bruce, Frederick F., 32, 37, 40, 61,
    73, 90, 104, 119, 138
Buckwalter, H. Douglas, 143
Burnett, Fred W., 108

Caesarea, 2, 6, 18–20, 24, 31–33,
    39, 41, 43, 50, 52, 54–58, 61,
    66, 81, 86, 88, 94, 98, 102,
    104, 110, 118, 120, 123, 125,
    128–29, 134, 140, 149, 160,
    163
characterization
    direct, 109–110, 116, 129, 171
    indirect, 109, 124, 129, 132–33,
        161, 172
character
    flat, 109, 126, 172
    round, 109, 116, 161, 173
    stock, 109, 129–30, 173
Chatman, Seymour, 11–13, 15–16,
    21, 82, 85, 107–8, 157, 177
Clark, A. C., 149

Index

Cohen, Shaye, 83
conversion, xiii, xiv, 78, 117, 152, 123, 135, 153, 155
Conzelmann, Hans, xiii, 22, 29, 38, 50, 58–59, 89, 94–95, 129, 135, 142
Crampsey, J. A., xiii
Crane, R. S., 84
Crossan, John D., 144
Cullmann, Oscar, 123
Culpepper, R. Alan, 13, 14–15, 17, 22, 25, 40

Danker, Frederick W., x, 112, 143–44
Darr, John A., 16, 107–8
Darton, Michael, 64
Dawsey, James M., 16–17
diegesis ("telling"), 21, 28, 32, 38, 53, 108, 158, 171, 174
discourse, 11–53, 133
    time, 25, 29, 32, 36, 38, 67, 71, 88, 171
Donfried, K. P., 122
Douglas, Mary, 75–76, 79
Dunn, J. D. G., 40–41, 68–69, 91, 93, 97, 99, 104
Dupont, Jacques, 99, 120, 139

earth, 23, 42, 54–55, 59, 62–65, 76–77, 81, 100, 135–36, 143, 145, 150, 160, 172, 174
Elliott, John H., 66–67, 74–75, 79
ellipsis, 24–25, 171
embedded narrative, 41, 45–47, 51–53
Esler, Philip F., 79–80, 91, 93,
extradiegetic, 46–48, 51, 53, 158, 172
Evans, Craig, 144

Fewell, Danna N., 83, 95, 98, 109–10, 126
Fianu, E. K., 71, 107
Finn, T. M., 113

Fitzmyer, Joseph A., 14, 29, 37, 40, 50, 52, 59, 61, 69, 72–73, 89–90, 97, 99–100, 102–3, 119, 121, 123, 135–36, 138, 142–44, 146, 153
focalization
    external, 21, 38, 41, 53, 158, 172
    internal, 21, 39–40, 48–49, 53, 158, 172
    zero, 21–22, 26, 40, 129–30, 174
focalizing process, 20, 171, 188
Foerster, W., 111
foils, 127–28, 130–32, 161–62
Fokkelman, Jan, 12, 15, 83
Funk, Robert W., 12–13, 18, 20–21, 37, 44–48, 171

Gaertner, D., 68
Gager, J. G., 113
Gaster, T. H., 64
Gaventa, Beverly R., 110, 123
Geer, T. C., 118
Genette, Gerard, 11–12, 21–22, 25, 46–47
Gilmore, D. G., 127
glossolalia, 91, 93, 105, 114, 141, 153, 159, 163
Gold, V. R., 56
Gowler, David B., 108, 116
Grant, R. M., 79
Green, Joel B., 142–43, 146
Grilli, M., 13
Gunn, David M., 83, 95, 98, 109–10, 126

Haacker, K., 32
Haenchen, Ernst, 26, 31, 38–40, 44, 50, 52, 61, 73, 89, 95, 110–11, 129
Hakola, Raimo, xiv
Handy, D. A., xiii, 18, 58, 69, 146–48
Harrington, D. J., 75
heaven, 23–24, 42, 54–55, 62, 64–65, 81, 87, 134, 136, 142, 147, 160

Index

Hensell, E., 63
heterodiegetic, 48, 51, 53, 158, 172
historical critical methods, xiii, 17
Hohlfelder, R. L., 57
Holladay, J. S., 66
Holum, K. G., 57-58
Holy Spirit, 7, 9, 26-28, 30, 33-36, 38, 40-41, 43, 50, 52, 56, 61, 65, 71, 81, 90-93, 95-98, 102, 104-6, 114, 116, 120, 129-30, 134, 136-42, 148-51, 152-56, 159, 163-64, 165, 169
homodiegetic, 48-49, 51, 172
Hoppe, L. J., 64
House, C., 76
Humphrey, E. M., 68
hypodiegetic, 47
hyperdiegetic, 47

implied author, xv, 13-15, 16, 40, 51, 53-54, 108-9, 116-17, 124, 132, 157-59, 160-66, 172
implied reader, xv, 13-14, 16-17, 116, 125, 132, 157-58, 162, 166, 172
intradiegetic, 46-49, 51, 53, 172
introductory formulae, 5-6, 10
Iser, Wolfgang, 17

Jakobson, Roman, 17
James (biblical), 101, 103-4, 106, 122
James, Henry, 107
Jeremias, Joachim, 68
Jerusalem, 2, 6, 35, 40-42, 44-46, 50-51, 53, 55-61, 63-64, 66, 71, 76-77, 80-81, 86, 91, 94-106, 117-18, 120-22, 124, 128, 130-32, 135, 137-38, 141, 143, 149-52, 154-55, 158-60, 163
Jerusalem Council (*see* Apostolic Council)
Jervell, Jacob, 77

Johnson, Luke T., 20, 26, 31, 37, 49, 58-59, 69, 72-73, 88, 93-95, 99, 103-4, 110, 119-23, 130, 146, 155
Joppa, 2, 6, 19, 23-26, 31-34, 36, 40, 42-43, 49-50, 55-58, 60-62, 66, 68, 81, 87-88, 123, 125, 128-29, 149, 152, 160, 169
Josephus, Flavius, 58, 73, 90, 111

Kaplan, J., 57
Kaplan, H. R., 57
Karris, Robert, xiii, 74
Kee, Howard C., 142, 150
kerygma, 40, 90, 119, 140, 151, 153
Kilgallen, John J., 50, 96
King, P. J., 58
Kingsbury, Jack D., xiii
Kirk-Duggan, C. A., 63
Kittel, Gerhard, xi, 152
Kort, Wesley, 75
Kraabel, A. T., 113
Kurz, William S., xiii, 14-17, 49-51, 121

Lee, David, xiii
Lenchak, Timothy, ix, 76
Levinskaya, Irina, 113
Licht, Jacob, 9
Liddell, H. G., 66
Lieu, J. M., 111, 113
Lincoln, A. T., 138
Longenecker, Richard N., 74
Lukasz, Czeslaw, xiii, 6, 18, 32, 52, 57-58, 110-11, 113, 115
Lukinovich, A., 66

Malbon, Elizabeth S., 55, 62, 65, 66
Malina, B. J., 71, 74-75, 78, 115, 127, 184
Marguerat, Daniel, 1, 4, 13-14, 17, 46, 48, 55, 67, 69, 71, 83, 85, 87, 90, 92, 98-99, 107-8, 109, 114-15, 125

191

Index

Marin, Louis, 45
Marshall, I. Howard, xiii, 97, 99–101, 134–35, 142, 152–53, 155
Matera, F. J., 120
Matson, David L., 111, 119
McCracken, David, 108
Merenlahti, Petri, xiv
Metzger, Bruce M., 29, 39, 49, 112, 118
mimesis ("showing"), 20–21, 28, 37, 45–46, 53, 158, 172–73
Mishnah, 68–69
mission, xiv, 59, 80–81, 101, 119, 147, 89, 123, 131, 140, 149, 151, 154
Mlakuzhyil, George, 5
Moxnes, Halvor, 79–80, 115, 127
Mowery, Robert L., 133
Murphy-O'Connor, Jerome, 113

narratee, 13, 16, 115, 173
narrative criticism, xiii, xiv, 2, 5, 11, 17, 158
narrator, xiv, 4, 6–7, 9, 11, 13–18, 20–23, 25–26, 28–33, 36–41, 44–48, 50, 53, 56, 60–61, 64, 67, 70–71, 77, 84–88, 90–91, 94–95, 100, 105, 108–12, 116–17, 124, 126, 128–29, 131, 137–39, 150, 157–59, 163–64, 173
  intrusive, 15, 53, 158
  omnipresent, 15–16, 29, 31
  omniscient, 15, 16, 26, 29–31, 40–41, 48, 50–51, 53, 108, 158
  unobtrusive, 48, 53
narratee, 13, 16, 115, 173
Navone, J., 145
Neyrey, Jerome H., 77, 79, 147
Nguyen, vanThanh, 143–44

Osiek, Carolyn, 127

O'Toole, Robert F., 120, 134–35, 137–38, 145, 155
Overman, J. A., 113

Parsons, Mikeal, xiii
paterfamilias, 115, 127, 132, 161
Peterson, David, 136, 146
plot, xiv, 1–2, 4–5, 10, 54, 81–107, 116, 125, 133, 158
  complication, 4, 83–84, 86–88, 92, 94, 96, 105, 159, 173
  climax, 68, 83–85, 88, 90, 92, 94–96, 99, 105, 130, 159, 173
  exposition, 4, 83–86, 105, 159, 173–74
  final situation, 4–5, 84, 92, 98, 105, 173, 159
  resolution, xiii, 53, 83–84, 87, 92, 94, 96, 98, 100, 105, 125, 159, 173
Plümacher, E., 39
Plymale, Steven F., 74
point of view, xv–xiv, 11, 15, 21–23, 25–26, 29–30, 33, 38–40, 48, 53, 74, 79, 95, 108–9, 113–14, 123–24, 137–38, 146, 158, 160–63, 165–66, 173
Pontifical Biblical Commission, xiv
Powell, Mark A., 11, 14, 17, 25, 55, 69, 72, 82, 85, 107–9, 114–15, 126, 129, 135, 138, 141
Prats, G. Haya, 138
purity and impurity, 75–76, 160

quinary scheme/plot, 4, 82–84, 159, 173

Rasco, E., 138
real author, 13–17, 117
real reader, 13–18, 44, 109, 115, 140, 164, 173
Rhoads, David, xiv, 15, 54, 87, 107
Richard, Earl, xiii, 139–40, 142

Index

Rimmon-Kenan, Shlomith, 12, 21, 25, 47–48, 82, 110
Robbins, V. K., 14
Robinson, W. C., 59
Rohrbaugh, Richard, 75
Rosner, Brian, 134–35, 138

Schrenk, G., 114
Schwartz, Joshua, 75
Schweizer, E., 9
Scott, J. J., 66
settings, xiv, 54–55, 81–82
  temporal, xiv, 4, 20, 24, 36, 44, 67, 69–70, 135, 160–61
  spatial, xiv, 4, 81, 161
Shepherd, William H., 107–108, 138, 141
showing (*mimesis*), 20–21, 24–25, 36, 38, 44–45, 109, 116, 124, 126, 131, 161, 172–73
Ska, Jean Louis, 2, 4, 10, 12, 14, 21–22, 25, 48, 69, 83, 85, 90, 92, 94–95, 98, 108–109, 125, 126
Soards, Marion L., 102–103, 119, 121, 135, 142, 150–51
space, 54–55, 81
  architectural, 65, 171
  geopolitical, 55–56, 81, 172
  topographical, 62, 160, 174
Speidel, M. P., 110
Squires, John T., 135–37
Sternberg, Meir, 12, 15, 85, 87, 108
Stuehrenberg, P. F., xiii
Sweetland, Denis M., 135, 142

table fellowship, xiii, 49, 93, 56, 62, 66, 71, 78–81, 94, 97–98, 100–101, 103, 105, 123, 130, 136, 140–41, 147, 149, 154, 159, 162–63, 166
Talbert, Charles H., xiii, 6, 90–91, 98, 137–38, 143–45
Talmud, 68

Tannehill, Robert C., xiii, 16, 40, 44, 49, 87, 91, 102, 113, 115, 119, 122–23
telling (*diegesis*), 21, 24–25, 29, 32, 36, 38, 44, 53, 108, 116, 124–25, 131, 161, 171, 174
Templeton, E., 120
Theophilus, 16–17, 113, 115, 145
Tiede, D. L., 76
time, 70–73, 81
  chronological durative, 70–71, 81
  chronological locative, 72–73, 160
  story time, 25, 36, 38, 67, 70–71, 88, 174
Trainor, Michael F., 66
transitional summaries, 5, 10
Trites, A. A., 73
Turner, M., 138, 141
Tyson, J. B., 146–47

Uspensky, Boris, 21

vision, 18–20, 23–27, 29, 31, 39, 41–42, 44–49, 51–53, 56, 63, 68–69, 73–72, 74–77, 86–89, 92, 95, 102, 118, 120–22, 126, 134–35, 137–38, 141, 153, 155–56, 160, 163, 165

Wall, R. W., 6, 57, 148
Walsh, Jerome, 1
Wenham, G. J., 77
Western Text, 39, 118
Wight, Fred H., 61, 88
Wilcox, M., 100, 102
Wilson, Stephen G., 101, 113
Witherington, Ben III, 44, 52, 68, 73, 88–89, 91, 94, 96–102, 113, 115, 119, 121, 123,146, 151
Witherup, Ronald D., 45, 52, 102

Yao, S., 79

Zerwick, Maximilian, 92

www.ingramcontent.com/pod-product-compliance
Lightning Source LLC
Chambersburg PA
CBHW051738230426
43670CB00012B/2066